Period Drama

TV Genres

Series Editors
Deborah Jermyn, University of Roehampton
Su Holmes, University of East Anglia

Titles in the series include:

The Quiz Show
by Su Holmes
978 0 7486 2752 3 (hardback)
978 0 7486 2753 0 (paperback)

The Sitcom
by Brett Mills
978 0 7486 3751 5 (hardback)
978 0 7486 3752 2 (paperback)

Reality TV
by Misha Kavka
978 0 7486 37212 5 (hardback)
978 0 7486 3723 2 (paperback)

The TV Crime Drama
by Sue Turnbull
978 0 7486 4088 1 (hardback)
978 0 7486 4087 4 (paperback)

Period Drama
by Faye Woods
978 1 4744 6281 5 (hardback)
978 1 4744 6282 2 (paperback)

Visit the TV Genres website at:
www.edinburghuniversitypress.com/series/EDTV

Period Drama

Faye Woods

EDINBURGH
University Press

Edinburgh University Press is one of the leading university presses in the UK. We publish academic books and journals in our selected subject areas across the humanities and social sciences, combining cutting-edge scholarship with high editorial and production values to produce academic works of lasting importance. For more information visit our website: edinburghuniversitypress.com

Edinburgh University Press Ltd
The Tun – Holyrood Road
12 (2f) Jackson's Entry
Edinburgh EH8 8PJ

Typeset in Janson and Neue Helvetica
by Cheshire Typesetting Ltd, Cuddington, Cheshire
and printed and bound in Great Britain

A CIP record for this book is available from the British Library

ISBN 978 1 4744 6281 5 (hardback)
ISBN 978 1 4744 6282 2 (paperback)
ISBN 978 1 4744 6283 9 (webready PDF)
ISBN 978 1 4744 6284 6 (epub)

Contents

List of Figures

Acknowledgements

I would like to thank the Department of Film, Theatre and Television at the University of Reading for the research leave that supported this book's completion. I would particularly like to thank Lisa Purse and Lisa Woynarski for their support during its final stages. My colleagues Simone Knox and Jonathan Bignell gave me valuable feedback at proposal stage. Many of the ideas in this book and the impetus for its existence came from my teaching on Popular TV Genres, so thanks to all the students who took that module and particularly my inspiring younger colleagues Delphi May and Anna Varadi who taught with me and from whom I learned a lot. The following friends gave me valuable feedback on this book at different stages: Courtney Brannon Donoghue, Lucy Donaldson, Amy Holdsworth, Beth Johnson and Zoe Shacklock. I also want to thank my personal librarian Sarah Currant, the ladies of the 'Backchannel' who keep me sane and support me on a daily basis, the Northern TV Research Group (honorary member) and Chris for giving me time. This book was completed during the coronavirus pandemic and the global lockdown, so I would like to thank the NHS and particularly the staff at Royal Papworth Hospital who put my dad back together again and cared for him during his long stay when we were unable to visit. This book is for Mum, Dad and particularly Hils, with her worn-to-shreds VHS of the 1995 *Pride & Prejudice*.

1 Introduction

Period drama recreates the spaces, people, society and politics of years past. The clothing and customs of these worlds are familiar yet strange, distant from those of the viewer at home. However, the genre is not a sealed time capsule; it draws the past close by constructing it, in part, in our image, tracing connections between the present and the past. As Pam Cook suggests, period drama 'looks backwards and forwards at the same time' (1996: 72). It is a genre shaped by expectations of authenticity and verisimilitude, particularly in terms of its mise-en-scène and costume. Press coverage frequently showcases the painstaking research and reconstruction involved in production teams' world-building. Questions of accuracy and interpretation shape the genre's reception, as both historical drama and literary adaptation hold expectations of fidelity. However, rather than searching for an ultimately impossible 'authentic' reproduction, we must recognise the genre's essential hybridity, its 'attempt to think historically and yet in the present tense' (Vidal 2012a: 34). Period drama reconstructs a past we can never truly know, whose documentation and preservation has itself been highly selective and political, so it needs to be understood as a blend of realism and fantasy.

Period drama is sometimes called 'costume drama', indicating the central role of bodies, mise-en-scène and material cultures in its storytelling and pleasures. It can present a lavish, sweeping spectacle, displaying houses and landscapes, balls and factory floors. But it can also produce an intimate encounter, drawing the past close to inspect the texture of fabric or the touch of a hand. Period drama is invested in the bodily and emotional experience of the past, a past it presents as strange yet familiar. It looks back and looks inward, building connections with the contemporary audience through its characters' emotional responses to historical, political and social dynamics, offering an affective experience of the past. As an introduction to the genre, this book challenges students to consider its expansive borders and contradictory ideologies and investments. Its thematic approach establishes key theories and emerging arguments, developing these through case studies that expand the genre's established 'canon'. I argue that fantasy, affect and emotion should have equal weight alongside the previously dominant frames of heritage, nostalgia and 'quality'.

Period drama is a genre shaped by prestige and pleasure. 'Prestige' refers to the elevated status acquired through the genre's associations with history, literature, politics and authorship, along with the high budgets needed to recreate its detailed images of the past.[1] This confers *legitimation*, a status as high culture, signalling period drama's value as prestige television (Newman and Levine 2011). 'Pleasure' refers to the genre's investment in spectacle, fantasy, melodrama, costume, romance and emotion. These elements are frequently *delegitimated* through their links with femininity. This leads to period drama's categorisation as a 'feminine' genre, separated from 'historical drama', which is viewed as a more serious, legitimate form (and therefore masculine) (Sargeant 2000; Vidal 2012b: 1–2). As Stella Bruzzi notes, unlike male-focused period narratives, historical romances are frequently charged with sidelining history in favour of 'far more trivial interests in desire, sex and clothes' (1997: 35). This book counters gendered separation by drawing both historical drama and literary adaptation under the wing of period drama, giving equal weight to prestige and pleasure.

Period drama attempts to balance a vision of the past as a foreign place, as distant and historically specific, with storytelling's need for identification and recognition. This tension between distance and closeness shapes its engagement with the past. It is why the genre is preoccupied with moments of rupture and social shift, such as the industrial revolution, the Edwardian era, and the First and Second World Wars. These were periods where nations and their people were confronted with wrenching change, when the past stepped towards the present (Vidal 2012b: 101). This is also why period drama returns to novels and authors (particularly Jane Austen and the Brontë sisters[2]) that can be interpreted as stories of proto-feminist protagonists straining at the constraints of patriarchal society. These people are like you but not like you, this story is distant from your experience but it feels close to you.

Distance and closeness are part of a collection of dualities that shape my exploration of period drama. The genre's interpretation of the past is shaped by the investments of the present. It blends realism and fantasy, interweaves the personal with the political, and trades on spectacle and intimacy, constraint and release. Period drama's doubled address is drawn out by Julianne Pidduck, who positions '[t]he contemporary viewer [as] at once inside and outside these mannered microcosms of the past', suggesting that 'the resulting play of surfaces and depth, witty remove and deep feeling provide some of the genre's greatest pleasures' (2004: 14). Positioning period drama as a genre of duality, ambivalence and hybridity enables me to look beyond frames of 'heritage' and nostalgia, presenting these dualities as its structuring forces.

Defining genre

This book defines period drama as television fiction engaged with representing the past. This definition collects a large amount of programming within its genre boundaries and allows me to trace connections, commonalities and contrasts across historical fiction, romantic melodramas, crime thrillers, action-adventures and literary adaptations. The latter incorporates the classic serial's canonisation of Western literature (Giddings and Selby 2000; Cardwell 2002) but also follows period drama's ventures into popular historical fiction and twentieth-century fiction. Jason Mittell presents genre as 'constantly in flux' (2004: xi), its boundaries, investments and representations shifting to reflect cultural and industrial contexts and the tastes of its audiences. This fluctuation and instability is also seen in a culture's relationship with its past, which is constantly shifting. Our interpretation of history is not fixed but malleable, and 'contemporary identities evolve in connection with a changing sense of historicity' (Vidal 2012b: 18). I have selected case studies that illustrate period drama's range of ideological investments and interpretations of national pasts. These are largely British and American, with some consideration of European nations. They highlight the genre's attempts to expand whose past we encounter and from whose perspective. But they also illustrate the ongoing limitations and absences in period drama's representations.

Genre definitions are not built solely by programmes themselves but through a discursive process that includes the perspectives of industry, audiences and the press, as well as government policies and historical contexts (Mittell 2004: xi). Our understanding of period drama is shaped by how we as a culture talk about the genre, and the programmes that get positioned as its defining texts. Charlotte Brunsdon charts an example of this discursive process in her analysis of 1980s British press and political discussion of public service broadcasting's value. She found that two ITV period dramas – *Brideshead Revisited* (1981) and *The Jewel in the Crown* (1984) – came to 'function as shorthand for taken for granted understandings of "quality"' in these discussions (1990: 82). This discourse repeatedly linked television 'quality' to four components: money, literary pedigree, 'the best of British acting' and heritage export (1990: 85–6). Brunsdon argued these were not innate components of 'quality' television but were shaped as such by this discourse, positioning the two period dramas 'as *uncontroversial* indicators of quality' (1990: 86). These components of 'quality' play a continuing part in period drama's positioning as prestige television.

Press coverage and promotional narratives frequently build a restrictive model of the genre, drawn from a period drama 'mainstream' rather than its variety. This defaults to a relatively conservative conception of the genre (which at times can misremember a programme's style and narrative to make it a more comfortable fit) and ignores the innovation, resistance or counter-narratives that were present in the period drama contemporary with a set of canonical texts. In the 2010s the canonical British period drama was *Downton Abbey* (ITV, 2010–15), moving back to the 1970s this would have been *Upstairs, Downstairs* (ITV, 1971–5), in the 1980s *Brideshead Revisited* (ITV, 1981) or *The Jewel in the Crown* (ITV, 1984), and in the 1990s *Pride and Prejudice* (BBC One, 1995). Both press and promotional discourse frequently define new programmes through this restrictive framework. A new programme will be claimed as 'not your normal period drama', a phrase that constructs the genre as conservative or feminised. Or it will be described as – or judged as attempting to become – 'the new *Downton Abbey*' when it bears little resemblance to this predecessor. As historian Hannah Greig notes, the 'new *Downton Abbey*' label produces a flattened and monolithic packaging of the genre and history itself, uncritically clustering a multitude of 'different dramas dealing with so many different historical periods, characters, narratives, contexts and formats' into a singular model (2018: 99). A sole programme becomes discursively constructed as *the* genre marker, in the process building a blinkered and forgetful vision of a genre which is inherently hybrid and slippery to define.

Scheduling plays a role in the discursive construction of genre (Mittell 2004: xi). British television's Sunday 9 p.m. slot has been understood as the 'traditional' home for flagship period drama since the 1960s. The 'cult of Sunday night' (Monk 2015: 40) contributes to the genre's position as prestige TV. In November 1999 this led to conflict between BBC One and ITV when both broadcasters scheduled new period dramas – *Wives and Daughters* (BBC One, 1999) and *Oliver Twist* (ITV, 1999) – in the timeslot, each arguing it held the legacy claim on the prestige slot (Thorpe 1999). Although period drama has strong connections to this slot in the UK, other scheduling slots highlight shifts in the genre's target audience, storytelling and tone. The BBC's Sunday teatime slot had a long history of adaptations of classic literature for family audiences, whilst the arrival of BBC Two in the mid-1960s saw a Saturday night slot identified for a more 'sophisticated' and 'adult' approach to the classic serial (Monk 2015: 33). In the 2010s BBC period drama appeared in weekday mid-afternoon slots where lower-budget dramas targeted retired audiences, including *Land Girls* (BBC One, 2009–11), *The Indian Doctor* (BBC One, 2010–13), *Father Brown* (BBC One, 2013–) and *The Moonstone* (BBC One, 2016). In turn, a mid-week BBC Two 9 p.m. slot signalled a more challenging or contentious interpretation of the past, such as the neo-Victorian *The Crimson Petal and the White* (2011) with its social-climbing sex worker heroine or *The Hour*'s blend of political thriller and workplace drama set behind the scenes of a 1960s news programme (2011–12).

This spread of scheduling spaces and programme styles illustrates why I chose a thematic approach, rather than a historical or genealogical (Mittell 2004) charting of a genre through developing 'eras'. A chronological approach can straightjacket a genre's televisual variety into dominant 'trends', ignoring the 'unruly diversity' (Monk 2015: 36) of programmes that do not fit into this mould and reinforcing a genre canon. For example, Claire Monk notes that academic histories of the genre ignore the contradictions and challenges of the range of period drama produced across Britain's 'long 1970s' as they cause tensions with tidy narratives of genre development (2015: 30). A thematic approach supported by a collection of case studies allows me to trace the genre's preoccupations, offering space for 'unruly diversity' whilst still highlighting the cultural or industrial context of individual programmes or genre trends. Themed chapters explore period drama's investment in race and nation; class and politics; space and place; gender and sexuality; and bodies and costume. Combining political and cultural analysis with close textual analysis, I draw out the genre's blend of intimate detail and social scope: the fragment and the sweeping gaze.

Aesthetics and formal judgements shape perceptions of period drama as conservative and undynamic. Writing about the British classic serial, Sarah Cardwell charts 'a pervasive generic style' across the 1980s and early 1990s, one drawn from 'highbrow' cinema and serving as a marker of 'quality' (2002: 80). This included 'the use of long-take, extreme long shots of grand buildings, or the preference for slow, smooth tracking shots over alternative shots which are more quickly and painlessly achieved' (Cardwell 2002: 80). This interpretation has solidified into a cultural stereotype of period drama as stilted and distant. This is evident in Jerome de Groot's assertion that 1990s and early 2000s classic serials 'peddle[d] lazy clichés about Englishness and present[ed] history in straightforward, unimaginative, elitist style' (2009: 188). Some programmes may retain such stylistic conventions, such as ITV's achingly conventional *Downton Abbey*, with its message of hierarchical respect and assertions of the importance of social order. However, as Cardwell's analysis of the energetic and bawdy *Fortunes and Misfortunes of Moll Flanders* (ITV, 1996) and gothic *Tenant of Wildfell Hall* (BBC One, 1996) demonstrates, 1990s period drama offered distinctive stylistic interpretations. An 'unruly diversity' of form and aesthetics has continued through the mobile hand-held camera of *Vanity Fair* (BBC One, 1998), the stark compositional imbalances of *The Crimson Petal and the White*, and the hyper-stylised slow motion of *Peaky Blinders* (BBC Two/BBC One, 2013–). This book's analysis illustrates period drama's stylistic diversity and hybridity. As a result, I offer no blanket stylistic or formal markers of genre, because the pleasure is in the divergence.

The weight of heritage

Period drama's position in popular culture blends high culture and the middlebrow. It is coded as prestige television, yet it is simultaneously culturally devalued for its associations with pleasure and its appeal to female audiences. This devaluing is also tied to its investment in the intimate lives of women and their lived histories. It is seen in press critiques of *Call the Midwife* (BBC One, 2012–) as 'cosy', rose-tinted nostalgia, which wilfully ignored the programme's politicised investment in post-war social structures and women's labour (Tincknell 2013: 774–5). The genre has always combined the popular and prestige, showcasing adaptations of classic and popular literature, modernist theatre and original stories. Yet until recently book-length studies of British period drama have tended to follow popular culture's preoccupation with the classic serial as the primary marker of the genre (Giddings and Selby 2000; Cardwell 2002). The classic serial's cultural dominance, together with the heritage debate's narrow focus on literary adaptations in film and television, has resulted in less prestigious period programming being written out of genre history. These are most often romantic dramas targeting female audiences, particularly those adapted from popular historical fiction, including BBC One's 1975 *Poldark* series (which Rachel Moseley (2013) and Julie Anne

Taddeo (2015) have recently explored), 1980s US mini-series such as *The Thornbirds* (ABC, 1984) and ITV's 1990s Catherine Cookson adaptations. Cultural attitudes to these dramas are illustrated by Sarah Cardwell's description of the Cookson adaptations as 'pulp fiction' (2002: 80).

As genre is discursively constructed, it is important to highlight how a set of critical and academic articles from the late 1980s and early 1990s have had a lasting impact on cultural perceptions of period drama. Centred in film studies and influenced by debates in cultural studies, the 'heritage debate' developed from wider press and cultural discussions during the 1980s.[3] It had permeable boundaries and at times folded in ITV dramas *Brideshead Revisited* and *The Jewel and the Crown*, but was focused on a cycle of 1980s and early 1990s 'heritage films' that were often adapted from Edwardian novels, which included *Chariots of Fire* (dir. Hugh Hudson; 1981), *A Passage to India* (dir. David Lean; 1984) and *A Room With a View* (dir. James Ivory; 1985). These 'screen fictions' were read as escapist, regressive reconstructions of the national past (Wollen 1991: 180), shaped by a seductive pictorial style and lavish 'nostalgic gaze' (Higson 2006 [1993]). As I discuss further in Chapter 2, these period dramas were viewed as offering a safe, conservative, elitist image of the British past, one that obscured the nation's pluralist history along with its tensions, contradictions and difficulties. Claire Monk argues that despite 'their frequently international origins, heritage films were conceived as a "genre" *centrally* engaged in the construction of *national* identity' (2002: 179). The heritage debate intersected with Fredric Jameson's (1991) characterisation of America's postmodern 'nostalgia film' as a glossy, depthless play of images of 'pastness' that displaced 'real' history. Jameson was echoed in Andrew Higson's influential 1993 essay that positioned British heritage film as a parade of static, seductive surfaces. Higson (2006 [1993]) argued that these films' fetishised period detail obscured and overwhelmed any social critique present in their narratives.

'Heritage' film and TV is a term at times used interchangeably with 'period drama' (Vidal 2012b), but it is important to recognise it as a critical construct, rather than a genre or cycle. Claire Monk suggests heritage film criticism was 'a historically specific discourse, rooted in and responsive to particular cultural conditions and events' (2002: 178). The heritage debate responded to the vicious polarisation of 1980s British politics and cultural debate, particularly the elitist visions of the national past promoted by Margaret Thatcher's Conservative government (which I discuss further in Chapter 2). Here nationalist political rhetoric blended with an increased commodification of the British past through tourism and preservation activities, which centred the homes and lifestyles of the upper class and aristocracy. This cycle of period dramas was charged with supporting the Thatcherite commodified fantasy of a British national past, one aimed at export and produced during a period of great social inequality and rupture.

Claire Monk highlights the monolithic nature of the heritage debate, where the 'heritage' character of these film and television programmes 'overrode any other possible sites of meaning or (by implication) sources of pleasure' (2012: 18). Significant differences in tone, style and narrative were ignored, and visual pleasure itself seemed to be politically suspect (Monk 2012: 21). By conflating aesthetic and ideological claims, the heritage debate took an ambiguous, non-political aesthetic and read it as a conservative nostalgia (Vidal 2012a: 18). Feminist and queer critics challenged the reductive, binary nature of the heritage debate, arguing its highly gendered critique othered the audience, and read period drama's engagement in formal spectacle, emotion and pleasure as inherently reactionary. They offered a counter-analysis that highlighted the films' tensions, nuances and ambivalence, as well as their sympathetic and detailed chronicling of women's lives and the experiences of lesbian and gay characters (Light 1991; Dyer 2001; Monk 1995, 2001).

Post-heritage and feminist film criticism brought greater nuance to period drama's complex engagement with mise-en-scène, costume and gender. This is seen in Julianne Pidduck's suggestion that the 'characteristic slowness and digression' of many period films and their representations of physical and social constraint are inherently interwoven with their investment in stories of 'female becoming against fraught backgrounds of class and colonial struggle' (2004: 16). Period films are understood as 'fantasy zones for the expression of national identity, gender and sexuality' (Pidduck 2004: 8), a space where 'identities (whether those of characters and nations within the film or the spectators viewing it) are shifting, fluid and heterogeneous' (Monk 1995: 122). Andrew Higson's later work (2003, 2010) assimilated some of these feminist and queer critiques, recognising the ambivalence and tensions present in period drama, whilst maintaining a lingering suspicion of its gendered spectacle.

Changing political backdrops and self-conscious 'post-heritage' (Monk 2001) trends in film and television have complicated the heritage debate's ideological claims. Yet its polemical critique remains an unavoidable part of discussions of period drama (Vidal 2012b: 19) and continues to shape public perceptions of the genre. This book counters the gravitational pull of heritage and nostalgia, which can smooth out period drama's complexity and ambiguity. I blend these established critiques with an intersectional approach that draws on gender and affect-driven readings of the genre from both film and television studies. This includes Julianne Pidduck's (2004) and Belén Vidal's (2012a) readings of affect, mise-en-scène and the intimate gaze as important period drama storytelling devices. I also engage with space and place, looking beyond the heritage debate's 'frozen' house museum and 'nostalgic' pastoral landscapes.

Belén Vidal highlights period reconstruction's balance of realism and spectacle, which are channelled through 'the fragment and the detail' (2012a: 11). Exploring the aesthetic hybridity of a post-1990s cycle of 'mannerist' period film, she suggests that '[r]ather than nostalgia, fantasy and its multiple spatio-temporal displacements might be . . . a more useful compass to guide us through the journeys of period drama' (2012a: 27). Period drama's intimate gaze can draw us close to inspect the fine weave of the past, which is enhanced by the intimacy of the televisual frame. This is seen in the intricate details of a reconstructed country house cleaned spotless by a silent servant's hand, or a crowded city street paved with grit and grime that cake travellers' boots; in the hot breath and sweat of sexually entangled or labouring bodies (in fields and factories as well as childbirth); in the social and emotional weight of a heavily layered dress or hairstyle, a glance, gaze or gesture. These create an 'affective engagement' between the past and the viewer, foregrounding intimacy and emotional histories. But, as Alison Landsberg highlights, whilst this can foster closeness it can also assert the past's alien nature, forcing distance (2015: 10). This push and pull produces a complex encounter, particularly within television's long form serialised storytelling space.

Selective histories

Period drama can rework, invert, challenge or settle comfortably within dominant narratives of the past. It can build partial images of national pasts through forgettings and selective storytelling. Period drama shapes popular understandings of the past, particularly through its representational and storytelling limitations. This contributes to perceptions of the British past as naturally white, compared with a multicultural present. The genre's stories are shaped by who commissions and makes programmes, in an industry with significant disparities in class and gender and a woeful record on race, particularly in the UK. In the late 2010s comments by filmmaker Ken Loach and actor

Riz Ahmed about the representational limitations of British period drama brought these concerns renewed public attention (Loughrey 2016; Singh 2017). These limitations in perspective are compounded by the funding and production practices of the international television market in the era of 'Peak TV'. This term was coined by US television executive John Landgraf to refer to the exponential growth in new US programming from the mid-2010s onwards, driven by the rise in new outlets for television in the age of streaming. Throughout this book, I use 'Peak TV' to periodise the late 2010s television industry and 'TV drama arms race' to refer to the highly competitive global television market of this period (Ryan and Littleton 2017).

In the second half of the 2010s the global television market was awash with a huge amount of programming as new streaming providers like Netflix, Amazon and Apple joined established television outlets in the competition for audiences' attention. This competition and the deep pockets of the international streaming giants have driven budgets and production deals to unsustainable heights in a bid to secure creative personnel and capture the eyes of audiences. The high budgets required for period drama's historical recreations mean that international co-production is now baked into the genre's funding model. This sharing of risk can produce innovative genre interventions in a bid to stand out in a crowded marketplace. However, it can also default to a safe investment, returning to an internationally marketable image of a familiar national past. As I discuss further in Chapter 2, both financing and a lack of diversity in creative personnel limit period drama's ability to produce intersectional histories, stories that challenge dominant national myths built around class, gender and notably race.

This is borne out by the streaming giant Netflix's choice of *The Crown* (2016–) as its first original drama commission from a UK production company, for which it aggressively outbid BBC and ITV, the traditional homes of UK period drama (Dowell 2017). It should be noted that despite its British production team, *The Crown*'s production company Left Bank is owned by Sony (following a period of mergers and acquisitions in the European independent production sector in the late 2010s) and is built on international financing. As a subscription video on demand service (SVOD), Netflix has consistently asserted itself as 'disrupter' of television's existing linear models, a narrative supported by favourable press coverage. The choice of a period drama chronicling the reign of Queen Elizabeth II and the lives of the British royal family, a programme created by white male filmmakers Peter Morgan and Stephen Daldry, could seem an oddly 'traditional' choice for a Netflix flagship programme. The commission made clear that for all its talk of disruption, the SVOD's focus was on British-made content that would draw and maintain subscribers as it expanded internationally. For Netflix this turns out to be period drama from established white male 'auteurs', chronicling white British aristocracy through the second half of the twentieth century.

Marketing and press coverage asserted the programme's prestige (and in turn Netflix's financial and industrial clout) through the much-touted £100 million budget for its first two seasons.[4] As I discuss further in Chapter 4, this financing signalled *The Crown*'s investment in verisimilitude and 'authentic' mise-en-scène, achieved through vast studio sets combined with international location filming. *The Crown*'s status as a flagship Netflix drama thus rested on period drama's possession of those qualities that Charlotte Brunsdon argues serve as '*uncontroversial* indicators of quality': literary source (here, historical fiction produced by film 'auteurs'), 'the best of British acting', money and heritage export value (1990: 85–6). A highly conventional British period drama helped assert an upstart US 'disrupter' as a space of prestige television and facilitated its global expansion.

As *The Crown* showed, where period drama has historically been considered the purview of the British public service broadcasters (a narrative which itself ignores the huge success of US television's historical mini-series), the genre has now become a key part of the international TV drama arms race. The 2010s boom in period drama, with its divergence of style, forms and investments, is shaped by industrial shifts which have been ongoing since the 1990s. These include deregulation, the increase of commercially minded commissioning and production cultures (particularly in British public service broadcasters), an increasingly globalised television industry and fragmenting audiences. Claire Monk suggests that period drama, long 'stereotyped as the preserve of a "discerning," culturally conservative niche audience', has become a mass-market genre (2015: 27). Alongside these industrial shifts came the adoption of self-conscious aesthetics and genre investments aimed at popularising the genre. This push to attract diversified audiences combined with a 'rising tide ... of critical, scholarly, and popular scorn for "heritage" television, "fidelity" adaptation, and the "*Masterpiece*" aesthetic' to push the genre into new directions (Monk 2015: 28). Although as Monk notes, many of these 'new' investments had been present in the period drama of the 1970s.

These post-1990s developments have accelerated in the era of Peak TV, where high-budget prestige drama is used to attract audiences and signal a broadcaster's or SVOD's cultural value (Ryan and Littleton 2017). Period drama is a key genre in this climate, as its high budgets and prestige associations help channels and SVODs worldwide signal their financial investment in drama. A flagship drama's distinctive interpretation of and attitude towards a national past can help signal its brand identity. These shifts have seen a breadth of period programming enter the market, which is reflected in my case studies. These strategically broaden the canon beyond the 1980s and 1990s dramas that have dominated existing scholarship, along with now extensively studied *Downton Abbey* and *Mad Men* (AMC, 2007–15). To keep its corpus manageable, this book focuses on British and US television with some address to Europe. However, the period drama boom has been international, in some cases continuing long-standing national television legacies. For example, East Asian period drama complicates the genre's links to prestige TV in the West, with the dominant markets of China and South Korea producing a wide range of popular historical drama and soap operas (Zhu 2005; Kim 2014). Lack of access to programmes and limited English-language scholarship on East Asian period drama has prevented me addressing this significant market. But this is a growing area of study, particularly as SVOD acquisitions begin to make these dramas more globally available.

Accessibility shapes my choice of case studies. Claire Monk warns of the losses to histories of period drama caused by 'short-termist amnesia', fed by 'the uneven selectivity of popular, critical, and institutional memory in relation to this history' (2015: 29). This is exacerbated by 'institutional marginalisation' of programmes whose recordings were wiped, or remain unreleased on VHS or DVD (Monk 2015: 31), and the further narrowing of available programmes in the streaming era. To facilitate this book's use for teaching, I have chosen case studies that are all available to view at the time of writing, but the chapter's wider discussions reflect the breadth of period drama in a bid to counter this amnesia.[5]

Where do I draw my historical boundaries of period drama? *The Crown* illustrates how recent years have seen the genre embrace the second half of the twentieth century, events within living memory of many audience members. In the UK this was catalysed by BBC drama executive Ben Stephenson's 2009 decision to refocus a portion of the corporation's period drama commissions towards the twentieth century. This was interpreted in the British press as 'the death of the bonnet' (Holmwood 2009), illustrating how popular perceptions of the genre were built around adaptations of classic nineteenth-century literature and preoccupied with feminine, intricately costumed, restraint.

Stephenson commissioned, amongst others, an adaptation of Andrea Levy's 2004 Windrush novel *Small Island* (BBC One, 2009) and *Call the Midwife*, adapted from Jennifer Worth's memoirs of her working life in the East End of London. These incorporated Afro-Caribbean and working-class women's experiences of post-war London into period drama's fold.

I include twentieth-century period dramas in this book and draw my boundaries at the 1980s. In the 2010s there was a marked turn towards the decade in British, US and European period drama. The 1980s now exists at thirty years' distance, allowing the era to be re-presented anew to audiences. Collective cultural memory has periodised the decade and solidified it into a set of cultural markers – costumes, cultural events and objects – that can quickly define a programme's setting. In turn, many of the decade's defining events speak closely to current cultural and political experiences. Many of these dramas rely on familiar popular cultural and political markers of the decade as a gateway for exploring less familiar perspectives, from East German espionage in *Deutschland 83* (RTL/Sundance TV, 2015), to the development of personal computing in *Halt and Catch Fire* (AMC, 2014–17), to New York's drag ball scene in *Pose* (FX, 2018–).

Shape of the book

The chapters that follow are organised by theme. Chapter 2 explores race and nation, highlighting period drama's ability to challenge or reinforce the images and myths that inform national identity. It questions whose past gets recreated and whose perspectives get centred. Case studies *Indian Summers* (Channel 4, 2015–16) and *Beecham House* (ITV, 2019) explore English encounters with India, and *Underground* (WGN, 2016–17) considers US period drama's representations of enslaved people.

Chapter 3 explores period drama's investment in class and politics. It considers the genre's potential to offer classed and feminist counter-histories by engaging with lived experience and the everyday as politicised narratives. Its case studies are *Shoulder to Shoulder* (BBC Two, 1974), *The Mill* (Channel 4, 2013–14), *North & South* (BBC One, 2004) and *Call the Midwife* (BBC One, 2012–).

Chapter 4 bridges the previous two and final two chapters, with its focus on space and place complicating the well-established critical frames of heritage, nostalgia, nation and class to approach period drama from new angles. It examines period drama's 'grand house', its rural spaces, and the city, with two case studies offering different interpretations of twentieth-century New York, *The Marvelous Mrs. Maisel* (Amazon Prime Video, 2017–) and *The Deuce* (HBO, 2017–19).

Chapter 5 is the first of two chapters that draw most prominently on feminist and queer perspectives on period drama to consider its affective, embodied experience of the past. Exploring gender and sexuality, it traces the genre's recent investment in women at work as well as the violent masculinities of action-adventures and crime thrillers, with the latter including a case study of *Peaky Blinders* (BBC Two/BBC One, 2013–). A look at queer desire in Victorian worlds includes discussions of *Fingersmith* (BBC One, 2005), *The Secret Diaries of Miss Anne Lister* (BBC Two, 2010) and *Gentleman Jack* (HBO/BBC One, 2019). The chapter concludes with a case study of *Pose* (FX, 2018–).

Chapter 6's focus on bodies and costume draws out tactile encounters with the past and considers the role of desire and pleasure, shaped by the genre's investment in constraint and release. Its case studies are *The Crimson Petal and the White* (BBC Two, 2011), *Outlander* (Starz, 2014–) and *Dickinson* (Apple TV+, 2019–).

Chapter 7 offers a brief conclusion, tying together the book's main threads of argument and considering recent developments in the genre as we move into the 2020s.

Notes

1. I choose the term 'prestige', used by US industry and television critics, over the academically prevalent 'quality television' because it more effectively signals 'prestige' as a construct, whereas 'quality' has the risk of signalling an innate value judgement. For more on the hierarchies and gendered discourse built into the term 'quality', see Newman and Levine (2011).
2. For example, Austen's *Pride and Prejudice* (1813) has been adapted for television six times (1938, 1952, 1958, 1967, 1980, 1995), and in 2017 ITV announced the commission of a new adaptation for future broadcast.
3. I use this term to refer to critiques that spread across journalism and academic work in film, sociology, history and cultural studies. See Monk (2002) and Vidal (2012b) for detailed charting of the nuances of this debate.
4. Prior to this era of Peak TV and the related escalation of drama budgets, the average price for US network drama was $3 million an hour. Looking back to the 1990s the budget for BBC One's 1995 adaptation of *Pride and Prejudice* was an at the time blockbusting £6 million.

5. I include a case study of suffragette serial *Shoulder to Shoulder* (BBC Two, 1974), which has remained unavailable for home viewing on DVD or streaming, as in 2019 it was added to the British educational streaming service Box of Broadcasts.

2 Race and Nation

This chapter explores one of the main frames through which period drama has been discussed, national identity, and considers the place of race in 'narratives of nation'. I use this phrase to recognise national identity as an (at times contested) process, and to allow me to incorporate different countries' programming into my discussion. Each country's national identity is shaped through different ideologies, histories and myths. Like history, national identity is always a narrative, created by stories we tell or are told about our nation's past. To draw on Stuart Hall, rather than thinking about national identity as an 'already accomplished historical fact' which period drama then represents, we should think of national identity 'as a "production", which is never complete, always in process' (1989: 68). Period drama can contribute to this production in process, as television is a 'primary site where the nation is imagined and imagines itself' (Malik 2001: 2). But period drama is a 'stage of competing memories and desires' (Vidal 2012a: 47). It can offer conservative visions of the past that are aligned with the status quo, contributing to myths of nation that mobilise the dangerous, non-existent 'phantom homeland' of nostalgia (Boym 2001: xvi). However, it also has the potential to present 'histories hitherto excluded from the national imaginary' (Burton 2017: 79) and explore tensions, critique or rewrite our perspectives on our national pasts, producing a playful or forceful challenge to myths of nation.

John Caughie suggests that '[t]he past and our relationship to it is not entirely stable nor is it lacking in its own contradictions and tensions' (2000: 212). Period drama's engagement with 'narratives of nation' often embodies these contradictions and tensions. It frequently struggles to bridge the competing concerns of social critique, disruption and difference on the one hand and marketability through familiar imagery and genre tropes on the other, with the latter blunting the force of the former. National identity provides a prime space to consider the racial investments of period drama. Who gets to be part of a country's narrative of nation? Whose history gets to be dramatised and through which perspective? Throughout this chapter I highlight the relationship between industry and ideology, showing how period drama's industrial contexts can shape and delimit the images it presents and stories it tells.

This chapter briefly sets out how the 'heritage debate' connects with national identity, thinking about how British period drama is charged with offering up a certain image of national identity for export. I then move to discuss international co-production and export, which are necessary components of period drama's funding due to its high budgets. As period drama's narratives of nation are in part shaped by these co-production partners and the export market, this can impact attempts to challenge familiar narratives. I sketch out the long transatlantic relationship British period drama has with US broadcaster PBS through its *Masterpiece Theatre* strand, then discuss European broadcasters' strategic use of period drama to compete internationally in the Peak TV era. This chapter's case studies consider British and US period drama's engagement with Black and South Asian experience, considering how this can contribute to and counter the centring of whiteness in narratives of nation.[1] I explore depictions of British colonial encounters with India with particular focus on how *Indian Summers* (Channel 4, 2015–16) and *Beecham House* (ITV, 2019) attempt to counter British period drama's colonial narratives of the region. I then look at how US period drama has presented the experiences of enslaved people following the blockbusting 1970s success of *Roots* (ABC, 1977). I position *Underground* (WGN, 2016–17) as a part of a wave of revisionist slavery stories in 2010s North American culture, looking at how it seeks to counter established narratives of enslaved lives in the antebellum South.

Heritage and nation

National identity was a key focus of the heritage debate, which charged period film and television with reducing British culture to a 'fantasy of Englishness, a fantasy of the national past' (Higson 2006 [1993]: 96). However, whiteness went largely unspoken in these critiques' preoccupation with class and nation, which 'did not devote too much space to the legacies of "race"' (Littler 2005: 5). Higson and others argued that these films and programmes projected a sanitised, nostalgic and marketable version of English national identity.[2] This vision of the past ignored fractured and contested narratives of nation in favour of a narrow, idealised upper-class 'Englishness', one aligned with the nationalist rhetoric promoted by the Conservative government of the 1980s and early 1990s. This was a commodified image of Britain's past that proved highly exportable in the international film and television markets, offering 'a certain image of England and Englishness (with little reference to the rest of Britain), in which national identity is expressed through class and imperial identity' (Brunsdon 1990: 86).

The heritage debate aligned period drama with the 1980s development of the British tourism and heritage industries. Both were viewed as privileging aristocratic lifestyles and houses in shaping an elite, conservative, saleable image of the national past. John Caughie suggests that '[a]t a time when Britain struggled to sell much else on the international market, it became particularly adept at selling the past' (2000: 208). The tourist pull of aristocratic properties such as *Downton Abbey* (ITV, 2010–15) location Highclere Castle – whose visitor numbers doubled following the programme's blockbusting international success (Brown 2015) – illustrates how period drama interweaves with the tourist industry's commodification of certain 'seductive' images of a national past. The mutual influence of the British tourist, film and television industries sees the preserved spaces of the heritage industry used as locations for period dramas. These buildings help assert programmes' historical authenticity and in turn the programmes help draw tourists to these sites. In recent decades the heritage industry's 'packaging of the past' has been expanded beyond the aristocratic mansions and estates celebrated by the Thatcher government, and now includes the industries and lives of working-class Britain. These have also been used as locations for period drama, with *The Mill* (Channel 4, 2013–14) filming at and drawing on the archives of Quarry Bank Mill in Cheshire (a National Trust property) and *Call the Midwife* (BBC One, 2012–) filming its exteriors in Chatham's Historic Dockyards museum in Kent.

As this book demonstrates, period drama has at times attempted to build a more complicated and questioning relationship with national identity. However, the dominant cultural status and significant export value of *Downton Abbey* indicates the persistent marketability of seductive images of aristocratic privilege and conservative narratives of nation. As Rosalía Baena and Christa Byker highlight, the country estate retains 'a powerful influence on the process of re-imagining Englishness' (2015: 264). Centred on the might and plight of the country estate, *Downton Abbey* asserts itself as 'a very powerful symbol of nationality and a heritage worth sacrificing for and preserving' (Baena and Byker 2015: 263). The programme illustrates how period drama intertwines with myths of nation, as the estate 'deliberately functions as a microcosm for the state' (Byrne 2014: 315). Its focus on a class-stratified household benevolently overseen by the aristocratic Lord Grantham communicates a preference for 'a hierarchical and patriarchal' organisation of British society (Byrne 2014: 315). This is significant as the programme debuted during a period of severe recession and stark income inequality in the UK, overseen by a Conservative coalition government whose Cabinet featured many politicians from aristocratic backgrounds. Katherine Byrne suggests that, despite its setting within an Edwardian era rife with social and cultural instability, *Downton*'s benevolent aristocratic household offers 'comforting cohesion and inclusion' (2014: 325). As I discuss further in Chapter 3, its upstairs–downstairs narrative includes working-class staff in its ensemble. However, the staff's narratives are structured within a narrative perspective whose sympathies lie with their employers and the concerns of their social class. The programme consistently challenges yet ultimate reasserts the power of a 'secure world of an earlier Englishness' (Craig 2001), an ideologically conservative narrative of nation.

Export and national identity

Export and international co-production play an essential role in the production of high-budget period drama like *Downton Abbey*. However, this funding model complicates narratives of nation. John Caughie warns of the dangers of 'reading a national identity out of images which function both as cultural representations *and* as tradeable goods' (2000: 208–9). International export has been part of the funding model of British period drama since the 1960s, whether through acquisitions of completed programmes or co-financing (where financial commitment comes in post-production or with little creative involvement). This was accelerated in the 1990s ratings-driven broadcasting culture where a more commercially minded BBC recognised period drama's value as an internationally saleable commodity (Cooke 2003: 177). This resulted in an industrial shift towards co-production (where financial commitment comes previous to production, with creative involvement), which bolstered budgets and produced a boom in classic serials that lasted into the 2010s. A few flagship British period dramas have been produced without international partners, such as BBC One's *North & South* (2004) and Channel 4's *The Mill*. Notably both dramas depict the struggle of working-class lives in Northern mill towns, a less exportable vision of the national past. (I discuss both programmes further in Chapter 3.)

The export value of British period drama has been shaped by a long-standing transnational distribution and co-financing relationship with the US public television service PBS. Its long-running anthology drama strand *Masterpiece Theatre* (renamed *Masterpiece* in 2008) has built its brand around the curation of imported British prestige drama. It later moved to co-finance and eventually co-produce these dramas, with *Downton Abbey* its biggest hit (Hilmes 2019). Produced by PBS's Boston affiliate station WGBH, *Masterpiece Theatre* debuted in 1971 with the 1969 BBC Two serial *The First Churchills*. This drama chronicled the late seventeenth-century lives of the Duke and Duchess of Marlborough and indicated the type of programming WGBH and PBS thought would appeal to their target audience. The strand has become synonymous with a 'safe', conservative taste for British prestige drama that is 'well acted, well crafted, attentive to detail and measured in its pacing . . . offering "the best of the past"' (Knox 2012: 31). However, Simone Knox suggests *Masterpiece Theatre* exhibits a tension between this homogenising 'heritage brand shorthand' and the actual range and diversity of its imports (2012: 34). These have included contemporary dramas and period dramas that problematise charges of 'nostalgic escapism', such as the Roman political intrigue of *I, Claudius* (BBC Two, 1976) (although this was edited for sex and violence) and the suffragette drama *Shoulder to Shoulder* (BBC Two, 1974), as well as post-heritage literary adaptations including *The Fortunes and Misfortunes of Moll Flanders* (ITV, 1996) and the controversial 1996 BBC One adaptation of *The Tenant of Wildfell Hall* (Knox 2012: 39; Monk 2015: 30).

Yet overall, *Masterpiece* maintains a brand of 'safe', conservative period drama. As my discussion of *Indian Summers* in this chapter shows, the *Masterpiece* brand can be at odds with attempts to challenge established narratives of nation. Its branding subsumes programmes from a range of UK broadcasters targeted at different demographics – from populist ITV dramas such as *Downton Abbey* to more challenging adaptations of experimentally tinged literature such as BBC Two's *Parade's End* (2012) – into a single articulation of prestige Britishness for the US market. Period drama contributes to how 'the nation is imagined and imagines itself' (Malik 2001: 2), yet its narratives of nation are shaped by the tastes of the international marketplace. The economics of the 2010s TV drama arms race exacerbated this issue, as national broadcasters (the traditional producers of period drama) had to compete with the deep pockets and international power of aggressive US SVODs. Co-production with US channels, SVODs or patchworks of European funders is now the standard model of funding all British prestige drama, not only period drama.[3] The national identity of period drama has become increasingly murky. However, this expanded market enables British broadcasters to look beyond *Masterpiece*, pairing with US cable channels whose brand identities are built on more challenging prestige drama, such as AMC, FX and HBO (and increasingly the broad audience targeting SVODs). These partnerships can support the production of period dramas that potentially contest established narratives of narration.

The lengthy history and international export of BBC and ITV period drama has tied the genre to certain articulations of Britishness. However, period drama has long been a part of US and European television industries, notably in the guise of 'historical drama' such as US multigenerational slavery drama *Roots* and *Heimat* (ARD, 1984), the German epic of twentieth-century village life. In the highly competitive television market of the 2010s international broadcasters looked to high-budget period drama to assert their national distinction both at home and in export, seeking to compete with Peak TV's flood of exported US prestige drama. Period drama is now a strategic, transnational genre, which allows different national industries to 'turn to the past at different moments in their histories in search of their own foundational myths' (Vidal 2012b: 3). Like in the UK, European broadcasters have shaped their national pasts through a dual national and international perspective. Unfamiliar national pasts can offer novelty and exoticism for international audiences, whilst period drama's familiar genre elements lessen the cultural discount (Hoskins and Mirus 1988) of subtitled programming. However, this dual address can raise concerns over homogenisation or the selective interpretation of distinct national identities for the international market.

Two recent European period dramas illustrate similar yet distinct approaches to mobilising the national past for export. *Versailles* (Canal+, 2015–18) debuted on BBC Two in the summer of 2016 in a swirl of performatively scandalised yet leering press reports documenting its sexual explicitness (with the *Daily Mail* branding it 'Primetime Porn' (Murfitt 2016)). Although press headlines labelled it a 'BBC drama', this was an acquisition of a French production devised explicitly for export to an international audience. A heavily fictionalised biographical drama about seventeenth-century French King Louis XIV, *Versailles* is a blend of royal romp and political thriller in the vein of Showtime's *The Tudors* (2007–10). Presenting a hyper-stylised imagining of an extravagant royal court immersed in sex, violence and political intrigue, it depicts the king as a Machiavellian twenty-something in the process of building the Palace of Versailles. The programme was seen as a defensive move by French broadcasters against the encroaching power of US-owned SVODs (Snoddy 2016). A French–Canadian co-production that aired on subscription channel Canal+ in France, *Versailles* was the most expensive drama made in France to date, at £25 million for season one's ten episodes. The production was built on strategic choices aimed at export. It was filmed in France but was created by British writers and starred European actors, with a British lead. It was shot in English, as English-language productions could draw twice as much from international buyers than French-language programmes (Sweney 2017). The strategy paid off as *Versailles* was eventually sold to 136 territories (Snoddy 2016).

A similar strategy informed the production choices of German period drama *Babylon Berlin* (Sky One/ARD, 2017–), made with international export in mind. But unlike the English-language *Versailles*, this was a German-language production, a noir thriller set in Weimer Republic-era Berlin. A rare co-production between subscription channel Sky Deutschland and national broadcaster ARD, *Babylon Berlin* was Germany's most expensive series ever, with a £33 million budget for its initial two eight-episode seasons. The project gambled on an increase in international interest in German history and German-language drama indicated by the 2015 international success of spy thriller *Deutschland 83* (RTL/Sundance TV, 2015), which followed a young East German soldier forced to become a spy in 1980s West Germany. *Deutschland 83* was a US–German co-production, debuting on the Sundance cable channel months before its German broadcast on RTL. It was more successful internationally than in Germany, suggesting a misalignment in its dual address (Oltermann 2016; Roxborough 2015).

Rather than attempt to appeal to international co-producers, who may have skewed its dense exploration of a pivotal moment in German history, *Babylon Berlin* kept funding within Germany. This was seen as a risky commercial venture, particularly for a complex German-language noir that confronted the country's dark past (Connolly 2017). Adapted from the crime novels of Volker Kutscher by a trio of German writer-directors (including film director Tom Twyker), the series follows German detective Gereon Rath who is brought to Berlin to investigate political corruption. Set in 1929, it explores the final throes of the Weimar Republic's fragile democracy. Its criminal underworld, glamourous nightclubs and opulent parties sit alongside depictions of extreme poverty and massacres of political activists. The social and political tensions that would pave the way for Hitler's Third Reich offered parallels with the rise of the 'populist' far right

in mid-2010s Europe and the US. As the programme began development in 2013 this was unplanned, but co-writer and co-director Henk
Handloegten explained that eventually '[t]he world seemed to be
catching up to our scripts' (Roxborough 2018). This illustrates how
period drama can speak to the present by tracing (at times unwittingly)
connections with a national past. Both *Versailles* and *Babylon Berlin*
drew on the international cultural reputations of their countries of
origin – a sex- and nudity-filled French royal romp and a decadent,
German expressionist-infused noir thriller – to shape a vision of their
national pasts for an international prestige audience.

National identity, power and race

I have highlighted how period drama's narratives of nation can be
shaped by industrial context and the influence of the export market.
These also arguably contribute to the overwhelming whiteness of the
representations of the national past in British and US period drama.
Stephen Bourne argues that Black history is largely invisible in British
period film, making 'whiteness' an unspoken genre marker (2002: 49).
Sarita Malik (2001) and James Burton (2017) have shown this extends
to television. If Black and South Asian histories are sidelined in British
and US period drama, then they are excluded from national identity.
This is because national identity is built from cultural representations
that bind the individual to the national story, so 'those who cannot
see themselves reflected in its mirror cannot properly "belong"' (Hall
2005: 22). This creates a cultural divide with a British past imagined
as white and a present defined by multiculturalism (Naidoo and Littler
2003).

These absences are compounded by the lack of diversity in British
and US television's creative and executive ranks, particularly at the
British public service channels and US subscription cable channels that
produce the bulk of internationally circulated prestige television. Here
Black and Asian writers remain trapped in a multicultural present and
are not given the tools to challenge visions of a white national past. For
example, the large budgets and co-production financing of UK-led
prestige drama creates a risk-averse climate that sees executives rely
on a small pool of experienced 'name' writers (Dams 2016). The need
for a safe pair of (white, largely male) hands to steer prestige projects
sees the same limited perspectives shape period drama's narratives of
nation.

We can also consider how history is 'narrated from the viewpoint
of the colonisers' (Hall 2005: 25). There is much selective cultural

amnesia about British and US national histories. To return to certain parts of these national pasts and events which shape national identity is to reckon with the trauma and violence from which these nations' power and empires were built. Period drama offers the potential to reconfigure our understanding of the past by discovering new stories and perspectives. Yet this chapter's case studies illustrate the challenging nature of this for a white-dominated, capitalist industry, even into the 2010s. Is there space for post-colonial period drama to challenge the centring of whiteness in the imagined communities of the past? Or to consider Black and South Asian histories beyond the limited narratives of slavery and service, colonialism and civil rights? Can period drama respond to Stuart Hall's challenge to revise mainstream versions of 'heritage' by rewriting 'the margins into the centre, the outside into the inside' (2005: 28)? Or will whiteness remain an unspoken genre marker?

Engaging with Black and South Asian history

As Stuart Hall notes, 'what the nation "means" is an on-going project, under constant reconstruction' (2005: 23). Black British history has been regarded as a segregated, 'ghettoised' narrative, one that positions 'The Windrush story' of the mid-twentieth-century migration of Commonwealth subjects as a mythic beginning for Black British history (Olusoga 2016). British period drama's limited depictions of Black British history have contributed to this shaping of national identity. The genre could respond to Hall's challenge to offer 'imaginative responses' that construct a more inclusive idea of Britishness by recognising '[t]he African presence in Britain since the sixteenth century, the Asian since the seventeenth century and the Chinese, Jewish and Irish in the nineteenth' (2005: 28). Rachel Carroll's (2019) discussion of *The Sailor's Return* (dir. Jack Gold; 1978) demonstrates period drama's potential to challenge received understandings of the British past. Part of ITV's *Armchair Theatre* strand, this single drama is adapted from David Garnett's 1925 novel. Set in early Victorian England, it follows Tulip, an 'African Princess' brought to England by her British sailor husband. Through Tulip's experience of England, her marital struggles and the hostilities of her new Dorset community, the drama recognises Britain's colonial role in the Black diaspora. Carroll suggests it challenges 'dominant narratives of English history' through Tulip's insertion into rural landscapes of Dorset, 'contesting the equation of Englishness with "whiteness"' (2019: 216). Yet this promise largely went unfulfilled in the decades that followed.

British period drama's encounter with the nation's colonial past has been dominated by the British Raj in India.[4] The empire's West Indian presence has received little attention beyond Dominica-set *The Orchid House* (Channel 4, 1991), whose narrative centres on the fading fortunes of a white plantation-owning family in the 1920s and 1930s. Windrush dramas *The Final Passage* (Channel 4, 1996) and *Small Island* (BBC One, 2009) also make Britain's colonial history visible through the trans-Atlantic journeys of their Caribbean protagonists, who hold an idealised vision of the Commonwealth 'mother country' (Mead 2009). These dramas integrate Black British history into narratives of post-war nationhood, and I discuss *Small Island* further in Chapter 4. *The Long Song* (BBC One, 2018) offers a rare centring of a Black enslaved protagonist in British period drama, countering cultural amnesia over the plantation history of the nation's West Indian colonies. A neo-slave narrative (Rushdy 1999) adapted from Andrea Levy's novel, the adaptation paired a white writer (Sarah Williams) and Black director (Mahalia Bello), offering some progression from *Small Island*'s all-white creative team. The drama follows the playfully defiant July, a house slave on a Jamaican sugar plantation ruled by her grotesque white mistress Caroline. It traces July's journey through the slave uprisings of 1831, charting the chaotic impact of the Empire's emancipation of the country's slaves.

The limited representations of Black and South Asian history in British and US period drama leads to a burden of representation on those programmes that do get produced. This was seen in the controversy surrounding John Ridley's *Guerrilla* (Showtime/Sky Atlantic, 2017), a US–UK co-production from a Black American writer which charted Britain's Black revolutionary movement in the 1970s through the perspective of a Black and South Asian couple. A rare Black-led period drama exploring an under-examined part of Black British past, Ridley's project drew fire for a perceived writing-out of Black women's role in the movement (Mohamed 2017). This was a doubly pained event due to the absence of Black women's voices in period drama. The genre's investment in women's voices and struggles against gendered barriers is rarely intersectional. James Burton traces the peripheral presence of Black, South and East Asian stories in *The Hour* (BBC Two, 2011–12), *The Bletchley Circle* (ITV, 2012–14) and *Call the Midwife* (BBC One, 2012–), contrasting this with these programmes' progressive gender politics. These dramas are set in a decade that saw Britain's Black population increase from 'an estimated 74,5000 in 1951 to 336,000 by the end of 1959' (Burton 2017: 72). Drawing on Allison Perlman's (2011) work exploring the peripheral black presence in *Mad Men*'s

(AMC, 2007–15) 1960s Manhattan advertising world, Burton notes the 'complex and somewhat contradictory ways' these British programmes deal with race, if at all (2017: 72). The earlier seasons of *Call the Midwife* offered limited depiction of the Commonwealth and immigrant communities of its London East End setting. But from season four onwards Burton identifies more developed characterisations that potentially reassert 'histories hitherto excluded from the national imaginary' (2017: 70). In season seven (set in 1963) the programme introduced West Indian midwife Lucille to its ensemble, belatedly recognising the contributions of Commonwealth nurses in the early years of the National Health Service (NHS). (I discuss *Call the Midwife* further in Chapter 3's case study and Lucille's journey in Chapter 4.)

In 2019 the US television industry showed glimmers of interest in expanding its representation of the national past to include untold stories of East Asian experience in hybrid period dramas. The action-adventure series *Warrior* (2019–) aired on pay cable channel Cinemax and moved to the streaming service HBO Max in 2021. The martial arts crime drama chronicles Chinese gang conflict in 1870s San Francisco. The second season of AMC's period horror anthology *The Terror* (2018–19) counters Second World War myths of the 'Greatest Generation' by following a Japanese American family who are imprisoned in a Californian internment camp following the attack on Pearl Harbor. The series considers the suddenly tenuous grasp minorities can have on national identity; a fear made intensely topical through the ideologies and policies of the Trump administration. It is interesting that both these representations of East Asian American experience frame this history within familiar East Asian genres of martial arts and folk horror. As my case study of *Underground* shows, US period drama seems more comfortable exploring Black and Asian experience through a frame of genre hybridity.

I now explore the intersection of race and nation in British and US period drama through two case studies. I consider the genre's investment in British encounters with India, focusing in detail on *Indian Summers* and *Beecham House*. I then examine US period drama's depiction of the lives of enslaved people in the antebellum South through an analysis of *Underground*. These programmes can give voice to those 'othered' in dominant narratives of nation and counter selective amnesia over the institutional oppression of colonialism and slavery. Yet as I demonstrate, any reckoning with the darkness of these nations' contested histories can sit in tension with period drama's production contexts and the long-standing centring of whiteness within the national imaginary.

India, Britain and the Empire

Stuart Hall posits that empire and colonialism are built into British national identity. He argues that '[t]he very notion of "greatness" in Great Britain is inextricably bound up with its imperial destiny' and colonisation, slavery and empire are 'deeply intertwined' with the everyday life of all classes of Britons (2005: 24–5). The political discourses of 1980s Thatcherism and the 2010s Brexit campaign mobilised myths of Britain's empire and its colonial past for Conservative political gain. However, these narratives of nation engaged in a selective historical amnesia over how Britain maintained its colonial power (Gilroy 2004).

A selection of recent British period dramas make visible the international reach of the nation's empire. Colonial dramas *Jamestown* (Sky One, 2017–19) and *Banished* (BBC Two, 2015) explore the struggles of settlers and convicts in seventeenth-century America and eighteenth-century Australia, respectively. The London-set *Taboo* (BBC One, 2017–) critiques the violent control of the East India Company across the Victorian empire. Europe's colonial exploitation of Africa haunts the shifting class dynamics of Edwardian society in Kenneth Lonergan's adaptation of *Howards End* (BBC One/Starz, 2017). *The Promise* (Channel 4, 2011) (which blends narrative strands set in present and post-Second World War Israel and Palestine) and *The Last Post* (BBC One, 2017) depict the British military's mid-century entanglement in the Middle East. The majority of these programmes attempt a degree of colonial critique, yet they centre white protagonists; the moral weight of empire is theirs to reckon with (if at all). Indeed, Australia's Aboriginal population is entirely absent from *Banished*'s vision of the British colony. British period dramas set in India consistently include non-white ensemble members, yet these programmes display an ambivalent engagement with the colonial project.

The British Raj has been the dominant colonial narrative in British period drama, presented largely through the perspective of the colonisers. Before I move on to my case studies of two 2010s India-set dramas, *Indian Summers* and *Beecham House*, it is useful to set out some of the ideological and narrative preoccupations of two 1984 India-set period dramas that were part of the 1980s 'Raj revival' (Rushdie 1992: 87). The ambivalent investments of *The Far Pavilions* (Channel 4, 1984) and *The Jewel in the Crown* remain present in *Indian Summers* and *Beecham House*, despite these programmes' ostensibly progressive goals. Paul Gilroy suggests Britain's amnesia over empire means the trauma and violence of imperialism has not been confronted or worked through; as a result, certain narratives of empire are returned to obsessively, 'recycled as fantasy', a 'lost greatness ... fleetingly restored' (quoted in Jeffries 2015). Raj revival dramas illustrate this cultural amnesia over the violence and oppression that maintained Britain's empire. Despite British period drama's frequent returns to the Victorian era, only *The Far Pavilions* is set during the height of the Victorian empire's colonial power. *Beecham House* is set in pre-Raj India of 1795, with the ascendant commercial coloniser the East India Company spoken of but unseen. *The Jewel in the Crown* and *Indian Summers* take place as British rule is coming to an end, with the colonial project given an air of impotent melancholy. Raj revival dramas rarely reckon with the trauma and violence of British imperialist reign.

Broadcast within weeks of each other in 1984, *The Far Pavilions* and *The Jewel in the Crown* joined films such as *Heat and Dust* (dir. James Ivory; 1983) and *A Passage to India* (dir. David Lean; 1984) in a 'Raj revival' trend that extended to food culture and home furnishing. The heritage debate connected the Raj revival with the nationalist rhetoric the Thatcher government had mobilised in response to the 1982 Falklands War. A political narrative of mythic Britishness evoked the country's colonial past in a conflict over a distant colonial outpost (Wollen 1991; Higson 2006 [1993]: 107). These film and television narratives are imbued with ambivalence, as their critiques of the empire's racial and political injustices are blended with the visual pleasures of an exoticised encounter with the colonial past (Oliete-Aldea 2015: 2).

The Far Pavilions is a four-part US–Italian–British co-production that aired on Channel 4 in the UK. Adapted from M. M. Kaye's 1978 historical fiction set at the end of the nineteenth century, it follows the adventures of Ash, a white British man who is immersed in Indian culture. Raised by an Indian family, he maintains a hybrid identity and marries Anjuli, a biracial Indian princess whose hybrid identity also makes her an outsider. Anjuli is played by a white American actress in brownface, a casting choice criticised at the time of broadcast. Hybrid and outsider identities are a feature of Raj revival narratives, distancing white leads (and by association, the audience) from the cruelties of colonial society (Oliete-Aldea 2015). The programme embodies bell hooks's assertion that 'imperialist nostalgia' presents a 'narrative fantasy of power and desire, of seduction by the Other' (1992: 25). Its adventure narrative and lush visual style evoke the empire adventure films of the 1930s and 1940s, which featured orientalist portrayals of the East as a 'place where Westerners' fantasies can be fulfilled'

(Oliete-Aldea 2015: 157). The orientalist adventure spectacle of *The Far Pavilions* was poorly received, particularly as press response contrasted its 'Hollywood' melodrama with the 'restrained' realist style and complex narrative of *The Jewel in the Crown*.

Broadcast on ITV and made by the same production company as the channel's 1981 hit period drama *Brideshead Revisited*, *The Jewel in the Crown* is adapted from Paul Scott's historical fiction *The Raj Quartet*. It is set amongst the families of the white British officer class during the last five years of British rule and concludes with the violence of Partition in 1947. *Jewel's* slow-moving and relatively sprawling story is initially centred on Hari, an Indian-born, English-educated man, and his brief romance with Daphne, an awkward, independent white English woman (serving as the proto-feminist heroine of period drama). Both are recently arrived in India and are positioned as outsiders, with Hari finding himself ignored by the whites he views as his countrymen (Oliete-Aldea 2015: 179). Hari's hybridity makes the Indian protagonist easier for British white audiences to identify with, as his upper-class 'English' identity presents him as an exception amongst an Indian community largely depicted as violent or voiceless (Oliete-Aldea 2015: 179).

At the time of its broadcast, *Jewel* was largely received as a liberal, anti-colonial narrative, critical of the Raj and its failings. However, as Sarita Malik asserts, 'it is worth asking liberal to whom, by whose standards and in comparison to what?' (2001: 145). Richard Dyer suggests that *Jewel* does not really critique the validity of British colonial rule; instead, it critiques imperialism's failure (1996: 227). Rather than depict violence and racism as embedded in the colonial systems and the upper-class men who maintain them, *Jewel* 'evades white complicity in imperialism' (Dyer 1996: 238). It focalises colonial violence and racism through the figure of Hari's abusive tormentor, police captain Ronald Merrick, a lower-middle-class English 'grammar school boy' and closeted gay man. Dyer notes that like other decline-of-empire texts, *Jewel* centres the blame for imperialism's failure on white women. The wives and daughters of British Raj society embody the institution's casual racism and social cruelties. The programme's liberal white protagonists Daphne, Sarah and Guy are depicted as helpless and impotent when faced with the cruelty and oppression of the Empire, as embodied in the repeated phrase 'There's nothing I can do!' (Dyer 1996: 226).

The cross-cultural romances of *The Far Pavilions* and *Jewel* are a recurrent feature of Raj revival narratives, embodying both their liberal perspectives and their edge of orientalised exoticism. *Jewel's* English–Indian romance ends in violence, a punishment for the couple

venturing beyond their racial boundaries. In events which catalyse
the serial's remaining narrative, Daphne is raped (and later dies in
childbirth) and Hari is falsely imprisoned for the crime. The tensions
between *Jewel*'s liberal, critical perspective and the conservatism
present in its storytelling and representational choices extend to the
2010s explorations of British encounters with India.

Indian Summers

Indian Summers chronicles the tail end of the British Raj, through
a largely Raj-critical perspective with elements of ambivalence.
Debuting in 2015, the Channel 4 drama was created by white writer
Paul Rutman, inspired by family travels in India. Its two seasons are
set in the town of Simla during the summers of 1932 and 1935. This
town in the foothills of the Himalayas was the summer home of the
government of the British Raj, who each year transferred their opera-
tions and families there to escape the Delhi heat. The programme
charts the racial and class dynamics of this community, which includes
civil servants and their families, club owners, missionaries and tea
planters. Indian civil servant Aafrin is positioned as its narrative pivot,
straddling the worlds of the rulers and the ruled. Aafrin works for
Ralph Whelan, Private Secretary to the Viceroy of India, and Ralph's
sister Alice is his slow-burn love interest. *Indian Summer*'s multi-racial
ensemble reflects Channel 4's public service remit for diversity and
offered the potential to correct the limited perspective of the 1980s
Raj dramas, which Sarita Malik argues did 'virtually nothing to tell
us anything oppositional, challenging, or otherwise about a silenced
colonial experience' (2001: 145).

Channel 4's scheduling of *Indian Summers* signalled it as both glossy
flagship period drama and political drama. Its Sunday 9 p.m. timeslot
had been established as the channel's home for imported prestige
political drama such as *Homeland* (Showtime, 2011–20) and *Deutschland
83*. Through this scheduling, Channel 4 positioned the programme as
a post-heritage challenge to the prestige period dramas that had long
claimed this slot on BBC One and ITV. The programme's post-
colonial politics are signalled by its interweaving of civil servants'
political manoeuvrings, the everyday brutalities of Britain's waning
colonial power and the struggles of the Indian political resistance.
These political strands sit in tension with its depiction of the seductive
glamour of the British Raj, producing an ambivalent address. This
conflicted identity was signalled by the involvement of US co-producer
Masterpiece. Channel 4's public service broadcasting remit for risk-

taking diverged from *Masterpiece*'s tendency to co-produce safer period drama from UK broadcasters, such as ITV hit *Downton Abbey*. The contrasting brand investments of the co-production partners resulted in narrative instability, confusion and inconsistency as *Indian Summers* progressed. The programme seemed unsure whether it wanted to be a prestige political drama confronting colonial darkness, a juicy, erotic melodrama or a feel-good tale of 'good whites' in India.

Indian Summers holds colonial guilt in tension with exoticism, producing an ambivalent 'imperial nostalgia' (Berghahn 2019: 41). The programme was filmed on location on the Malaysian island of Penang rather than Simla itself, and the landscape's vibrant colours are presented with a high colour saturation that shapes the town as an exoticised 'Other' (Berghahn 2019: 41). Colonial architecture sits amongst lush tropical foliage whose vibrant colours are pulled through in the saris of Indian women and the mise-en-scène of Aafrin's neighbourhood. The audience is introduced to Ralph's colonial mansion through Alice's wondering, contemplative gaze as she returns to her childhood home after decades spent in England. Mist wafts across its grounds, creating a dreamlike atmosphere. The mansion's large doors and windows are constantly open, constructing visual contrasts between the Indian natural world framed against the palatial colonial interiors. The boorish and cruel behaviour of the British community explicitly undercuts this natural beauty, yet the programme's aesthetic choices evoke and fulfil a 'desire for "otherness"' (Schwander 2019: 136).

Figure 2.1 The natural world of Simla, India, is framed against colonial interiors in *Indian Summers* (Channel 4, 2015–16)

The programme presents a limited attempt to counter the conservative undercurrent of 1980s Raj revival dramas. Its opening minutes show the human impact of the glamorous British Raj life, tracking an endless procession of Indian workers in the white-hot sun, struggling to transport the heavy possessions of the British community to Simla by road whilst the Brits travel by train. Yet the narrative swiftly shifts to centre the travellers' perspectives, with the workers relegated to the narrative background. Indian opposition to colonial rule is presented through the resistance politics of Aafrin's wilful sister Sooni and his friend Naresh, an Indian Nationalist. But the programme has difficulty maintaining consistency in Sooni and particularly Aafrin's involvement in the resistance movement. For large stretches of season two the widespread resistance to British rule is narrowed down to the individual terrorist actions of a now unstable Naresh. His violent extremism and threat to the British community can be easily dispatched and resolved. The impact of colonial rule on India is embodied by Simla's ostracised biracial population, including schoolteacher Leena and Ralph's illegitimate biracial son, Adam. This illustrates period drama's preference for reading history's political events through interpersonal storytelling. Adam and his mother 'haunt' Ralph as an unwanted reminder of his past and his somewhat divided identity. The hybrid or outsider identity of much of *Indian Summers*'s ensemble is less pronounced than *The Far Pavilions*'s Ash or *Jewel*'s Hari, but the programme consistently highlights the entanglement of British and Indian identity in Simla's colonial community.

As white, Indian-born Brits, Alice and Ralph exhibit elements of hybridity. Their classed and raced privilege allows them to maintain an ambivalent relationship with Raj society, retaining its power whilst viewing its segregation, racism and social climbing with a degree of distaste. At the programme's outset, young mother Alice returns from England to her childhood home of Simla, secretly fleeing an abusive husband. Her position as an outsider is emphasised by her conflicted attraction to Aafrin. Like other period drama heroines, Alice voices some of the progressive perspectives of the contemporary audience, but like the white women of *Jewel*, her critique of the Raj and her community is largely impotent and passive. Anti-hero Ralph is cruel and manipulative with ruthless ambitions for colonial power, but he somewhat distances himself from boorish colonial society. He refuses to contemplate returning to England and embraces India as his home, wearing Indian slippers and linen pyjamas at home and eating curry with his hands seated cross-legged on his porch. Yet he unthinkingly presents his hands for washing by his manservant Bhupinder, who also washes him by hand in the veranda bathtub. Unlike Scottish tea planter Ian (or Ash in *The Far Pavilions*), Ralph's hybridity is not the white Western man 'gone native', a figure present in Raj narratives as far back as Kipling's novel *Kim* (Oliete-Aldea 2015: 164). He does not covet an exoticised, free India; instead, he values his version of colonial India, where he has the power as a white man to take from the culture, yet social barriers remain.

Indian siblings Aafrin and Sooni are the critical products of empire, who Lisa Schwander (2019) suggests are sympathetic 'anti-imperialist heroes' challenging the power and social divisions of British colonial rule. Schwander argues the programme practises exceptionalism, distinguishing the siblings from many of its other Indian characters (including their parents) through their British-educated critical minds and border-crossing romances (2019: 138). Sooni is active in the Indian freedom movement and involves Aafrin in her cause, but as the narrative progresses *Indian Summers* reduces its engagement with the wider political resistance. It instead shifts its focus to a critique of colonial and ethnic social divisions through cross-cultural romances. These romances are a feature of Raj revival narratives, embodying an exoticised desire for 'otherness'. They are the dominant romantic connections in *Indian Summers*, with any relationship that does not cross racial or religious boundaries (Ralph's romance with American socialite Madeline, Alice's abusive marriage and Dougie's loveless marriage) depicted as doomed. Schwander suggests these cross-cultural romances symbolise the borderless, 'hybrid state' that the programme positions as the idealised post-colonial society (2019: 129–31). Yet this 'romanticised' approach blunts the programme's critical engagement with the Raj's racist colonial systems (Schwander 2019: 121–2). These romances attend to period drama's sensual pleasures, which I discuss in Chapter 6, but risk eroticising Indian cultures. They contribute to the programme's slide from a Raj-critical stance into an 'apologetic vision of the British imperial past' (Schwander 2019: 131).

This illustrates the seemingly irresolvable tensions at the heart of *Indian Summers*, which is pulled between political drama, society melodrama and exotic romance. As a Channel 4 prestige drama with Indian protagonists, it had the potential to take risks in offering Raj-critical perspectives that decentred the 'good whites' who evade complicity with imperialism. However, Channel 4's contribution to the programme's rumoured £14 million cost (O'Connor 2015) took up a significant part of its yearly drama budget and necessitated high audience ratings. Chasing popular audiences was an ill fit with a politicised critique of one of Britain's central myths of nation – a recurring bind of period drama's economics. These contexts combined to produce an ambivalent encounter with the complex politics of colonial India, one whose exoticised gaze is tinged with the Raj revival's seductive glamour of empire, despite the programme's progressive politics.

Beecham House

ITV's *Beecham House* also exhibits tensions between ideology and industrial contexts. It attempts to expand beyond familiar narratives of the British in India but is constrained by the demands of ITV Sunday night flagship period drama. *Beecham House* was shaped by the broadcaster's position as Britain's most popular commercial channel and the legacy of its hit period drama *Downton Abbey*, which had ended its run in 2015. Created, directed and co-written by veteran British-Asian filmmaker Gurinder Chadha, the programme follows a white British trader's encounters with Indian aristocracy in 1795 Delhi, before the country became part of Britain's empire. Instead of the colonial visual spectacle prevalent in British period drama's visions of the country, it showcases a sumptuous, spectacular India of self-rule. Featuring aristocratic Indians bedecked with gold and jewels and a parade of majestic palaces (with exterior filming taking place in Jaipur, doubling for Delhi), it presents an intensely exoticised vision of India. This projects 'fantasies of authenticity, abundance and sensuous intensity onto Other cultures' (Berghahn 2019: 37). Eighteenth-century India had not been previously represented in British period drama, so *Beecham House* sought to make the 'Other' familiar for the mainstream ITV audience. The widowed John Beecham's palatial Delhi mansion and devoted Indian servants are presented through upstairs–downstairs dynamics familiar from *Downton Abbey*. Press headlines positioned the programme as the 'Delhi Downton' (Cooke 2019; Singh 2019a; Wilson 2019)

Where *Indian Summers*'s fading days of the British Raj echo *The Jewel in the Crown*, *Beecham House* evokes the adventurous action and Indian royal splendour of *The Far Pavilions*, including its white British hero's romance with an Indian princess. Like *The Far Pavilions*, it presents India 'as a place of adventure, a place where Westerners' fantasies can be fulfilled, far removed from the rigidities imposed by European society' (Oliete-Aldea 2015: 157). A deserter from the East India Company's private army, John Beecham is a capitalist version of the white Westerner gone native. His post-desertion travels and immersion in India have enabled him to become a wealthy independent businessman trading in the products of the country's skilled craftsmen.

The programme ties itself in knots trying to free its progressive white hero from the taint of colonial exploitation. Beecham presents himself as 'a fair trader, not a pillager', who supports Indian self-rule, framing his own exploitation of India as altruistic and ethical.

Chadha's status as a veteran filmmaker of popular British cinema that addresses the 'diaspora paradigm' (Aftab 2019: 34) positions her as a 'culture broker' in a similar fashion to her protagonist. Daniela Berghahn notes that diasporic creatives are 'expected to provide "authentic" accounts of their culture of origin' (2019: 35). Although Chadha originates from colonial Kenya and grew up in the UK, she is part of the Indian diaspora. In a cultural context where British period drama's visions of India have been shaped by white creatives, Chadha is positioned as a 'native informant' (Berghahn 2019: 35), translating India's history for a British mainstream audience. *Beecham House*'s promotional discourse positioned Chadha's British-Asian identity as an authenticator of the programme's depiction of Indian history and its dramatisation of an era of colonial expansion little explored in British period drama. Berghahn suggests diasporic creatives are expected 'to articulate anti-imperialist resistance' rather than present exoticised tropes (2019: 35). In press coverage Chadra sought to present *Beecham House* as a response to Britain's amnesia surrounding empire, particularly in the context of the Brexit 'leave' campaign's mobilisation of its myths (Noor 2019). Yet she was also careful to assure potential viewers that the programme was a 'genially subversive' emotion-led story that used 'soap-like' emotional realism to shape India's national history for British audiences (Wilson 2019). Chadha's reputation for warmly comic filmmaking and a Sunday night slot on Britain's most populist channel did not offer much potential for challenging the country's colonial amnesia and the British empire's place in myths of nation.

Chadha's suggestion that the Indian characters' 'lives and loves [would be] as important as their white counterparts' (Noor 2019) indicated a challenge to the Raj revival's patterns of storytelling. Yet this proved unfounded as white perspectives are centralised, with the stories of the Indian house staff, royalty and aristocracy interwoven with and in support of the perspective of John Beecham, his family, friends and his British governess love interest. With British-Asian representation in ITV prime time largely limited to soap operas and terrorist-driven glossy thrillers like *Next of Kin* (2018), Chadha argued that the presence of 'Indians in period costumes on primetime British TV' was a 'flipping radical thing" (Noor 2019). *Beecham House* does expand ITV period drama's representations of the past to include Indian lives, offering a spectacular vision of India's past that was notably foreign to a mainstream white British audience raised on myths of British empire. Yet this was circumscribed by centring the white gaze of Beecham's capitalist adventurer. India is presented as an exotic world where Westerners' fantasies can be fulfilled, shaped by Chadha's self-orientalising gaze (Dirlik 1996: 99). *Beecham House*'s narrative focus showed that 'whiteness' maintains its hold as a genre marker (Bourne 2002: 49) and highlighted the tensions between expanding period drama's perspectives on the past and serving a prime-time ITV audience. The programme's unfamiliar world is made safe through its mapping onto *Downton Abbey*'s familiar classed dynamic with its Indian characters orbiting Beecham's benevolent colonising master. *Beecham House* was still history from above, not below; from the centre, not the margins.

America and stories of slavery

Just as Britain engages in selective amnesia to avoid confronting the violent shame of empire, Laura Dubek argues that America is 'a country whose people seem intent to remain in perpetual flight not just from their past, but from any understanding of the deep and enduring contradictions at the core of their national identity' (2018: 69). Imported Raj revival narratives allowed US audiences to engage in 'guilt-free nostalgia' as they did not feel implicated in British imperialism's violent sins (Hipsky 1994: 102–6). However, America's own guilty history of oppression in slavery's 'commodification and subjugation of the black body' and its foundation in the 'making of a (white) nation' (Dubek 2018: 70) allows no such distance. US period drama's avoidance of a reckoning with this guilt has led to a lack of engagement with Black American history. As cultural representations bind the individual to the national story, 'those who cannot see themselves reflected in its mirror cannot properly "belong"' (Hall 2005: 22). Through these absences, period drama contributes to assumptions of whiteness 'as universal, neutral and, therefore, quintessentially American' (Dyson 2016). Within the genre's limited representations, the 1960s civil rights movement and chattel slavery are offered as the dominant facets of Black American experience. However, in situating racism in the antebellum South or mid-century America, period dramas risk allowing liberal white viewers to believe that racism is in the past and moved beyond (Hesse 2002: 157–8; Dubek 2018: 69). I focus here on cable drama *Underground*, which debuted in 2016 and presented a revisionist, genre-hybrid account of enslaved people in the antebellum South. First, though, I briefly set out how the blockbusting success of the mini-series *Roots* incorporated 'people of African descent into the founding mythology of the nation' (Ball and Jackson 2017: 6–7).

The 1974 CBS TV movie *The Autobiography of Miss Jane Pittman* (dir. John Korty) reframed American history through the Black American experience, charting one woman's long life from Civil War-era slavery to the civil rights era (Gray 2005: 161). The 1977 mini-series *Roots* expanded this approach to a multigenerational family. Airing six months after America's bicentennial celebrations, it presented a 'pluralist ethnic history' and was a cultural phenomenon (Ball and Jackson 2017: 6–7). Adapted from Alex Haley's novel, itself a block-busting success, *Roots* was broadcast across eight consecutive nights. ABC chose this scheduling to mitigate the risk of a Black-centred American history, but the series became 'event' television, drawing 140 million viewers. *Roots* begins in Africa and follows Gambian man Kunta Kinte, who is captured and sold to slavery in 1750. He endures the Middle Passage crossing then life on a Virginian plantation. The series follows generations of Kunta Kinte's descendants through to the Civil War and freedom from slavery, concluding with the family as land-owning farmers in 1870s Tennessee. Herman Gray suggests that the programme's focus on a multigenerational family contributed to its populist success, as it developed emotional attachments that connected viewers to the brutality of chattel slavery and the struggle for freedom (2005: 161). However, both the novel and mini-series were critiqued at the time for conservative perspectives that shaped the story of Kunta Kinte's family through the 'reassuring, traditional values of the domi-nant white culture of the 1970s' (Lambert 2017: 99). This avoided any parallels with contemporary Black radicalism in order to smooth its acceptance within the 1970s climate of conservative backlash (Lambert 2017: 99).

Roots allowed Black Americans to encounter representations of their shared history outside of the 'white gaze' that had previously depicted the antebellum South through the perspective of the white plantation (Ball and Jackson 2017: 8). The mini-series showed the influence of the revisionist 'history from below' movement, which since the mid-twentieth century had reconsidered the interior lives, personal worth and strivings of enslaved Black Americans (Stevenson 2018: 504). But the project's potentially radical intervention in American history was limited by the middlebrow storytelling of 1970s network television, its white creative team and its address to a largely white mass audi-ence. Eric Pierson (2012) notes that in adapting Haley's novel for this broadcast context, the mini-series softened its depiction of the harsh realities of the slave trade and life of enslaved people in America. *Roots* characterised slavery as a practice of 'evil' white individuals rather than an American institution and economic system. These individuals were contrasted with 'good' white characters given prominence alongside the perspective of the Black protagonists. These storytelling choices made *Roots* a more familiar, palatable and 'universal' narrative for network television's audiences (Pierson 2012: 23–4).

The programme's key storytelling device was to frame Kunta Kinte's multigenerational family as the classic immigrant story, 'rationalis[ing] the suffering of blacks as an inevitable step towards acceptance' (Tucker and Shah 1992: 333). Slavery's oppression and dehumanisation was reworked as the 'boot strap' immigrant narrative of economic mobility, the unifying assimilationist myth of the American Dream (Pierson 2012: 28). The programme's conservative subtext privileged generational endurance, 'rising above' instead of revolt (Ball and Jackson 2017: 12). Herman Gray argues that the programme's huge popular success came at the cost of this minimising of 'the social organisation of racial subordination, the cultural reliance on human degradation, and the economic exploitation of black labour' (2005: 161). All these aspects helped to make *Roots*'s depiction of chattel slavery a more comforting experience for white viewers, reassured that the events and racism depicted were safely in the past.

Roots reworked the complexity of Black American history to fit the mass audience and storytelling model of 1970s network television. Forty years later the WGN series *Underground* demonstrates how recent industrial shifts have impacted period drama's representational possibilities. A thriller about runaway slaves in the antebellum South, *Underground* debuted in 2016 as one of a slate of original dramas produced by basic cable channel WGN in an attempt to rebrand itself as a prestige TV outlet. The programme was part of a boom in US period drama during the 2010s as new SVODs and rebranded channels like WGN sought to use innovations in the genre's form and representations to stand out in the crowded television marketplace. This industrial context combined with a relatively small increase in Black creative voices in the US industry in the late 2010s to open up space for a story of enslaved people that privileged revolt over 'rising above'.

Underground was part of a wave of revisionist slavery narratives in North American culture across 2015–16. This included Canadian mini-series *The Book of Negroes* (CBC, 2015), Nate Parker's film *The Birth of a Nation* (2016), the History Channel's new adaptation of *Roots* (2016), Ava DuVernay's documentary *13th* (2016) (which connected slavery and mass incarceration), and Colsen Whitehead's much-celebrated novel *The Underground Railroad* (which Barry Jenkins adapted for television and debuted in 2021 on Amazon Prime Video). This wave was catalysed by two distinctly differently cinematic slave narratives that have a clear influence on *Underground*: Quentin Tarantino's controversy-baiting *Django Unchained* (2012) and Steve McQueen's Oscar-winning *12 Years a Slave* (2013). Alongside this wave was a swell of cultural interest in the Underground Railroad, a secret network that helped conceal and transport escaped slaves to freedom in the North. The Underground Railroad enabled Black Americans to be presented as heroes, emphasising courage and rebellion rather than subjugation, offering 'the possibility of moral comfort in a profoundly uncomfortable past' (Schulz 2016).

Where *Roots* was produced by a white creative team, reflecting the racial demographics of the 1970s US television industry, *Underground*'s vision of the antebellum South was shaped by a Black co-creator (Mischa Green, a rare Black female showrunner) and a Black director (Anthony Hemingway) who helmed its pilot and early episodes. Where the multigenerational narrative of *Roots* emphasised endurance as part of the long route to freedom, promotional interviews positioned *Underground* as 'the "revolution" not the "occupation"' (Herzog 2016). The programme's 1850s setting meant audiences knew the American Civil War was on the horizon and the battle for freedom was within reach. *Underground*'s first season interweaves the stories of the 'Macon 7' runaways, the slave catchers that hunt them, those they leave behind at the Georgia plantation, and a white abolitionist couple who become involved in the Underground Railroad. The programme blends a period drama grounded in oral history – inspired by first-hand accounts of enslaved people held in the Library of Congress – with an action-packed thriller of revolution and revenge. This genre hybrid challenged standard narratives of chattel slavery, which emphasised Black subjugation and suffering (Dubek 2018: 70–1).

Alfred L. Martin (2018a) suggests *Underground*'s high budget required 'dualcasting' to draw both white and Black audiences. Including sympathetic white protagonists in its Black-dominated ensemble helped 'make its story particular to blackness, yet universal enough so as not to exclude white viewers' (Martin 2018a). The myth of the Underground Railroad offers 'one of the few narratives [of slavery] in which white Americans can plausibly appear as heroes' (Schulz 2016). In abolitionist lawyer John and his wife Elizabeth, *Underground* presents the standard empathetic 'good whites' familiar from *Roots* and the British Raj's colonial narratives. Although, in a development from the impotent white women of Raj narratives, season two sees Elizabeth take up arms in the fight against slavery.

Karen Schulz highlights how the fugitive-slave narrative offers a paradox as it represents 'one of the darkest eras of American history' yet it is also 'the perfect American story of a hero's journey' (2016). *Underground*'s promotional discourse framed the Underground Railroad and runaway slaves as 'American heroes who were the first superheroes' (Swinson 2017). This positioned the 'foreign country' of the past and the devastating history of chattel slavery in familiar terms. Using period drama's blend of realism and fantasy (Vidal 2012a), the drama shapes the familiar tropes of slave narratives – the white-pillared plantation home, the endless cotton fields, the cruel mistress, the frantic runaway pursued by dogs – through a fast-cut editing style, dynamic camerawork and a soundtrack of hip-hop, electronica and R&B. Just as *Peaky Blinders* (BBC Two/BBC One, 2013–) makes connections between the present and the past by soundtracking its working-class Birmingham gangsters with the jagged, rasping contemporary rock of Nick Cave, The White Stripes and PJ Harvey, *Underground* uses hip-hop to draw connections between these historical Black bodies and contemporary Black lives.

The programme uses 'the sonic elements of hip-hop – both rappers' voices as well as their instrumental accompaniments' to 'validate the traumatic lives of enslaved blacks' (Bradley 2016: 5). This contributes to *Underground*'s communication of the affective experience of enslaved people: their scars, wounds and whippings, and the tough, ragged physicality of the escapees on their panicked journey North.

Figure 2.2 Noah crouches hidden in the undergrowth in *Underground* (WGN, 2016–17)

From its opening moments the programme uses hip-hop to position itself as a revisionist slave narrative, blending the fanfare, drums and yelping vocals of Kanye West's 'Black Skinhead' with the sounds of barking dogs and the heaving breath of runaway slave Noah as he crashes through dark woods. The propulsive soundscape is matched with a dynamic following camera and choppy editing. The intense drum rhythms combine with the anxiety and conflicted self-image of West's lyrics to communicate Noah's state of mind as he frantically scrambles through the undergrowth. The loop of West's rhythmic breathing is layered onto and speaks for Noah's own ragged breath as he crouches hidden in the undergrowth, his eyes bright in the darkness. West breathes *for* Noah, the connections made between Black men across centuries.[5] Here hip-hop binds Black lives past and present, but also serves to 'defamiliarise the familiar' (Bradley 2016: 5). From the outset *Underground* seeks to destabilise cultural conventions of chattel slavery narratives, presenting the runaway's flight for freedom and mortal danger as a dynamic action thriller.

Underground 'provide[s] an alternative imagining of a slave plantation' that complicates 'racial identity politics' associated with the plantation in American culture (Bradley 2016: 8). It repeatedly draws attention to the army of Black hands and bodies required to maintain the Macon family's plantation and privileged lifestyle; bodies often erased in plantation tourism's chronicling of the heritage of 'Dixie'. Bradley suggests that the American South's heritage industry works alongside popular culture to construct national myths. Centred on the antebellum plantations, 'Dixie' heritage presents a selective and white rendering of a 'South of the imagination' (Cox 2011: 8). Like Britain's amnesia over the violence of empire, this 'racially splintered relic of southern identity' removes or waters down the role of slavery through a selective memory that presents plantations as farms with 'black and happy workers' (Bradley 2016: 7–8). *Underground* counters these myths of the American South by foregrounding the economic workings and exploitations of chattel slavery; the 'occupation' of Black bodies as a capitalist system. The programme uses the genre conventions of melodrama and the action-adventure thriller to depict the visceral, daily horrors of the lives of enslaved people, presenting the plantation's brutality as an economic and psychological system.

The explicit villains of *Underground*'s melodrama are the plantation owners, who display the dehumanising beliefs behind 'thingification' (Césaire 2000: 42), viewing enslaved people as both commodities and objects for sexual exploitation. The programme presents cotton farming, the plantations and the bodies they own as a carefully calibrated system supported by the politics of the state. The Macon 7's heist sees them steal their own bodies from the Macon's master but as they scramble to find their route North, the team is progressively picked off by slave hunters. A failed escape attempt by Rosalee's brother Sam is punished by his murder through lynching. This is staged as part of the plantation master's grandstanding speech for election to government. As the speech reaches its climactic defence of the South's 'heritage', the camera cuts from the plantation house's balcony to a wide shot, revealing Sam's dead body hanging from the porch beneath his declaiming master, surrounded by drapes of fabric in red, white and blue. The moment foregrounds the 'racial politics of nation-building' that 'explain our current historical moment as much as the period preceding the Civil War' (Dubek 2018: 71). I return to *Underground*'s representation of Black bodies and the plantation house in Chapter 4's discussion of space and place.

Underground's novelty as a revisionist period thriller shaped by anachronistic aesthetics and music blended prestige and risk for cable channel WGN. Kristen Warner has argued that subscription cable channels like HBO and FX use their few Black-cast programmes to signal the risk-taking that is key to their prestige channel brands. She notes that 'risk is a way to draw an audience and earn critical attention' (2016). For channels with a marked lack of diversity, the Black showrunners and casts of *Insecure* (HBO, 2016–21) and *Atlanta* (FX, 2016–) are signals of risk-taking, helping to assert the channels' prestige value. As a hybrid period drama with a Black cast, *Underground* presented a risk for WGN, a channel not known for Black-targeted programming or prestige drama. The programme's high budget and its prestige status was a rarity in US television's Black-cast dramas. Alfred J. Martin notes these tended to be characterised as lower-status melodrama or soap opera; for example, *Empire* (Fox, 2015–20), *Queen Sugar* (OWN, 2016–) and *Being Mary Jane* (BET, 2013–19). This gave *Underground* an added burden of representation as a Black period drama (Martin 2018a). WGN's risk paid off and the programme was a critical hit, producing marked improvements in WGN's ratings. However, by season two the ratings had dropped and when the channel was bought by Sinclair Media Group, *Underground* was cancelled in favour of cheaper, more profitable reality programming. At a rumoured cost of $5 million per episode, it was unable to find a new home on Black-focused cable channels OWN and BET, whose smaller budgets relied on lower-cost genres. Here we see again how period drama's economics can impact its ability to draw stories of the marginalised to the centre.

Conclusion

Indian Summers, Beecham House and *Underground* offer varied – at times limited – attempts to push beyond whiteness as a genre default and reposition 'othered' voices from the margins to the centre. In doing so they challenge the selective amnesia over colonialism and slavery that has helped support British and American myths of nation. But challenges to both entrenched narratives of nation and the tenacious hold whiteness has on British and US period drama sit in tension with the economics of the genre. Period drama's blend of historical verisimilitude and spectacle requires significant budgets, which in turn requires co-production partners and needs large viewing numbers to justify its costs. Yet programmes that challenge accepted myths of nation, offer discomforting representations of the past or delve into the experiences of minority populations can struggle to draw large audiences. This also makes them challenging to export to or attract suitable co-production partners in an international television market accustomed to more comforting, easily commodified images of national pasts. If commissioned at all, more challenging period dramas that question narratives of nation tend to receive smaller budgets and rely on public service channels or prestige cable channels where their 'risk' can support a channel brand and their costs can be offset against more popular programming. Few US and UK channels seem able to take on the risk of producing Black and Asian histories that challenge existing conceptions of national pasts. As Karen Schulz argues, the problem 'is not the stories we tell; it's the stories we don't tell' (2016). These untold stories help to maintain whiteness as a 'universal' part of Britain's and America's national identity.

Notes

1. Throughout this book, I refer to 'South Asian' ethnicity and use 'Indian' to describe characters in British programmes set in the subcontinent. I use 'Black' to refer to both African American and Black British ethnicity. When talking about specific British representations, I use 'British Asian' and 'Black British'. British and US dramas offer extremely limited representations of East Asian experience.
2. For more detailed discussion of the nuances of this debate, see Monk (2002) and Vidal (2012a: 8–20).
3. Ofcom's 2019 Media Nations report highlighted that 'third party' funding – co-production, deficit funding by production companies

and tax credits – now made up 54 per cent of the total spend on drama by the UK's public service broadcasters – BBC One, BBC2, ITV, Channel 4 and Channel 5 (Ofcom 2019a).

4. The official British rule of India – known as the British Raj – ran from 1858, when the subcontinent passed from the hands of the British East India Company to Queen Victoria. It ceased in 1947 with Indian independence and Partition, when the country was split into Pakistan and India.

5. See Bradley (2016: 3–5) for a detailed close analysis of this sequence and the relationship of visuals and soundscape.

3 Class and Politics

Season two of runaway slave drama *Underground* (WGN, 2016–17) features a showcase episode consisting entirely of a monologue from Harriet Tubman. The hero of the Underground Railroad is giving a speech to abolitionists that builds to a passionate call to arms against the system of chattel slavery (02: 06). In a programme built around dynamic action, the episode's physical stillness and singular focus on Black female voice makes a spectacle of Tubman's political rhetoric. The monologue brings to the foreground *Underground*'s tracing of connections between the antebellum South and contemporary American politics. This is made explicit in the episode's closing moments when Tubman's determined gaze shifts to direct address (a non-naturalistic device otherwise absent from the programme). She breaks the fourth wall to align the audience with the abolitionists in her final call for action. Evoking the nostalgia of the Republican sloganeering of President Trump, she declaims, 'You gotta find what it means for you to be a soldier. Beat back those that are tryin' to kill everything that's good and right in the world and call it "makin' it great again".' The episode concludes with Tubman's challenge, "Aint nobody get to sit this out, y'hear me"; the war for the freedom of enslaved Black Americans is directly connected to a contemporary fight for America's soul.

This striking moment of non-naturalism presents a didactic illustration of period drama's investment in social and political concerns. In these moments period drama builds connections between the present and the past, rather than presenting the past as a 'foreign country', eroticising or fetishising its difference, or viewing it as a more settled world to escape to. Television outlets frequently commission literary adaptions and original dramas whose plots can be read through current cultural and political preoccupations. This can sometimes be accidental, as when *The Americans*'s (FX, 2013–18) story of Russian spies working undercover in 1980s America became unexpectedly topical with the exposure of Russia's interference in the 2016 US elections (Jeffries 2017). Period drama looks to the past to explain our present or makes a 'foreign' past recognisable by connecting the audience's own experiences to the events that shape its characters' lives. Here history is not a linear journey towards 'progress' but a form of echo chamber.

Iris Kleinecke-Bates suggests that this move to identify the 'the modern in the old' exists alongside period drama's desire to deconstruct and re-evaluate the past (2014: 101). This illustrates the genre's duality, the tension between closeness and distance. Period drama has the potential to reawaken submerged pasts and write those excluded – through class, gender or race – back into history, but it can also work to preserve and reinforce classed hierarchies and ideologies. This chapter explores how period drama speaks about class and politics, focusing on programmes that serve as a 'mode of public history'. Here the genre draws on television's role as an unofficial source of historical knowledge and cultural memory (Long 2017: 169). As part of this book's project to expand the period drama canon, its case studies examine how politics intersects with women's and working-class histories, focusing largely on dramas that make 'visible the contours of life for everyday people as they were shaped or circumscribed by historical parameters and conditions' (Landsberg 2015: 69). It briefly looks at three dramas that explore life above and below stairs in grand houses – *Upstairs, Downstairs* (ITV, 1971–5), *Servants* (BBC One, 2003) and *Downton Abbey* (ITV, 2010–15) – to consider how authorship can shape period drama's classed investments. It then moves on to three case studies that explore the intersection of class and politics. Suffragette drama *Shoulder to Shoulder* (BBC Two, 1974) documents key moments in the campaign for women's right to vote. *The Mill* (Channel 4, 2013–14) and *North & South* (BBC One, 2004) chart the impact of the industrial revolution on the people of Northern mill towns. *Call the Midwife* (BBC One, 2012–) blends women's and working-class history in the post-war East End of London. This chapter's examples draw nearly entirely from British programmes, as 'class is a structuring feature' of British television (Wood 2017: vii) and period dramas are one of the primary places for contemporary television's discussions of class (Long 2017: 169).

The lasting influence of the heritage debate has shaped cultural perceptions of period drama's classed dynamic. The assumption is that it reproduces 'class exclusion and misrepresentation' as part of its privileging of 'conservative myths of privileged Englishness that [gloss] over class struggle, past and present' (Piduck 2004: 123). The perception of period drama as inherently conservative was arguably shaped by British television's reliance on the classic serial from the 1980s into the early 2000s. Jerome de Groot argues that 'the Austen adaptations above all ... have given rise to a sense of the costume drama being comfortable, bourgeois and politically modest' (2009: 191). This has been compounded by the blockbusting success of *Downton Abbey* in the 2010s, reflected in its dominant presence in academic discussions of the genre (Tincknell 2013; Byrne 2014; Baena and Byker 2015; Taddeo 2018b; and Hilmes 2019 are just a few examples). *Downton Abbey*'s international success shows how dramas exploring worlds of privilege continue to be valued by the export markets that are essential to the genre's structuring economies.

Period drama chooses narratives and historical moments that speak to, work through, or worry at contemporary concerns. For example, Claire Monk found 1970s British period drama responded to the decade's 'democratising impulses' through investments in class, gender and regionality (2015: 41). The genre has tended to centre a 'top down' perspective. Julianne Pidduck suggests film and television adaptations practise a 'systematic erasure of working people from the frame' or present domestic servants as the 'silent counterpoint[s]' to the romance and self-discovery of middle- and upper-class protagonists (2004: 123). However, the explosion of original dramas and adaptations across the 2000s and 2010s has offered space for broader perspectives. Paul Long highlights how the classed investments of gangster drama *Peaky Blinders* (BBC Two/BBC One, 2013–) were influenced by creator Steve Knight's working-class Birmingham background and his desire to bring an under-represented regional history to life (2017: 168–9). Gemma Goodman and Rachel Moseley suggest that *Poldark* (BBC One, 2015–19) presents Ross as an egalitarian hero despite his position as landed gentry (2018: 58). He is depicted as an outsider to his class who instead aligns himself with the workers he toils alongside at his Cornish mine. Yet long-running successes such as these remain relatively rare, emphasising television's 'continuing under-representation of ordinary and extraordinary working people – whether located in the past or present' (Long 2017: 177).

Above and below stairs

Chapter 2 showed how the whiteness of British and US television's creative teams has in part shaped the racial dynamics of period drama. This can also be extended to the genre's classed representations, as who gets to make period drama shapes the kinds of stories that are told and whose perspective is privileged. Period drama's upstairs–downstairs narratives illustrate how the backgrounds and classed (and in some cases gendered) investments of creative teams can shape a programme's depiction of domestic servants and the privileged families they serve. The differences in depictions of class-divided grand households in *Upstairs, Downstairs*, *Servants* and *Downton Abbey* illustrate how storytelling is shaped by the classed investments of creators and writers.

Upstairs, Downstairs is a prime example of 1970s British television's blockbusting popular period dramas. The programme ran for five seasons, and the shifting narrative focus across its lengthy run of sixty-eight episodes illustrates how its classed and gendered investments were shaped by different creative voices. The 'auteur' status regularly assigned to the television writer or the writer-producer figure of the 'showrunner'[1] is muddied by television's collaborative production culture. *Upstairs, Downstairs* was devised by actresses Jean Marsh and Eileen Atkins, who sought to move servants' narratives from the edges of period drama to the centre. For D. L. LeMahieu, the programme's success was linked to the 'active presence of three-dimensional working-class people', breaking with period drama's representational silence (1990: 248). Marsh's mother had worked in service during the early twentieth century, and the women conceived a drama that explored the lives of the domestic staff of a grand Edwardian town house, centred on two young female servants. Edith P. Thornton (1993) suggests that during the programme's production creative control moved to executive producer John Hawkesworth and script editor Alfred Shaughnessy. The programme's narrative was progressively shifted to reflect their own backgrounds. Having grown up in upper-class Edwardian homes, they orientated *Upstairs, Downstairs* 'toward the upstairs rather than the down', centralising the perspective of the aristocratic Bellamy family (Thornton 1993: 28). Thornton presents the programme's earlier seasons as fast-paced and less rigidly hierarchically structured, with a raucous, disruptive female-centred ensemble built around maids Rose and Sarah. Both Thornton and Helen Wheatley (2005) connect this to Marsh and Atkins's concept and writer Fay Weldon's feminist influence in early seasons. However, Thornton argues that across its run the drama transitioned into a more subdued story centred around an elite male protagonist in the Bellamy's son James and his experiences in the First World War. A female-centred 'grand soap opera' (Thornton 1993: 42) became a male-centred prestige drama, illustrating how the classed and gendered investments of creatives can shape stories of upper-class households.

The extended runs of 1970s mass-audience original period dramas such as *Upstairs, Downstairs* required a team of writers; however, the short serial or season written by a single writer has long been British television's dominant production model. The 2003 drama *Servants* was created and written by Lucy Gannon, who had an established career in popular television drama. Gannon contrasted her own work with the higher cultural status of prestige drama: 'I'm not sitting in an ivory tower. I've never had awards because I don't write for critics or accolades. I write for people sitting at home' (quoted in Rampton 1999). *Servants* is distinct in this trio of dramas as in it the upper-class family of an 1850s country house are rendered as background figures in favour of a focus on the everyday life of its domestic staff. Here the family are the marginal and anonymous 'silent counterpoints' (Pidduck 2004: 123) to the staff's bawdy behaviour and jovial, competitive community (Kleinecke-Bates 2014: 128–9). Gannon wanted the drama to draw connections between the audience and its working-class protagonists, whom she presented as 'ordinary people' (Kleinecke-Bates 2014: 124). The programme cast actors largely familiar from popular television drama and soap opera and was marketed as a 'period soap', playing up its popular appeal and alternative perspective on the past (Kleinecke-Bates 2014: 127). Iris Kleinecke-Bates suggests the programme's aesthetics, modern tone, and performance style deliberately collapsed the Victorian age into the present (2014: 134) and suggests its lack of ratings success was due to this play with genre expectations. A playful relationship with the past became more common in late 2010s period drama. But in 2003 viewers' expectations of period 'authenticity' were tied to an invisible 'realist' aesthetic and a centring of the middle and upper classes that was read as a depoliticised norm (Kleinecke-Bates 2014: 141). *Servants*'s anachronistic tone and bawdy working-class ensemble presented a disruptive, politicised intervention into period drama's visual and classed norms.

Servants disrupted the genre's conventional depiction of the master–servant relationship as one built on trust, friendship and devotion (Kleinecke-Bates 2014: 129–30). Nevertheless, friendships between the elite and their devoted servants are at the heart of *Downton Abbey*'s recuperative, conservative storytelling. Despite its international reputation as prestige drama, *Downton Abbey* functions, like *Servants*, as popular television drama. It is a prime-time ITV drama built around the serialised narratives, melodrama and interpersonal dynamics familiar from soap opera. However, this is clothed in the aesthetics, performances and export value that Charlotte Brunsdon identifies as signifying 'quality' (1990: 85–6). Its stately, lush cinematography, detailed attention to verisimilitude in costume and production design and its location filming offer 'a combination of restraint and uncommon spectacle' linked to upper-middle-class taste codes (Brunsdon 1990: 85). *Downton Abbey*'s catalysing plot pivots around class, as the British rules of succession designate that Lord Crawley's country house cannot be passed down to his eldest daughter Lady Mary. Instead a distant cousin, middle-class lawyer Matthew, will inherit the estate.

In contrast to Lucy Gannon's positioning of herself as the voice of 'ordinary people', the class background of *Downton Abbey*'s creator and writer Julian Fellowes brought connotations of prestige. Fellowes had served as screenwriter and technical advisor for Robert Altman's period film *Gosford Park* (2001), a satirical murder mystery set in an Edwardian country house. An actor and novelist, Fellowes's 'technical expertise' drew from his own elite social position: he married into the aristocracy and became a Conservative peer in 2011, sitting in the House of Lords.[2] His frustrations over the British rules of succession preventing his wife from inheriting her family title influenced *Downton*'s central conflict over the future of the Crawleys' estate. Brunsdon identifies 'literary source' as a 'quality component' (1990: 85). As *Downton Abbey* is an original drama, Fellowes's 'expertise' derived from his elite social position works in a similar manner to assert the programme's historical 'authenticity'.

Although *Downton Abbey* is heavily indebted to *Gosford Park*, it offers a much more supportive staff and sympathetic portrait of the aristocracy than the 'narcissistic culture of the upper classes' exhibited in the film (Pidduck 2004: 130). *Downton* presents a top-down classed perspective that centralises the paternalistic Lord Crawley and offers a romanticised vision of domestic service. It depicts the relationship between master and devoted servant as one of loyal close friendship and obscures the gruelling labour of the domestic service needed to maintain the Crawleys' vast house and glamorous lifestyle. This privileges a 'very conservative view of a rather coherent world in which everyone knew their place' (Baena and Byker 2015: 267), one that values and requires 'obedience and loyalty' and rewards this with Lord Crawley's benevolent support (Byrne 2015: 9). In this way the programme acts as 'a fable for modern society . . . acting as a mouthpiece for the Tory-led Coalition government' (Byrne 2015: 9) whose Cabinet was filled with those from elite and aristocratic backgrounds yet which preached a politics of austerity for the masses. *Downton Abbey* presents a world where the English country gentleman serves as the figure of 'natural order' (Pidduck 2004: 123).

Downton Abbey's success during a post-recessionary period of austerity and income inequality illustrates Colin McArthur's (1980) influential assertion that at a time of disenfranchisement and social unrest, period drama offers a vision of a more settled, optimistic past. He suggests this has a 'restorative, conservative and potentially ameliorative' effect on the viewer's feeling of alienation and class inequity (1980: 40). *Downton Abbey* is set during the Edwardian era, which was a period of significant social change that included the reconfiguration of the English aristocracy. This social change frequently impacts the world of the estate, yet the programme repeatedly 'makes safe' and assimilates challenges to conservatism, maintaining a classed status quo (Tincknell 2013: 776).

Upstairs, Downstairs also tracks the social changes of the Edwardian era, and it is useful to return to it as a transition into my case study of *Shoulder to Shoulder*. Critical orthodoxy has read *Upstairs, Downstairs* as a conservative 'drama of social harmony' (Wheatley 2005: 150), with histories of British drama positioning it against the more radical historical dramas of the 1970s. Yet Helen Wheatley's feminist re-reading draws out the programme's gender politics, arguing these 'worry at' the concerns of the early 1970s women's liberation movement contemporary with its broadcast (2005: 143–4). *Upstairs, Downstairs*'s serial narrative produces dramatic conflict 'by characters serially challenging, rejecting, or speaking up against the status quo' of conservative containment (Wheatley 2005: 150). Wheatley argues that Fay Weldon played a significant role in the programme's early years, writing its first episode and others across its first two seasons. Weldon used the programme to 'work though' or worry at feminist issues in a covert way (Wheatley 2005: 151). This thematic investment in 'issues relating to women and equality' (Wheatley 2005: 152) aligns its interest in Edwardian women's domestic lives and domestic labour to the concerns of second-wave feminism.

Feminist histories: *Shoulder to Shoulder*

The connection between 1970s second-wave feminism and Edwardian women's challenge to society's gendered status quo was expanded by *Shoulder to Shoulder*. The drama documents the campaign for women's right to vote, focusing on the increasingly militant actions of England's largest suffragette group, the Women's Social and Political Union (WSPU). The progression of the movement is developed through six seventy-five-minute episodes, each focused on a particular figure within the movement. The Pankhurst family – the widowed mother

Emmeline and her daughters Christabel and Sylvia – are centred, with episodes also featuring former Lancashire mill worker Annie Kenney, aristocrat Lady Constance Lytton, and the direct actions of Emily Wilding Davison and Mary Richardson.

The serial is the collaborative creation of three women, actress Georgia Brown, filmmaker and feminist activist Midge Mackenzie and powerful TV producer Verity Lambert. It grew out of Mackenzie's documentary work on the 1968 Golden Jubilee celebrations of women's right to vote, and her frustration that the story of the women who fought for the vote 'had vanished from our history' (1988: ix). Lambert positioned the serial as an explicitly feminist project, a counterpoint to the media's misrepresentation of the 1970s women's movement (LeMahieu 1990: 250). However, Janet McCabe and Vicky Ball (2014) suggest the serial was a site of feminist struggle at a production and institutional level, illustrating the power dynamics of 1970s British television. Mackenzie's research and story outline was ultimately translated by a nearly entirely male creative team and she felt a 'sense of feminist betrayal' (McCabe 2014) of her vision of an all-female production. The creative team featured some of the most prominent writers of British television's 'golden age', including Ken Taylor and Alan Plater, with directing duties divided between Waris Hussein and Moira Armstrong, the sole prominent female creative beyond the producers (with Mackenzie credited as script editor). As McCabe (2014) notes, these production choices illustrate 'the culturally awkward relationship between what a feminist drama might look like and the institutional space which will make that possible in the first place'. We see again how representations of the past and which voices that get to shape it are affected by 'what is possible within a particular media ecology' (McCabe 2014).

Shoulder to Shoulder benefited from the 'romantic nostalgia' for the Edwardian era that permeated 1970s culture (Giddings and Selby 2000: 27–8) but also complicated it. Rather than a vision of a settled past, the serial positioned the Edwardian era as a period of struggle, with characters rejecting and speaking against the status quo of patriarchal society. Katherine Cockin notes that since the formation of the WSPU, the suffragettes 'have been mythologised and reinvented for different purposes' (2004: 17). In the 1970s they provided historical antecedents for the decade's countercultural feminist and socialist movements, cushioning the 'shock of the new' (LeMahieu 1990: 251). The concerns of the suffragettes mapped onto the contemporary women's movement and its struggles 'over questions of inequality, images of woman as Other and the culturally awkward position of women within the public sphere and their right to speak' (McCabe and Ball 2014). In turn, the contemporary actions of the IRA (and in the US, the radical left's militant organisations such as the Weather Underground) made familiar the WSPU's tactics of property damage and bombings, along with prison hunger strikes as a form of political action (McCabe and Ball 2014). The past was brought close through its links with the present.

Shoulder to Shoulder builds a female ensemble drama focused on 'a cross-section of feminine types' (Ball 2013: 246) although it centralises the actions of the WSPU. Here it relies on the Pankhurst family's status as the recognised 'brand' in popular culture's limited awareness of the suffragettes. As McCabe and Ball (2014) note, 'committee work and letter writing is far less televisual than the drama of arson campaigns and bruising clashes with the police'. In a contemporary article Claire Johnston charged that this 'bourgeois' focus on the family reads the movement's deep divisions between feminism and socialism as sibling rivalry (1974: 83). Yet the programme's socialist sympathies are clear, aligning *Shoulder to Shoulder* with the politics of 1970s British television's radical drama (Cooke 2003: 90–103; Monk 2015). Early episodes see the Pankhurst family repeatedly position working-class women as the key beneficiaries of the right to vote and throughout the serial working-class women are presented as sympathetic yet sceptical audiences for suffragette speeches. However, outside of Annie Kenney, working-class women's struggle is relayed through the voices of privileged women: Christabel's early speeches, Sylvia's work in the East End and Lady Constance Lytton. The latter disguises her aristocratic status in order to experience the violent force-feeding ordinary suffragettes endured in prison.

Episode five demonstrates a reflexive awareness of this classed dynamic, interweaving the stories of the two women who perpetrated the most famous direct actions of the militant campaign with Sylvia's socialist-driven interactions with the women of the East End. It features Emily Wilding Davison who died at the 1913 Epsom Derby, trampled in a collision with the king's racehorse, and Mary Richardson, who claimed to witness her death and later slashed the *Rokeby Venus* painting in the National Gallery. The episode is perhaps the most dynamic of the serial as it depicts the peak of the suffragettes' campaign of property vandalism and direct action. As Davison's eventual ambiguous death happens offscreen, the episode's primary set piece is her violent force-feeding in prison after a silent campaign of defiance. This is one of *Shoulder to Shoulder*'s multiple scenes of force-feeding, with the rattle of the instrument trolley along the prison's

Figure 3.1 *Shoulder to Shoulder* (BBC Two, 1974) depicts the force-feeding of an imprisoned suffragette

metal walkways becoming a sound of terror for the imprisoned women. Davison's force-feeding unfolds without diegetic sound; it is accompanied by an abstract male voice clinically reading a parliamentary report on the practice. The detached voice of patriarchal authority detailing the physical damage of nasal force-feeding is layered onto the violent struggle of Davison and the prison staff, depicting it as an act of state violence.

The episode's physical dynamism and the largely silent characterisation of Davison are interwoven with a relatively static series of conversations between Sylvia and local East End citizens at her new WSPU outpost. These repeatedly highlight the struggles of cross-class understanding, with an extended conservation between Sylvia and local woman Maisy Dunn forming the episode's other set piece. This scene sets out the barriers to political action for working-class women, showcasing *Shoulder to Shoulder*'s use of conversation and debate as somewhat didactic devices to communicate and work through conflicting ideological and political positions. Maisy is interested in yet sceptical of the suffragette cause but explains her situation as a working mother in substandard housing. She asserts that despite Sylvia's socialist sympathies, she is an upper-class interloper who can never fully understand the lives of the East End women. Maisy's explanation that '[i]deas aren't enough, not when you're hungry' brings into focus the episode's juxtaposition of the lived experience of hunger through poverty with the choice of hunger as a political action. Through such interweaving of action and debate, the programme repeatedly represents the divisions and conflicts – over tactics and ideologies – within the movement for women's suffrage.

Although *Shoulder to Shoulder* revels in the transgressive power of Edwardian women's bodies pushing beyond social restraint, Sylvia and Maisy's conversation illustrates the programme's focus on women's voices. It depicts them sharing, listening and asserting their beliefs in intimate conversations, passionate debates and public speeches. This aligns the programme with 1970s radical drama, which 'dramatised, rather than efface[d], the processes of debate and conflict, collective decision making, and dissent' (Monk 2015: 37). The programme stages repeated conflicts within the campaign, including debates over gender or class equality as the greater barrier to social change and disagreements over property vandalism or hunger strike as the more appropriate form of direct action. Its depiction of conversation, debate, sharing and listening as forms of consciousness-raising were familiar to 1970s audiences as central practices of second-wave feminism, tracing connections between the past and present.

Shoulder to Shoulder's use of conversation and debate is partly a rhetorical and storytelling device and partly a function of the programme's filming processes. It is a predominantly studio-set drama, using the then industry-standard combination of studio interiors shot on video and exteriors shot on location on more costly film. These production practices necessitate a focus on events relayed through speech in interior spaces rather than directly experienced. Directors Hussein and Armstrong present these interiors – sitting rooms, halls, courts and prison cells – through the 'meaningful and expressive' studio mise-en-scène of 1970s drama (Wheatley 2005: 145), using deep staging, high angles, cross-fades and layering to display emotional and physical dynamics. This makes the moments of location-filmed direct action – repeated sequences of smashing windows and violent tussles with police, including the assaults of 'Black Friday' – all the more dynamic.

Claire Johnston's 1974 critique expressed disappointment at the programme's use of 'the traditions of bourgeois realism' that aligned it with the classic serial rather than radical drama (1974: 83–5). However, I would suggest *Shoulder to Shoulder* draws its political power from working *within* period drama's established conventions.

The serial utilises period drama's investment in women's voices and experiences and its familiar spaces of the upper middle class and aristocracy. The serial's first half plays out in these sitting and receiving rooms familiar from period drama's depiction of privileged society's intricate codes of social visits, romantic manoeuvrings and genteel philanthropy. In *Shoulder to Shoulder* these become sites for women's conspiratorial discussions, passionate speech and debate, reworking domestic space as political space. As the WSPU's power grows, the serial moves into spaces unfamiliar from period drama's stories of privileged women's lives. The spatial shift to wood-lined offices and stone prison cells illustrates the suffragettes' challenge to the gendered norms of Edwardian patriarchal society. Similarly the physicality of women breaking windows, setting fires, enduring and administering (as prison guards) violent force-feeding pushes the boundaries of a genre typically characterised 'by limited character mobility or physical, social and corporeal constraint' (Pidduck 2004: 16). Through this manipulation of the genre's gendered dynamics, the programme signals the transgressive impact of WSPU's social and political actions.

Shoulder to Shoulder provided the suffragettes with new historical stature (LeMahieu 1990: 250); however, the programme has remained largely unseen since its broadcast, rarely repeated and never released on VHS or DVD.[3] This 'organised forgetting' (Monk 2015: 31) stands in contrast to its period drama contemporary *Days of Hope* (BBC One, 1975). Ken Loach and Tony Garnett's controversial socialist serial charted the British labour movement through the male members of a working-class family from 1916 (when conscription was introduced) to 1926 (the year of Britain's general strike). *Days of Hope* is part of the British television drama canon due to its status as radical drama, its 'auteur' creators, and its role in 1970s academic debates over progressive drama and the use of 'classical realism' in the representation of history on screen, now known as 'the *Days of Hope* debate' (Cooke 2003: 100–3). Claire Johnston's 1974 *Screen* article critiquing *Shoulder to Shoulder* for its use of realism and identification echoed many of Colin MacCabe's catalysing arguments in the journal earlier that year. Yet the programme played no part in the debate that followed. Vicky Ball asserts that *Shoulder to Shoulder* proves 'that it is not only "boys' stories" that engage with the class-based politics of the 1970s' (2013: 244). Yet its absence from the accessible archive, television history's canon and accounts of the 1960s and 1970s 'golden age' of radical British television drama reaffirms gendered hierarchies of cultural value and ignores period drama's ability to present political and classed critique.

Working-class histories and the factory floor: *The Mill*

Period drama's engagement with the industrial North offers space for working-class histories beyond those of loyal servants familiar from upstairs–downstairs narratives. Julianne Pidduck points out that the genre's pastoral settings of country estates and village life exclude 'modernity, urbanisation, industrialisation and the industrial worker' (Pidduck 2004: 123). However, these elements are central to period dramas set in the nineteenth-century mill towns of the North of England. *The Mill* and *North & South* chronicle the shifts in population, power and labour produced by the region's booming manufacturing base during the industrial revolution. As Beth Johnson and David Forrest note, British 'television dramas frequently draw upon regional iconographies to organise class identity' (2017: 6), and both programmes depict the industrial North as 'a place constantly at work and as a consequence as resolutely *working*-class' (Long 2017: 171). Through programmes like *Days of Hope*, *When the Boat Comes In* (BBC One, 1976–81), *North & South*, *The Village* (BBC One, 2013–14) and *The Mill*, period drama writes the nineteenth- and twentieth-century working class back into British history.

The Mill and *North & South* present the factory floors of Lancashire cotton mills as spaces of working-class 'heritage', expanding the term's limiting use in genre discussions. Rather than period drama turning its 'back on the industrialised chaotic present' to 'nostalgically reconstruct an imperialist and upper-class Britain' (Higson 2006 [1993]: 93), these programmes reconstruct Britain's chaotic industrialised past. They showcase how 'England is founded on a violent past' and 'the forceful suppression of dissent' (Ken Loach quoted in Lyndon 1975: 66). The struggle of mill workers' everyday lives – where child labour, poverty and death are ever present – is blended with the dynamism of both the factory floor machinery and the collective action of workers unions. These dramas draw on social realism's connection with class and 'the real' (Rolinson 2011) to suggest their interpretation of the past is 'a darker and because of that perhaps more "real" place' (Kleinecke-Bates 2014: 101).

Jerome de Groot positions *The Mill* as 'misery programming', aligning it with BBC One's *The Village* as 'actively anti-conservative' period dramas which serve as 'social-history documents that strive to show a more authentic life, particularly revising idealised versions of the 19th century' (2016: 166, 163). *The Mill* is written by Jon Fay, who had a background in evening soap operas *Coronation Street* (ITV, 1961–) and *Brookside* (Channel 4, 1982–2003). Its storytelling draws on these programmes' blend of social realism, melodrama and the mundane everyday, tracing connections between the Northern working-class past and present. A co-production between Channel 4's drama and 'specialist factual' departments, *The Mill* was marketed as the channel's first 'factually-inspired period drama', demarking its difference from docudrama. With its teenage protagonist and focus on child labour, it was targeted at a younger audience and scheduled at 8 p.m. on Sundays rather than competing with BBC's and ITV's 9 p.m. prestige slot. Surrounding paratexts clearly signalled *The Mill*'s educational role, and its dialogue is frequently didactic, using historical drama's conventional practice of evoking 'points of historical significance' through dialectical exchanges (Forrest 2011: 225).[4] Its storytelling draws on the archives of Cheshire's Quarry Bank Mill, a cotton mill owned by the regionally powerful Greg family, now a National Trust property (acquired in 1939, it was opened to the public in 1958). Programme makers used the vague phrasing of 'broadly truthful' to encompass *The Mill*'s blend of fact and fiction, with largely fictional characters and chronologies devised from the fragments of workers' lives found in Quarry Bank's archived documents. Esther Price was one of the mill's most well-documented workers as she was a runaway who was used as a case study in the political campaign for the ten-hour day (Matthews-Jones 2013). *The Mill*'s Esther is a bolshy, hard-working teenage protagonist whose everyday experiences as a mill worker are intertwined with the region's shifting political landscape. Through the perspectives of the child and teenage workers, the mill-owning Greg family and the campaigners for workers' rights, the cotton mill is presented as an industrial and economic system.

Promotional discourse framed *The Mill* as 'showing history from the worm's eye of the working class' (Dams 2013). Its sympathies lie with the workers, yet it presents an ambiguous portrait of the Greg family's conflicted role as 'paternal employers' to their young workers. The programme highlights the challenges they face navigating the new middle class as business owners who still, as the Greg patriarch asserts, 'get their hands dirty'. *The Mill* consistently illustrates the workers' conflict between trying to survive daily working life and the desire to challenge the status quo through political protest, union agitation and Esther's small acts of rebellion. Set across 1833–42, *The Mill*'s two seasons feature important political moments in the history of the British working class during a period of massive growth in Manchester and the surrounding Lancashire cotton industry. Season one weaves the campaign for the ten-hour working day into its storytelling, and season two features the Chartist movement for political reform and the campaign for the working-class vote. *The Mill*'s factual origins work to substantiate the historical and political dimensions of its narrative, as 'fidelity to chronologically accurate detail is the logic that undergirds historical re-enactment more broadly' (Landsberg 2015: 93). By dramatising lives and events that are not part of the national imaginary of the nineteenth century, like the vast rally for the vote at Kersal Moor in 1838, *The Mill* writes working-class history back into national history.

E. Deidre Pribram argues that one of period drama's strengths is its 'capacity to explore the felt experiences of what it might mean to live through an era of historical significance' (2018: 767). *The Mill*'s location filming produces a tactile investment in the affective experiences of the harsh life of mill work. The production combined studio interiors with exteriors filmed on location at Quarry Bank Mill, with Murray Mill in Manchester providing the interiors of the 'mule room' where the young apprentices work the machines spinning the cotton. The clattering, whirring machines are depicted in fragmented close-ups of spinning wheels, cotton reels, and threads strung tightly. This displays the beauty of industry, but also its threat. Episode one opens with a mutilating injury as a child worker is caught up in a machine's belt and drawn instantly to the ceiling, his hand crushed in its wheel. The programme emphasises the physicality of the apprentices' labour as Esther and her teenage co-workers wrench the machines forward and back. In constant motion they clean spindles whilst children scamper underneath to clean cotton fluff, barely escaping the moving machinery. Later in episode one the mill's pre-dawn streets are filled with the clatter of clogs on cobbles as the young workers trudge to work in the dark. We see the sheen of ice on outdoor bathing water and the sharp cracks as it is broken for morning washes, steam rising from bodies amidst foggy, frozen breaths. Here period drama's sensory experience, its close engagement with history 'by means of the fragment and the detail' (Vidal 2012a: 11), is brought to working-class history.

The Mill's first season was one of Channel 4's highest-rated dramas of 2013 with 3.2 million average viewers, yet television critics complained about the programme's worthiness (Dent 2013) and 'relentless misery' (Dempster 2013). *The Village*, which also critiqued British class structures by exploring the hardship of lives beyond the aristocracy, met with a similar response (Wollaston 2013; Lawrence 2013). These critics' complaints are echoed in Jerome de Grout's (2016) labelling of *The Mill* and *The Village* as 'misery texts'. He suggests their storytelling presents a potentially problematic binary, 'as misery is represented as working class and realistic, splendour as aristocratic and pleasurable'

(2016: 163). Yet the assertions by middle-class newspaper critics that realist representations of working-class history are 'worthy' and incompatible with the conventions of Sunday evening period drama illustrate the delimiting cultural perceptions of the genre; one of conservativism and safety, with pleasure only considered part of representations of privilege. Ratings successes such as *North & South* and *Call the Midwife* challenge such assumptions of period drama's classed investments and representational politics.

The industrial city, capitalism and romance: *North & South*

BBC One's *North & South* is also situated in the industrial North and invested in the ethics and human costs of the industrial revolution's accelerated progress. The drama adapts Elizabeth Gaskell's 1854 industrial novel, set in the cotton mills of 1850s Milton (standing in for the Lancashire boom town of Manchester). Following the classic serial model, romance is a central feature, with the conflicts between the mill owners and workers layered onto John Thornton and Margaret Hale's relationship. The most traditionally romantic of Gaskell's novels, it presents a familiar period drama love story between a strong-willed heroine and darkly passionate hero. This romance makes safe the narrative's investment in industrial unrest and its questioning of the morality of the capitalism that was driving the expansion of the Victorian empire. These are both topics rarely addressed in the Sunday 9 p.m. timeslot and classic serial form.

Gaskell was invested in working-class struggle at a time of social and cultural upheaval, and as a result sits apart from the canonical authors of British literature to whom period drama has repeatedly returned. *North & South* had previously been adapted in 1975 by an all-male production team, and Gaskell's last novel *Wives and Daughters* was adapted in 1999 by Andrew Davies (BBC One). The classic serial had dominated the BBC One period drama since the success of 1995's *Pride and Prejudice*. These were largely adapted by male 'auteur' television writers, particularly Davies, whereas 2004's *North & South* was adapted by Sandy Welch, a female writer new to the classic serial. Its industrial North setting signals a post-millennial shift in the dominant representational tendencies that had shaped the post-*Pride and Prejudice* classic serial boom (Kleinecke-Bates 2014: 93). Notably it is one of the few BBC classic serials of this period that is not a US co-production, perhaps because its classed investments trouble the marketable vision of the British past. The drama challenges perceptions of 'the classic television serial as a homogenous group of texts lacking either the distinctiveness or artistic merit of their literary sources' (Butt 2014: 27). *North & South* unsettles the aesthetic conventions of the classic serial through its use of an expressionist and subjective aesthetic. This highlights Margaret's misplaced nostalgia for the pastoral South by self-reflexively quoting but also questioning 'heritage aesthetics'. As Iris Kleinecke-Bates suggests, the programme questions, challenges and destabilises geographic, gender and class polarities (2014: 86).

North & South provides the viewer with 'history from below', albeit through the perspective of a gentlewoman. Forthright vicar's daughter Margaret is transplanted from the lush pastoral village of Helston in the South to the North's dark and crowded industrial town of Milton. Her distaste for the practical, capitalism-focused lives of the manu-facturing class and her nostalgia for the South are gradually shown to be misplaced. Conflicts of class and gender together with the strug-gle between the individual and society are embodied in Margaret's fractious relationship with the stoic yet passionate middle-class mill owner Thornton. Their central conflict and eventual romance links 'the plight of workers with that of women' (Sali 2014: 126). Margaret's ethical and charitable world view (shaped by her father's intellec-tual questioning) positions her as innately empathetic to the town's workers, in opposition to Thornton's pragmatic approach to the mill business. She is structured as the voice of the workers, asserting their plight to Thornton and questioning the morality of Milton's industrial economy. Margaret's friendship with mill worker Bessie Higgins helps her recognise her privileged naivety and understand the economic necessities of working within the unsafe conditions of Thornton's mill. In contrast to *The Mill*'s centralising of the workers' perspective, *North & South* echoes *Shoulder to Shoulder* in its use of an upper-middle-class woman to assert the rights of the working class. However, *North & South* gives equal weight to the fiery rhetoric of Bessie's father Nicholas, a union leader.

Margaret and Thornton's potential romance is impaired by a blend of class and regional polarities. Despite her own fallen circumstances after her father leaves the Church, Margaret's upper-middle-class upbringing feeds her dislike and rejection of Thornton. She views his Northern bluntness, his anger, physicality and passion as ungen-tlemanly. Thornton illustrates the unstable class status of the new middle class of Victorian manufacturing families within Britain's long-established pre-industrial class structures. Margaret views his capitalist ideologies and new money status with distaste, but *North & South* ultimately valorises Thornton's position as a 'self-made man'. The adaptation shapes the mill owner as an entrepreneur, mapping the perspectives of the present onto the past. Thornton embodies social mobility and economic success gained through focus, hard work and self-sacrifice, qualities valued by contemporary audiences and neoliberal society (Fanning 2018: 100).

Margaret and Thornton's conflicting world views are illuminated by the programme's blend of the emotional investments of melodrama and expressionist elements derived from poetic realism. Richard Butt argues that the adaptation follows Gaskell's investment in melodrama as a mode of social criticism, using moral frames to generate emotional responses to 'the social injustices of mid-nineteenth-century England' (2014: 28). In *North & South* the cotton industry drives progress and creates wealth, but it is also depicted as a site of moral horror, creating unhealthy and exploitative working conditions whose human costs are shown through Bessie's illness and death. The programme presents Thornton's mill as an ambiguous spectacle, shaped through an expressionist alignment with Margaret's perspective on her first visit. This is a space of work and hard labour, with *North & South* sharing *The Mill*'s fascination with the fearsome machinery of industry. Where that programme's worker protagonists enabled a tactile closeness with machinery, *North & South* presents the machine room of Thornton's mill through the outsider perspective of upper-middle-class Margaret. It is a dizzying mass of activity that she gazes upon in wondering horror; the space is presented as fearful, foreign and fascinating. The subjective aesthetic of these scenes illustrates Margaret's perception

Figure 3.2 Margaret stares at the industrial spectacle of the cotton mill's machine room in *North & South* (BBC One, 2004)

of Thornton and his machines as the embodiments of modernity's brutality, where workers are disposable components in the mill town's economic system.

In shots of the machine room the frame is densely packed in strikingly composed images. Workers attend to rows of clattering, whirring machines arranged deep in the frame, the air a haze of cotton dust. This is a spectacle of industrial power, but also a vision of horror in both the deafening speed of the steam-powered machines (which children scramble underneath to clean) and the deathly cotton that floats through the air, clogging the workers' lungs. When Margaret first enters the mill the cotton drifts like snow, caught in light shafts and cloaking the workspace in a beautiful soft-focus haze. The programme presents the mill as a spectacle of fearful, thundering beauty, a hell – as Margaret describes it – that is 'snow-white'. As Iris Kleinecke-Bates suggests, 'The idealised notion of beauty representing beauty is continuously questioned and undermined', with the 'surreal beauty' of the mill floor suggesting that in *North & South* things are not what they seem (2014: 94). This depiction of the mill's beautiful horror aligns with Margaret's subjective perspective of Milton and her eventual 'realisation of the incompleteness of her understanding of her surroundings' (Kleinecke-Bates 2014: 93). The complexity of this deathly beauty counters Jerome de Groot's categorising of 'misery programming' in binary opposition to aristocratic splendour and pleasure, where working-class history is aligned with a realist mise-en-scene of 'bleached austerity, dark greys, and shadows' (2016: 163). *North & South* depicts Milton as a town of austere dark greys and shadows but also through the expressionist wonder of its dynamic yet threatening industrial splendour.

Like *Shoulder to Shoulder* and *The Mill*, *North & South* builds scenes of passionate political rhetoric, particularly the union speeches of Nicholas Higgins. The first half of the serial is driven by the mill workers' threat of labour action over wages, which culminates in a strike. Here the narrative divisions that align Margaret with the workers are compounded by spatial divisions that position her and the workers below Thornton and the watchful mill owners. Episode two builds to two connected sequences, the angry protest of the strikers at Thornton's mill and Thornton's declaration of love and failed proposal to Margaret. This illustrates the narrative's intertwining of its labour and romance plots and the use of sweeping emotional expression in both. Richard Butt describes the protest as the 'sensation scene' of the melodrama mode, where Gaskell and the adaptation use mise-en-scène to assert passionate emotions (2014: 40). Margaret declares the moral right of the workers to Thornton and demands he face them. She is then drawn to defend him from their anger first through passionate speech and then with her body. The scene's impact is drawn from Margaret's 'exemplary ethical action [and] the melodramatic staging of her virtue', which is reinforced by the mise-en-scène's stark black and white colour palette and polarised lighting that casts Margaret as a vision in white (Butt 2014: 39). The emotions of the event and Margaret's break from social conventions in her public defence of Thornton lead to his thwarted declaration of love. The programme here uses the stark sensation of the melodrama mode to interweave the sweeping affective pleasures of its central romance (which I discuss further in Chapter 6) with the dynamic energy of union protest.

Thornton's love and respect for Margaret draws out his compassion for his workers. Yet it is the respectful bond he develops with Nicholas Higgins that completes his transformation into a caring capitalist. The contradictions of this figure draw connections between Gaskell's vision of the 'caring manufacturer' as the answer to the industrial revolution's moral failings and the neoliberal political ideologies of 2004's 'New Labour' government (Sali 2014: 137). Thornton comes to symbolise the industrialised nation's struggle between capitalism and morality. Through his growing friendship with Higgins, Thornton shifts to an egalitarian position. Together with Margaret's recognition of Milton's dynamism and the value of the mill's work, this clears the path for the couple's eventual romantic pairing. Margaret's planned financial investment in Thornton's mill sees *North & South* position caring capitalism and the couple's marriage of equals as a resolution to the industrial revolution's moral murkiness and the narrative's mapping of gender onto classed conflict.

If *North & South* reworks its romantic hero in line with an idealised version of contemporary neoliberal ideologies, then *Call the Midwife* shows how period drama can be used to work through or 'worry at' (Wheatley 2005: 15) contemporary political tensions. Broadcast during a period of intense press and political attacks on the welfare state across the 2010s, the programme presented a vision of British post-war society indelibly shaped by the National Health Service.

Women's labour: *Call the Midwife*

Some British television critics have positioned *Call the Midwife* as comforting, 'cosy' nostalgia (Tincknell 2013: 774; Rolinson 2017a). This is echoed by Charlotte Brunsdon's description of the 'warmth of its evocation of female agency' within 'a long line of comforting Sunday night television drama' (2018: 78). It was created by Heidi Thomas, a writer with an established reputation for BBC period drama, including the 2007 adaptation of Elizabeth Gaskell's *Cranford*, which also centred on a female ensemble with elderly characters. Running since 2012, the series is one of the public service broadcaster's longest-running prime-time dramas (currently recommissioned for thirteen seasons running until 2024) and key prestige drama brands. Its BBC One 8 p.m. Sunday timeslot signals it as family viewing, yet the programme offers a 'sneaky radicalism' (Nussbaum 2016) and 'social anger' (Rolinson 2017b). This is channelled through the work of a quartet of National Health Service (NHS) midwives who support the Poplar community of London's East End, working alongside an order of nuns. The long-running programme charts the working-class Docklands community from 1957 into the 1960s, taking the neighbourhood from post-war poverty into a period of progressive change. It illustrates the social impact of Britain's post-war welfare and housing systems, the neighbourhood's shifting demographics, and the beginnings of challenges to class and gendered dynamics. The programme blends class and politics through its 'compelling defence of socialised medicine as central to the transformation of the health and happiness of ordinary people' (Tincknell 2013: 780). By embedding its stories in Poplar's working-class community, *Call the Midwife* offers a 'history from below' that blends public and medical history.

Call the Midwife illustrates how period drama traces connections between the past and present, returning to historical moments that speak to contemporary viewers' cultural context. The programme debuted in a 2012 Britain suffering the effects of the Great Recession along with the austerity policies and anti-welfare state agenda of the Conservative-led coalition government. This period saw escalating attacks on the health service from Conservative politicians and parts of the press, illustrating the crisis rhetoric that Hannah Hamad argues has 'characterised mediation of the NHS since its inception' (2016: 141). In this climate a programme showcasing the value of socialised medicine was inherently political. Yet Hamad suggests that despite its championing of the NHS's social interventions, the programme unwittingly contributes to the contemporary discourse of NHS critique. In asserting the value of nursing's affective labour, *Call the Midwife* offers a nostalgic vision of the 1950s as a golden age of NHS care. Hamad argues its midwives embody an irretrievable ideal of nursing as young, white, feminine and middle class, depicting an idealised version of 'care' that contemporary attacks on 'falling standards' in the NHS claimed was irretrievably lost (2016: 146).

The programme's medical procedural structure uses patients to explore particular topics and issues. It is particularly focused on the gendered labour of women both inside and outside the home: labour both domestic and vocational, the labour of childbearing, along with the physical and emotional labour of women's lives. Moya Luckett connects *Call the Midwife* to other 2000s and 2010s period dramas about mid-century working women, suggesting these build connections between past and present by linking work to 'female emancipation, agency, self-fulfilment and even glamour', whilst also recognising the 'contradictory pleasures and pressures of female labour' (2017: 15, 16). By centralising women's labour, *Call the Midwife* frequently contrasts the challenging yet fulfilling professional lives of the midwives with the domestic labour of their working-class patients struggling to raise large families in poverty. In some ways the programme aligns the sacrifice of motherhood with the sacrifice of the working woman, with both the nuns and the young midwives living a sacrificial and frequently monastic life (Luckett 2017: 29). Yet their single, middle-class lifestyles allow them freedoms and social pleasures often out of reach of the working-class mothers they serve.

Call the Midwife's attention to another form of female labour breaks the 'aesthetic taboo' (Fitzgerald 2015: 253) of childbirth. It presents the physicality and visceral nature of birth, its sweat and blood, and the midwives' intimate, skilled ministrations. This 'unusual bluntness about how the female body operates' (Nussbaum 2016) centralises an affective experience of women's history, particularly in the home births that are the dominant experience of its earlier seasons. The programme frequently brings the midwives and the audience into the cramped, dark homes of working-class women, crammed with families and evidence of domestic labour. These are spaces infrequently seen in British period drama and assert that 'domesticity *is* valuable history' (Fitzgerald 2015: 253). The programme's East End setting and its 'radical nostalgia for the newly created welfare state' (Luckett 2017: 21) foreground the social barriers caused by poverty. By depicting the high maternal mortality rates in the post-war period as well as the impact of childbirth on working-class women's daily lives, desires and freedoms, the programme 'implicitly endorses the virtues of safe birth control and family planning' (Tincknell 2013: 780).

Call the Midwife's depiction of mid-century Poplar is shaped by ambiguity. Its 'material social conditions' depict the starkness of poverty, yet the programme also 'contains a powerful nostalgic appeal for the community values which it espouses' (Tincknell 2013: 771). These values are embodied by the multigenerational female collective of Nonnatus House, whose working women assert a vision of 'capable, progressive femininity' (Luckett 2017: 19). The midwives' caring vocation and the NHS itself are aligned with the nuns' Christian humanist values of love, tolerance and compassion (Tincknell 2013: 779–80). The programme frequently sets these beliefs and viewpoints in tension with the challenges and lived experience of the women's working-class patients. Yet the narrative ultimately asserts a progressive, compassionate view of society, one that understands the actions of individuals as the result of their circumstances; a world view in tension with twenty-first-century neoliberal rhetoric of individual blame. The Nonnatus House dinner table features discussions that repeatedly return to issues of poor housing, welfare support, employment and family dynamics. The midwives present these as the cause of their episodic caseloads, drawing connections and contrasts between mid-century and contemporary struggles.

The programme was commissioned following a 2009 refocusing of the BBC's period drama away from the classic serial towards less explored eras of British history, particularly the twenty-first century. *Call the Midwife*'s late 1950s and early 1960s setting positions it within lived memory of a portion of its audience, with the programme drawing on and at times challenging cultural memories of the period. Initially based on the memoirs of midwife Jennifer Worth – fictionalised in the young middle-class protagonist Jenny – the programme's narrative is 'animated via recollections' (Luckett 2017: 18). Each episode's themes are shaped by the opening and closing voice-over of Mature Jenny (played by Vanessa Redgrave), which continue even when Jenny departs the programme after three seasons. This voice-over, along with the *Call the Midwife*'s investment in women's lives, arguably influences press readings of the programme as 'cosy' despite its frequently stark emotions, visceral physicality and sense of social justice. The voice-over frames the programme as memory, conveying a sense of nostalgic reminiscence and safety. Where an episode focuses on the difficulties of women's lives, the framing voice-over can provide comfort through an implied assurance that these issues are now located securely in the past. For example, episode 02: 05 features a desperate mother of eight resorting to an unsafe backstreet abortion. The episode's closing voice-over asserts that the introduction of the contraceptive pill will revolutionise the future lives of her daughters. In such moments the programme 'reminds women of what has been achieved in the fifty years since the NHS was established and what now is endangered' (Tincknell 2013: 780).

The voice-over's omniscience can also be foreboding, challenging this 'nostalgic' safety. Season five's premiere centres on local woman Rhoda, who gives birth to a baby with severe birth defects. The episode's closing voice-over sees Mature Jenny obliquely warn of society's coming reckoning with the fallibility of the medical profession, which viewers understand as referring to the worldwide thalidomide scandal. Born without limbs and with malformed hands, baby Susan's body shocks the midwives and horrifies her father, illustrating how the impact of disability can overwhelm families 'with few resources to care for children who are viewed by a frightened public as monsters' (Nussbaum 2016). The closing voice-over signals that Rhoda and Susan's story is not yet complete and tees up the thalidomide scandal as the long-arc storyline of the season. This storyline centres Doctor Turner's guilt as the medical profession deals with further birth defects and investigates their mysterious cause, eventually revealed to be a medication prescribed for morning sickness. Rhoda and her husband's experiences are returned to in two more episodes across seasons five and six to illustrate the human cost of such medical actions within Poplar's community.

Here the programme's medical plot modifies the duality that Belén Vidal reads in period drama's relationship with the past, the careful balance between 'reassuring recognition and uncanny strangeness' (2012a: 204). Baby Susan's body is viewed as fearful and strange by the characters in 1961, but the contemporary audience recognises and understands it. Here the programme reads the past through the present-day knowledge of a large section of the audience. The viewer's awareness that the episode's single case will become a generational scandal settles a pall of tragedy over Susan's story and the season to come. Here the programme's focus on bodies and emotion brings 'a personal, felt connection to the past' (Landsberg 2015: 3) by centring the affective experience of living through medical history and the personal impact of medical progress.

Call the Midwife illustrates how period drama 're-dramatis[es] the past as an emotionally charted space, and shows a preference for affective rather than intellectual histories' (Vidal 2012a: 21). By centring the communal hands of women (and one community-based male doctor), it illustrates the everyday, personal impact of small medical advancements. Across its long run the programme charts developments in medical provision and the increasingly centralised structure of the NHS. These are constantly held in tension with the midwives' knowledge and their devotion to community care. The programme repeatedly asserts 'women's values' (Tincknell 2013: 780) and the midwives' presence in their community over the cold, clinical gaze of the male-dominated, hospital-centred NHS. Here *Call the Midwife* contrasts with the pioneering surgeons of US period drama *The Knick* (Cinemax, 2014–15). Set at a hospital in early twentieth-century New York, the US prestige drama's medical professionals similarly serve a poverty-ridden community during a period of medical advancements. However, its narrative focuses on the innovations of the operating theatre and the boundary-pushing activities of its male protagonists, the 'difficult' men familiar from 2000s and 2010s prestige television (Martin 2013). In contrast, *Call the Midwife* presents its medical procedural stories through lived experience, embedded in the homes of Poplar's working-class women.

The midwives and nuns hold a privileged social position as holders of medical knowledge. They bring new social and medical developments to the community, from teeth brushing to family planning. Discussing the programme's earlier seasons, Louise Fitzgerald argues the middle-class midwives are frequently presented as holding progressive views that align them with the contemporary viewer, whereas the uneducated working-class women are positioned as ignorant or prejudiced (2015: 259). Yet across the programme's long run a form of exchange has emerged as the primary relationship between the midwives and their community. The young women are challenged by both their patients and the nuns to build a fuller understanding of the community they serve. *Call the Midwife*'s procedural structure positions the working-class community as guest stars in the middle-class medical ensemble's ongoing arcs. However, its editing interweaves its guest and lead characters through visual connections and comparisons that develop 'our understanding of characters in their social environment and at times even complicates the position of the midwives in that environment' (Rolinson 2017b).

In season six new midwife Valerie integrates Poplar's working-class perspective into the central ensemble. A local barmaid and former Army nurse, she represents the view from within as Sister Monica Joan delivered her as a baby. Her personal and professional connections to the community become entangled in the long-arc storyline of season eight. The midwives deal with life-threatening illnesses caused by the infected instruments of a back-street abortionist, whom Valerie eventually discovers to be her grandmother. Set four years before abortion was legalised in the UK, the arc illustrates women's need to resort to illegal medical treatments, with back-street abortion a recurring single-episode plot across the programme's run.[5] It also shows how care for the community's women has long existed beyond the official figures of Nonnatus House.

Call the Midwife's political potential lies in its prioritising those whom feminism has been accused of leaving behind. Noting that the wombs of poor women are the most political place on earth, Louise Fitzgerald argues that the programme humanises and individualises the pregnant working-class woman, who in wider culture is frequently framed as a parasitic object of horror (2015: 255). This forms part of the programme's address to and representation of groups and topics often absent in period drama. Yet some women are more invisible than others. The programme's early seasons lack representations of the racial diversity that has historically been part of the London Docklands community (Burton 2017: 73–5). Here *Call the Midwife* plays into cultural and political structuring of British working-class history as white. This illustrates how period drama's images of the past are built to accommodate flawed cultural memory as much as historical fact (Fitzgerald 2015: 258). The programme eventually makes steps towards an intersectional understanding of class, as once its narrative departs from Worth's memoirs the programme begins to integrate the experiences of immigrant women into the community. From season four onwards, it begins to 'reassert histories hitherto excluded from the national imaginary' (Burton 2017: 79) by including more fully drawn West Indian, South Asian and Chinese families, as well as adding Jamaican midwife Lucille in season seven. (I discuss Lucille further in Chapter 4.)

Call the Midwife illustrates how period drama can shore up or challenge existing perceptions of Britain's past. The programme draws affective connections between the past and the present through its focus on women's labour – vocational and domestic, physical and emotional – and the social impact of the young NHS. It explores the challenges of life in post-war working-class communities whilst asserting the value of its multigenerational female collective, who are presented as embodiments of its compassionate, idealised vision of the welfare state.

Conclusion

This chapter's focus on class and politics has shown how period drama can reinforce existing top-down narratives of the past, yet also has the potential to challenge them. Looking beyond the upstairs–downstairs narratives that have often been the focus of discussions of period drama's classed dynamics, it has illustrated Belén Vidal's assertion that period drama is a 'stage of competing memories and desires' (2012a: 47). It has foregrounded programmes that illustrate struggles against the status quo as well as the politics of the everyday. The case studies show how period drama can write women's politics and the lived experience of the working class back into history. We can also see period drama's investment in an affective experience of the past. These programmes draw the viewer close whilst also presenting discomforting experiences that can challenge perceptions of the genre's cosiness, exhibiting period drama's tension between distance and closeness.

Notes

1. See Michael Newman and Elana Levine's *Legitimating Television* for in-depth discussion of television authorship (2011: 38–58).
2. Julian Fellowes's class status is elite even by the standards of the British television industry, which, as an Ofcom report (2019b) highlighted, is dominated by those from privileged, privately educated backgrounds.
3. In 2019 *Shoulder to Shoulder* was added to the British educational streaming service Box of Broadcasts, which is not available to the general public.
4. Online paratexts show how Channel 4 framed the programme as an education text for schools, producing short videos as discussion prompts that were 'designed to reveal the impact of issues portrayed in The Mill on young people in the UK today, raising important questions about how society has progressed since the 1830s' (Channel 4 2014).
5. See Rolinson (2017b) for a detailed close textual analysis of an abortion sequence in episode 02: 05.

4 Space and Place

Period drama's encounter with the people and places of the past is frequently discussed in terms of mise-en-scène and location, particularly its grand houses and pastoral scenes. This is illustrated in Sarah Cardwell's outlining of the genre conventions of classic novel adaptations, which includes 'generic "heritage landscape" long shots' along with set piece scenes of 'ballroom, or at least "dancing", sequences; scenes of refined conversations over afternoon tea; sequences where characters travel by carriage or horseback across rolling countryside' (2002: 121). The heritage debate's reading of 1980s period drama asserted that period film and television's settings and visual style were frozen, inherently 'nostalgic' and conservative, a reading that retains a tenacious hold on discussions of the genre. Andrew Higson diagnosed a preoccupation with the visual splendour of privileged lifestyles, arguing this overwhelmed the films' narrative critique of these worlds or their storytelling alignment with outsiders' discomfort (2006 [1993]: 96). As Claire Monk highlights, this 'fixation upon the "fetishization of period details" . . . shaped a critique which seemed to treat visual pleasure itself as politically suspect' (2012: 21). Subsequent programmes and post-heritage scholarship problematised these readings, and Cardwell asserts that '[w]e cannot assume that nostalgia is the only possible response to the gaze as re-presented in classic-novel adaptations, just as "heritage" is not intrinsically reactionary' (2002: 138). This chapter's focus on space and place leaves behind, or at least complicates, the well-established critical frames of heritage and nostalgia to approach period drama from different angles.

I use 'place' to refer to locations and settings – a mansion, a factory, an office, a farm, a living room, a village street and a city – and 'space' to refer to how place is organised through mise-en-scène, movement and narrative. This chapter expands beyond the dominance of the grand house and rural space in existing work on period drama, drawing out the genre's engagement with urban space. It also offers some consideration of the gendered and racial politics of space. I demonstrate how period drama's rendering of space and place blends the 'visual (and aural) spectacle of pastness' (Vidal 2012a: 9) with television's intimacy and its serialised returns. This chapter considers period drama's space and place through the grand house, rural spaces and the city. It then moves on to two case studies that offer different interpretations of twentieth-century New York, *The Marvelous Mrs. Maisel* (Amazon Prime Video, 2017–) and *The Deuce* (HBO, 2017–19).

Grand houses

The grand house is a recurring spatial motif of period drama. This can be a mansion nestled in a landscaped English estate or overlooking a plantation in the antebellum American South. It can also be a townhouse facing onto a bustling city street or quiet square. The grand house performs a dual role, serving as visual spectacle and creating period drama's 'affectively charged interiors where intimate dramas of desire and mannered social critique unfold' (Pidduck 2004: 45). As Belén Vidal explains, the grand house of period drama is 'poised between the shifting meanings of "home", "property", and "museum"' (2012a: 65). It can embody social standing or the contested inheritances of the upper classes (*Sense and Sensibility* (BBC One, 2008), *Downton Abbey* (ITV, 2010–15)). It showcases the spoils of capitalist colonial oppression (*Indian Summers* (Channel 4, 2015–16), *Howards End* (BBC One/Starz, 2017)) or wealth to be exchanged in marriage plots (*Pride and Prejudice* (BBC One, 1995), *Vanity Fair* (BBC One, 1998; ITV, 2018)). It can also socially and emotionally entrap women in melodrama and gothic narratives (*The Tenant of Wildfell Hall* (BBC One, 1996), *The Crimson Petal and the White* (BBC Two, 2011)).

The grand house serves as the object of the camera's gaze, as a site of visual pleasure and desire both inside and outside the narrative. The heritage debate characterised it as a frozen house-museum version of the past. Here the house was 'caught in a critique profoundly suspicious of the visual artefacts and practices of heritage culture' (Vidal 2012a: 67). The grand house embodies period drama's interdependence with the tourist industry. The 'cult of the country house' (Cannadine 1997) makes period drama part of a tourism cycle as preserved buildings can be used as locations for programmes. In return this display draws visitors to the sites. 'Prized as living links to the past' (Samuel 1994: 39), the preserved grand house signifies the permanence of a privileged world. It embodies classed wealth and power both in its original construction and in its ability to be preserved where other structures and homes have not. Julianne Pidduck complicates the concept of the house-museum, highlighting the expressive and storytelling dimensions of the grand house's mise-en-scène, such as the 'panoply of detail' in the sumptuous interiors of 1990s Austen adaptations. Pidduck suggests this evokes the 'oppressive patriarchal laws of inheritance', the social codes of comportment and the weight of history that shape the female characters' lives and actions (2004: 29).

The spatial dynamics of *The Crown* (Netflix, 2016–) illustrate 'the ambiguity of visual spectacle' (Vidal 2012a: 18) common to the grand houses of period drama. The drama tracks the Windsor royal family and the reign of Queen Elizabeth II across the second half of the twentieth century. It uses a slow pace and static framing of vast rooms in wide and long shot to encourage a lingering gaze on these ornate, spectacular and at times cavernous interiors. This mise-en-scène produces the fetishised, frozen, 'orderly spectacle of the house-museum' that the heritage debate read as unambiguously conservative (Vidal 2012a: 18). However, Will Stanford Abbis suggests the programme's interrogation of this world, its self-consciousness and ambiguity allow 'a post-heritage point of view to consistently dominate the more conservative heritage visuals' (2019: 8). *The Crown*'s visual storytelling depicts the physical and emotional isolation of the Windsor royal family. This is embodied in the tensions produced by the grand house serving as both museum and family home. The scale of these royal spaces is used to depict Queen Elizabeth's isolation and to separate the royals from the changing world outside: post-war austerity, the social changes of 1960s and the political strife of the 1970s. Within Buckingham Palace shots are frequently composed at a distance, framing the space rather than the character. Square or high-angled compositions dwarf the royal family (and the occasional servant) as they work or attempt to perform domesticity within ornate expanse. Medium shots of Elizabeth in meetings with visitors are composed at a slight distance to isolate her in the frame and fill the space around her with walls and surfaces that are covered with antiques. Shots are frequently composed in depth, with characters framed in front of a procession of doorways or pushed to the side of a frame filled with an expanse of extravagantly decorated table. This communicates the isolation of royal life and a marriage under the strain of unbalanced power dynamics. The distancing effect of this visual system means it is hard to gain access to Elizabeth's interiority as the viewer is rarely in intimate contact with her (in contrast to the programme's investment in the struggles of Prince Philip, Prince Charles and occasionally Princess Margaret). *The Crown*'s grand house illustrates how period drama's spectacle is most productively read as ambiguous, at once visual pleasure and an affective critique of social constraint.

To depict the day-to-day life of the royal family *The Crown* needed to recreate existing royal residences. The production team drew on Britain's stock of stately homes and palaces preserved by class privilege and tourism, using Lancaster House and Wilton House along with a selection of preserved and abandoned stately homes. These were patchworked together to construct the 'professional' spaces of Buckingham Palace and other royal residences. Expansive sets create an imagined version of the palace's private royal apartments. Rather than exacting reconstruction of these spaces (as there is no access to the private royal spaces for research and these are rarely photographed), *The Crown*'s production designer sought to create the 'feel' of a palace through 'a healthy mix of historical accuracy and creative interpretation' (Ivie 2017). This relied on the audience's familiarity with the classed spatial markers of extravagant wealth, built in part through previous period dramas. The scale of the royal households was emphasised in a promotional discourse that foregrounded production design, touting the 398 sets used across eight months of filming season two (Boone 2018). *The Crown* was in part marketed on the $130 million budget that Netflix provided to enable this scale of production across the programme's first two season. This was asserted as a 'type of scale and historical recreation from locations and sets ... unprecedented in television' (O'Falt 2017). To draw on Charlotte Brunsdon (1990: 85), this promotional discourse presents the vast sums of money used to reconstruct royal space and place as a marker of *The Crown*'s – and by extension Netflix's – 'quality'. This was particularly important for a streaming platform whose brand was still being built in 2016 and that lacked a reputation for prestige drama.

I have noted British period drama's symbiotic relationship with British tourism. The preservation practices of the American South's heritage industry enabled runaway slave drama *Underground* (WGN, 2016–17) to reconstruct a plantation's grand house on location. The 'big business' of the South's plantation tourism sells a 'South of the imagination ... created by the industries of popular media' (Cox 2011: 8). A selective and white rendering of 'Dixie' is commodified as a 'fetishised memory of white supremacy' (Bradley 2016: 8). *Underground* counters this vision of the South by bringing to life the army of enslaved Black bodies required to maintain its grand houses and effortless life of privilege. The production recreated interiors on a soundstage and filmed exteriors on location at Felicity Plantation near Baton Rouge, Louisiana. Rebuilding its facade to create the Macon

Plantation's 'big house',[1] the production added the sweeping staircases and picturesque verandas common to those of the programme's Georgia setting. However, slave quarters have not been preserved like plantation houses, which helps plantation tourism to erase or water down the region's painful history (Bradley 2016: 7). The Rural Life Museum at Louisiana State University included rare, preserved slave quarters. These enabled *Underground* to reproduce the communal and family spaces largely absent from the plantation house-centred national imaginary of the antebellum South (Sisson 2016).

Underground reproduces the spectacle of the 'South of the imagination' but shapes it through the perspective of those who labour to maintain its riches. The Macon Plantation's 'big house' is introduced in a sequence that draws on the selective white 'heritage' gaze that has shaped the antebellum plantation in popular culture (Cox 2011: 8). But it blends this with a dynamic visual style that reorientates the perspective on this space (01: 01). The plantation is introduced in a series of sweeping aerial shots that display the building and its bordering cotton fields, accompanied by the non-diegetic sound of a Black woman gently humming a melody. This sequence follows a dynamic pre-credits action sequence scored to a contemporary hip-hop track. In contrast, these shots bring a peaceful pause and an edge of romanticism to this initial sight of the house, presented through the genre's conventional visual dynamics. Yet the woman's voice makes an aural connection to the enslaved people who maintain this grand space and the voice becomes atonal as the sequence transitions to the cotton fields. Here low angles and close-ups centre the cowed, nervous field slaves stooping to pick cotton. The plantation's visual splendour is immediately connected to the violent system that maintains it. An edit contrasts these hardened hands with those of light-skinned house slave Rosalee who is planting flowers in a manicured garden at the front of the 'big house'. The sequence suddenly shifts to a faster pace with shots of a running boy (James) accompanied by driving drums on the score. A cut to an arcing extreme long shot of the front of the house displays its sweeping driveway, landscaped lawns and pond. This conventional 'heritage' long shot (Cardwell 2002: 140–1) centres Rosalee, tiny in the middle of the frame, displaying the grandeur maintained by many hands like hers. In a spectacular long take the programme then situates the geography of the house by tying it to Rosalee, the programme's protagonist, rather than its white masters. From this extreme long shot the camera swiftly arcs around the driveway, reframing to a long shot of Rosalee and James as he delivers his message. The camera then tracks quickly backwards through the house's porch in a steadicam

Figure 4.1 Rosalee runs through the hall of the 'big house' in an *Underground* (WGN, 2016–17) long take

shot that keeps Rosalee in the centre of a long shot as she gathers her skirts and runs into the house. This long take is reframed to a medium shot as the camera continues backwards through the house propelled by Rosalee as she runs through the spacious hall, passing an array of house slaves maintaining the grand space, and out its back door. The camera disconnects from Rosalee and rises up into a crane shot revealing the columned rear of the house framed by the branches of a huge tree as she runs out of frame. The sequence continues with a series of edits that follow Rosalee as she runs into the slave quarters to assist her mother with a birth. This visually dynamic long take establishes the world of the plantation and *Underground*'s rhythm and pace. It upsets the conventional visual dynamics used to depict both period drama's grand house and the world of the antebellum South. Instead, it centres the plantation's enslaved workers, signalling the narratives is theirs.

Rural spaces

Where period drama's grand house combines spectacle and constraint, its rural spaces – pastoral countryside, rugged moors and windswept highlands – combine spectacle and freedom. This is a space that can be bucolic or bleak. A pre-industrial space largely emptied of people is unspoilt, absent the signs of modernity communicated by the city. The landscapes of British period drama are shaped by regional distinctions: the gently rolling hills of the English home counties, the stark and windswept Yorkshire and Derbyshire moors, the sublime mountains and glens of the Scottish Highlands. Like the grand house, rural space illustrates period drama's interconnection with tourism and ideologies of nation. Period dramas utilise Britain's country estates, national parks and Areas of Outstanding Natural Beauty (designated as National Scenic Areas in Scotland). The preservation of these 'unspoiled' natural spaces facilitates the genre's presentation of picturesque and spectacular landscapes emptied of signs of modernity. 'Imagined and idealized versions of the English countryside play a prominent role in constructions of national identity' (Carroll 2019: 215), leading period drama's rural space to be read through certain cultural and political frames. Andrew Higson describes the picturesque pastoral imagery of Austen adaptations as a 'surface prettiness' (2010: 208), whilst Katherine Byrne constructs *The Village*'s (BBC One, 2013–14) Peak District landscapes as an idealised, seductive beauty. She argues that this is at odds with the programme's harsh and bleak view of humanity and its 'general refusal of nostalgia' (2015: 150–1). In both cases the visual pleasure of these landscapes is read as romanticised and inherently conservative.

Julianne Pidduck highlights the increasing deployment of 'iconic English landscapes' (2004: 29) in 1990s period drama. Austen adaptations used pastoral imagery centred on the Georgian houses, landscaped estates and picturesque countryside of England's southern home counties. These spaces are frequently read as conservative visions of England, 'heritage' landscapes whose rural space is 'controlled, peaceful, unthreatening' (Cardwell 2006: 26). BBC One's 1995 *Pride and Prejudice* reworked some of period drama's spatial dimensions to emphasise characters' dynamic movement within this English countryside. The adaptation was given an 'energy and youthfulness' through physical exercise, riding, dancing, walking and running (Kleinecke-Bates 2014: 99). Pidduck points out that movement – coach rides, horse rides, picnics and country walks – is a recurring feature of narratives set in the English countryside, offering 'respite from the pressures of social convention' (2004: 29). *Pride and Prejudice*'s opening sequence introduces us to Elizabeth Bennet engaged in a country walk. She watches Darcy and Bingley gallop across the fields on horseback, set against a green and brown patchwork of farmland. Turning in a circle to contemplate the country view, she then gambols down a hillside. Pidduck notes how nearly all episodes of the serial begin with Elizabeth or her sisters engaged in a country walk, and Elizabeth's enjoyment of walking was 'set against costume drama's predominant physical compression' to present her as an 'independent, dynamic, freethinking force' (2004: 34).

The dynamic walking woman positioned within rural landscapes is a key component of Sally Wainwright's Brontë sisters biopic *To Walk Invisible* (BBC One, 2016). The literary legend of the Brontës is intertwined with the Yorkshire moorland. 'Brontë country' and its 'romance of the marginal rural otherness' (Helsinger 2014: 177) is used to promote the South Pennines area surrounding the family's Howarth home. *To Walk Invisible* depicts the moorland just beyond the gates of the Brontës' parsonage home as both everyday and sublime. Expansive aerial shots and intimate medium shots depict the sisters confidently traversing the rocky moorland on regular walks and seeking respite from family conflict nestled in blankets of heather. The moorland evokes these women's practicality and endurance. Their comfort within and easy traversal of its stark, difficult beauty suggests that it is this landscape (along with their brother Branwell's alcoholism) that drives their gothic literary imaginations (Woods 2019: 361). Emily Brontë's 1847 novel *Wuthering Heights* along with its film and television adaptations have contributed to the cultural image of the Yorkshire moors as a space of wild, harsh beauty. The programme strongly connects her to these moorland landscapes, with both Emily and the moors figured as ruggedly everyday and wildly sublime. The drama depicts her as practical and brusque yet uses the Romantic trope of landscape signifying wild interiority to connect Emily's creative voice to this rural space. One intensely affective sequence sees Charlotte discover and read the poems that Emily has secretly written.

Figure 4.2 An aerial shot sweeps around Emily Brontë standing on a rocky outcrop in *To Walk Invisible* (BBC One, 2016)

Her voice unfolds over images of Emily striding determinedly across craggy moorland, tracked by driving drone shots. The sequence's racing, swirling camerawork ultimately breaks free from Emily, propelled by the passion in her words, and speeds out across the moor. The poem climaxes in a sweeping circular aerial shot that frames Emily against a majestic rocky outcrop. This sequence produces an affective experience of the landscape that is aligned with the urgent, passionate, earthy sensuality of Emily's poetry (Woods 2019: 363). *To Walk Invisible* uses sublime images of the wild, uncultured moorland to evoke the unbounded emotions of her hidden creative interior.

Like *To Walk Invisible*, *Outlander* (Starz, 2014–) offers a sensual engagement with rural space, centred on an 'active exploration of land, presenting the experience of walking on the land, touching and feeling it' (Cardwell 2006: 31). Scotland is depicted as a space of sublime landscapes, to be 'gazed at and admired' (Cardwell 2006: 25) in extreme long shot, with the spectacular Glen Coe mountains featured in the programme's opening credits. However, the narrative primarily presents this as a 'land that must be worked, lived with, and respected' (Cardwell 2006: 25), offering a tactile engagement with this environment of sumptuous spectacle and intimate beauty. Duncan Petrie argues that screen representations of Scotland frequently invest it with 'a spiritual power drawn from the landscape and natural phenomena' (2000: 171). As a hybrid period fantasy, *Outlander* centres the spiritual power of this land through its time-travel conceit. It follows former Second World War Army nurse Claire Randall, who is whisked back in time from 1945 to 1743 when she touches a stone circle while on holiday in Scotland with her husband. Transported into the middle of the conflict between the occupying British Army and the local clansmen, she enters into a marriage of convenience with Scottish highlander Jamie Fraser and the pair fall in love. As a romantic-adventure narrative, *Outlander* offers the twin pleasures of female desire and Scottish landscapes, presenting Claire as both a romantic and action heroine in an epic adventure across the landscapes of the Scottish Highlands.

Outlander's extensive location shooting presents Scottish rural space as everlasting and unspoiled, drawing on an established tradition that presents the country through 'the romantic and elemental appeal of the beauty and remoteness of the landscape' (Petrie 2000: 155). The programme is made for US subscription channel Starz, adapted from a series of historical fantasy romance novels by US author Diana Gabaldon (with the first book published in 1991), and has a US showrunner and creative team. However, it is a transnational product, produced by British production company Left Bank Pictures (which is owned by media giant Sony) and filmed in Scotland using an English and Scottish cast and large amount of local crew. This hybrid outsider–insider identity produces a romantic image of highlander culture tinged with mysticism. This vision of Scottish rural space is targeted at the tourist gaze of the international audience. The Scottish clanspeople are depicted as intimately connected with the unforgiving land, unlike the occupying British Army. Despite her English identity marking her as an outsider, Claire's knowledge of botany also ties her to the land. The standing stones that transport her back in time are tied to a female-centred ancient pagan ritual. *Outlander* possesses an 'awareness of the politics of place' (Goodman and Moseley 2018: 68) through its focus on the Scottish highlanders' conflict with the British Army over control of the land and the latter's brutal oppression of the Scots. Season one and two's narrative trajectory leads to the Battle of Culloden, imbuing the landscape with a tragic romance through Claire's knowledge that the Highland clans will imminently be 'lost', wiped out by the battle and the Highland clearances that will follow.

Dynamic and overwhelming cities

When Claire travels back in time in *Outlander*'s opening episode, her confusion is signified through the surrounding landscape, which is suddenly rendered uncanny to her, in part through the absence of the lights of Inverness on the skyline. The absence of the city as a site of modernity is a key part of the representation of space and place through the grand house and rural space. Yet period drama has expansive engagements with city space, from Dickensian London to Weimar Berlin to mid-century Manhattan. As Charlotte Brunsdon argues, television has played a central role in 'the apprehension of cities and how they are inhabited since the mid-twentieth century – so central, and so taken for granted, that it has been almost invisible' (2018: 27). In particular the wealth of Dickens adaptations have shaped televisual understandings of the Victorian city, particularly London. Here city space embodies 'a past that was turbulent in its pace of change, rather than achieved in its pastness', possessing a 'sense of the excitement and terror of modernity' (Brunsdon 2018: 61). This also shapes the Northern English industrial city of *North & South* (BBC One, 2004), which is manifested as a fearsome, oppressive example of modernity's cruelty. However, this representation of space and place is shaped by the programme's use of a subjective aesthetic connected to its protagonist Margaret Hale, whose 'nostalgia for the past and the south gives colour to her memories [and] makes her perceive her present as drab and grey' (Kleinecke-Bates 2014: 90).

North & South uses stylistic juxtapositions to contrast the urban Milton of Margaret's present – associated with people, machinery and money – and the rural Helstone of her past – associated with nature and comfort (Kleinecke-Bates 2014: 89). Episode one presents the pastoral South through Margaret's memories, where its lush greenery and extreme saturation of colour has a dreamlike feel, whereas the North she arrives in has a desaturated, monochrome palette and a crowded mise-en-scène. Iris Kleinecke-Bates argues that the Helstone sequences build on familiar 'heritage' tropes, yet their visual excess breaks with 'what can be perceived as a realistic visualisation of space' (2014: 89). This signifies the pastoral beauty as subjective and Margaret's vision of the South as an unstable fantasy. In contrast, Milton's dark, monochrome palette, crowded frame and persistent smog draws on the North's association with realist narratives, yet this is eventually also revealed to be a subjective vision (Kleinecke-Bates 2014: 90).

Margaret's perspective pervades all of Milton's spatial dynamics, with the town presented as a threatening space from the Hales family's night-time arrival at the train station. On the platform the distressed family are hemmed in by people and machines. The camera's view is constantly obstructed and the soundscape is filled with an oppressive blend of steam, clanking and banging machinery, and the shouts of the crowds that jostle them. In the town views are constantly obstructed by houses, people and industrious activity. However, as Margaret comes to appreciate Milton's people and the town's dynamism, the aesthetic subtly brightens and opens up. Kleinecke-Bates (2014) argues that the series builds a reflexivity into its spatial dynamics, as Margaret comes to understand that her vision of the pastoral South – presented through heightened 'heritage' visual tropes – is an idealised, nostalgic memory. This illustrates the mediated nature of period drama's encounters with the past (Kleinecke-Bates 2014: 82).

North & South's spatial dynamics may be shaped by its heroine's subjectivity, but its visions of the Victorian city align with period drama's representation of this world as an overwhelmed space of conflict and bewildering detail, particularly in neo-Victorian dramas. Programmes such as *The Crimson Petal and the White* (BBC Two, 2011), *Ripper Street* (BBC One/Amazon Prime Video, 2012–16) and *The Alienist* (TNT, 2018–) present London and New York as fast-paced, gothic cities that are at times on the edge of chaos. Working-class spaces such as London's East End and New York's Lower East Side present a heightened vision of this chaos. These dramas engage with what Tamara Katz (2010) describes as 'urban nostalgia'. This counters assumptions of nostalgia's conservatism, instead communicating a 'desire [for] less traditional communities and forms of social convergence imagined through conflict rather than consensus' (Katz 2010: 814). Through genre hybridity and a self-conscious stylisation, these programmes present the city as a harsh, fearful, modern place. Their cities are a spectacle of dense detail and a muscled grotesquery. This 'dirty' vision of city space is constructed by a 'profusion of material details [that] creates a kind of excess which we read as authenticity' (Katz 2010: 832).

Katz describes the New York of *The Alienist* novel as a 'bewildering phantasmagoria and . . . a case study in knowable, socially determined behaviour' (2010: 832). This extends to the TNT adaptation, whose gruesome crime story depicts New York as familiar yet strange. *The Alienist* illustrates how US basic cable channels that lacked a reputation for prestige TV used innovations in period drama to draw attention in the crowded television market of late 2010s Peak TV. These expensive flagship dramas frequently offer unusual or unfamiliar representations of the past. The jagged, skyscraper-filled skyline of New York is etched on the cultural memory, yet in wide shots of the city *The Alienist*'s Victorian skyline feels uncannily empty, despite being crowded with buildings. This absence is signified through an as yet unfinished Brooklyn Bridge, whose rickety, windswept scaffolding must be scaled by a sketch artist to view a victim's body in episode one. Like Dickensian London, this New York is a harsh world of 'fleeting human connections, the inexorable machinery of capital and the law, and the random and not-so-random connections between characters' (Brunsdon 2018: 67).

Charlotte Brunsdon suggests the Dickensian vision of London is widely recognisable, giving the city global reach and export value (2018: 80). The East End of London depicted in BBC One's *Ripper Street* is shaped by period drama's Dickensian city. The police drama blends this with the borough's criminal mythology built from the Victorian Jack the Ripper and the twentieth-century Kray twins, producing a space of muscular masculinity, dirt and disorder. The East End is figured as London's Wild West, a space of sexual violence and perverse killings, gore and body horror.

Where the Dickensian city has long been period drama's dominant city image, however, the 2010s have seen a rise in representations of twenty-first-century cities, including the London East End of *Call the Midwife* (BBC One, 2012–) and the Birmingham gangsters of *Peaky Blinders* (BBC Two/BBC One, 2013–). The twenty-first-century city is shaped by demographic change, with Jerry White suggesting that post-war migration of '[t]he West Indian diaspora of the late 1940s and 1950s was the key event in the remaking of the Londoner' (quoted in Brunsdon 2018: 69). *Small Island* (BBC One, 2009) and select storylines in *Call the Midwife* – particularly those of Jamaican midwife Lucille in season seven – use city space to show West Indian settlement 'as a story of quotidian strangeness, hostility, difficulty and accommodation' (Brunsdon 2018: 69). Brunsdon notes that 'the city also has an inside, which comes in forms of both public and private' space (2018: 35). Period drama's limited depiction of the 'Windrush generation' has used domestic city space to embody these British citizens' struggle to find a home in an inhospitable mid-century London.

Small Island is adapted from Andrea Levy's novel and follows the interconnected lives of Jamaicans Gilbert and Hortense – who migrate to London after the Second World War – and their white English landlady Queenie. Both Hortense and Queenie have made practical choices to marry men they do not love, and their containment and thwarted ambition is personified in the domestic space of Queenie's London house. After she marries Bernard to escape life as a pig farmer, Queenie's married home becomes a drab, empty space of routine and suffocating isolation. Back home in Jamaica, Hortense imagines the 'mother country' will welcome her with a comfortable professional life as a teacher. But the spare, cold room Gilbert rents from Queenie (having met her whilst stationed in Yorkshire during the Second World War) signifies the stark reality she is confronted with on arrival in post-war England. The small, dim room with its bare lightbulb, peeling wallpaper, single sink and rats in the ceiling embodies the broken promises of the mother country. The couple realise that rather than the mythical 'home' they have been rigorously taught about as colonial subjects, this bombed-out London is hostile and unwelcoming. It is as poor, parochial and small-minded as the country they left behind. Due to a friend's good fortune, Gilbert eventually rents a dilapidated house, fulfilling Hortense's dream of her own home, with her own doorbell. The couple's identity as British citizens was unstable in the porous, cramped space of the rented room. Their status is transformed by their escape from the racism of Queenie's husband and neighbours and their possession of their own space as homeowners, which signifies their settlement.

Domestic space is central to *Call the Midwife*'s representation of working-class lives in London's East End. The programme avoids the aesthetic conventions of social realism, the mode most prevalent in stories of working-class life. Its tight framing of domestic spaces evokes the limited and constrained lives of the midwives' working-class patients. But it combines this with a vivid colour palette that evokes 'an energetic and positive femininity that refuses fully to comply with those limitations' (Tincknell 2013: 775). Colour and domestic space play a part in the season seven storyline that tracks Lucille's desire for a welcoming religious community when she is made to feel unwelcome at her local church choir. Lucille's arrival in the Poplar community sees only a fragment of the daily experiences of racism Black midwives recounted in BBC Four documentary *Black Nurses: The Women Who Saved the NHS* (2016). However, this storyline signals the difficulty of settlement for the West Indian migrants who supported the NHS during this period. Lucille's salvation comes in a patient's invitation to join her husband's small Black house church, run from the couple's living room. The spiritual warmth that Lucille has sought is embodied in both the gospel hymn sung by the Black community she finds crammed into the Palmers' living room and the rich colours of the congregation's clothing. *Call the Midwife*'s constrained domestic space is here used to fill the frame with a vibrant profusion of community. Lucille is enclosed in a 'black abundance' (Laymon 2019) that erupts from *Call the Midwife*'s largely white vision of the London East End. Both *Small Island* and *Call the Midwife* use domestic space to illustrate how West Indian settlement 'both transforms and must be accommodated in the streets of London' (Brunsdon 2018: 69).

I now move to consider twenty-first-century New York in two case studies. These showcase distinctly different interpretations of the spatial dynamics of the city's recent past. *The Marvelous Mrs. Maisel* and *The Deuce* figure period drama's televisual city as a layered space, illustrating how across history and through progressive remakings cities 'accrue resonances and layers of meaning' (Geraghty 2008: 170).

Fantasy New York: *The Marvelous Mrs. Maisel*

Midge Maisel stands at the door of a New York butcher shop, her jewel-toned swing coat, hat and coordinating handbag making her pop against its weathered wood and windows crowded with posters. Framed to dominate the space despite her petite size, she proudly throws a hand in the air and yells to the street, 'We got the Rabbi!' This moment early in the show's pilot illustrates the wealthy Jewish Upper West Side world its protagonist inhabits in 1958 New York. In the pilot Midge's comfortable, perfectly maintained life as a young, upper-middle-class housewife is derailed when her husband Joel announces he is leaving her. Left alone and in shock, she boards a subway train and stumbles, dripping wet and drunk, onto the stage of the bohemian Gaslight coffee house. Shambolically commanding a space where she had earlier watched Joel's disastrous amateur stand-up set, Midge pours forth her outrage at her husband's betrayal. Her improvised comic monologue culminates in her flashing her breasts and immediate being arrested for obscenity. The arrest leads her to meet legendary comedian Lenny Bruce, and the improvised set gains her a manager in coffee house employee Susie Myerson. Midge transfers her focus from a perfect family life to a thirst for success on the New York comedy scene. A 'show about the oppressive weight of feminine perfection at mid-century becomes a show about the obsessive quest for artistic perfection' (Maciak 2017). *Mrs. Maisel* expands its world in seasons two and three, to Paris, Miami, Las Vegas and the Jewish holiday resorts of the Catskills 'Borscht Belt' of upstate New York, but I focus here on season one's navigation of New York city space.

Mrs. Maisel was the breakout hit for the relatively young, US-based SVOD Amazon Prime Video, with its fleet of Emmy wins helping to establish the platform in a crowded marketplace. Like Netflix's deployment of *The Crown*, the detailed period construction and location filmmaking of *Mrs. Maisel* signalled Amazon's intimidatingly deep pockets. Its high budget, together with Amazon's investment in 'auteur' showrunner Amy Sherman Palladino (although best known for female-centred, hyper-verbal family dramedy *Gilmore Girls* (WB, 2000–7) rather than prestige drama), signalled Amazon Prime Video's arrival as a space of prestige drama.

Mrs. Maisel is characterised by the propulsive movement of its comic ensemble and the fluid, extended steadicam shots that dance around them. This fluidity aligns with the pace of its screwball-paced dialogue and Midge's comic monologues to present a vision of the late 1950s in New York as a period of optimism, promise and anticipation. It signifies the upper-middle-class privilege of Midge and her parents, who stride assured and unencumbered through life, as well as the hard-scrabble hustle of her working-class manager Susie. *Mrs. Maisel* creates a glamorous, fantasy vision of a New York permeated with musicality, cut through with Susie's dark cynicism and the sharp social critique of Midge's early stand-up routines. The programme evokes mid-century Hollywood's visions of Manhattan and echoes its largely whitewashed image of the borough (a smattering of Black and East Asian extras populate the audiences of its coffee houses and jazz clubs, signalling these spaces' bohemian cool). This outsized, fantasy vision of New York normalises its protagonist's forceful, dynamic personality. Midge is depicted as period drama's favoured woman out of time: a glamorous, hyper-confident, fast-talking comedian who pushes gendered and social barriers.

Mrs. Maisel maps out late 1950s New York as a city of defined neighbourhoods, drawing comedy from the heightened portrayal of the lifestyles and social rituals of these spaces. These small, defined worlds allow Midge to conceal her comedy career from her family and her new job in a Midtown department store. The programme charts the city through its public and private spaces. Its blend of spacious Upper West Side apartments and the scrappy bohemia of the Village counters the dominant cultural memory of 1950s America as a suburban world. In place of the suburbs' idealised yet constraining space of stable (white) families, commodities and conservative social structures, *Mrs. Maisel* offers 'alternative visions of urban married life and child rearing' (Robertson Wojcik 2010: 5). Its image of 1950s New York is shaped by what Pamela Robertson Wojcik calls the 'apartment plot' film, which is 'centred on values of community, visibility, contact, density, friendship, mobility, impermanence, and porousness' (2010: 5). Midge's sophisticated upbringing and dabbling in downtown bohemia echoes the imagery and spatial investments of these mid-century films, whose optimism 'cemented New York's position as a glamour capital' (Robertson Wojcik 2010: 16). The pop culture of the 1950s shaped a vision of the single-family suburban home and the world of the suburban housewife as one of privacy and containment.

Figure 4.3 Susie is shocked at the size of Midge's apartment in *The Marvelous Mrs. Maisel* (Amazon Prime Video, 2017–)

In contrast, Midge's Manhattan is characterised by mobility and porousness. Her privileged class status allows her to effortlessly move between her own and her parents' spacious Upper West Side apartments, her job at a Midtown department store and stand-up gigs in the Village. In contrast, working-class Susie must scrabble and graft, her frustration and limited opportunities embodied in her tiny apartment. However, when Midge's stand-up set evolves beyond the Gaslight she discovers New York's comedy world is less porous, as she comes up against the gendered barriers erected by the patriarchal entertainment industry. Her slow progress through the lowest ranks of this world is defined spatially, as her gigs creep slowly up Manhattan towards Midtown, the promised symbol of success.

The spatial dynamics of Midge's comfortable Upper West Side family world are set out in episode 01: 02 through a series of long steadicam tracking shots. These take Midge and Susie around her spacious, high-ceilinged, double-aspect 'classic 6' apartment – whose size shocks Susie – and on to her parents' matching apartment to collect her children, only a short elevator ride away. This is depicted as an effortless routine for Midge, edited to evoke one continuous movement between the two spaces. To Susie, the size of these apartments showcases Midge's privilege, in contrast to her own studio apartment whose Murphy bed leaves her unable to open her door to visitors. However, this spatial privilege is rendered unstable, as early in season one it is revealed that Midge and Joel's apartment was paid for by his father and she is forced to move back in with her parents. The size of these apartments communicates class status and they are well appointed with antiques and now-classic mid-century modern design. Yet these spaces are not displayed through a lingering, acquisitive 'heritage gaze'. Instead, this square footage is the stage for the choreography of the household. A spectacle of performance and camera movement (in complex steadicam shots) displays Midge and her mother's constant movement and the family's fast-paced, sharp, screwball dialogue.

Season one's most theatrical space is not the grimy, smoky Gaslight coffee shop where Midge develops her stand-up act. Instead, the Midtown department store B. Altman is presented as a theatre of glamour and refined consumption. The make-up counter becomes another stage for Midge as she fast-talks her way to sales, deploying her expert knowledge of highly constructed 1950s femininity. The shop floor is a fully dressed set built into a former bank in Brooklyn, with high windows, wood panelling and sumptuously merchandised glass counters. This space allows shots to be composed in depth with layers of movement. The complex flow of customers and staff around the shop is often staged by the show's choreographer (Gordon 2019). The spectacle and rituals of feminine consumption are showcased with a knowing wink of camp theatricality and musicality as the camera repeatedly swirls through the store's centre aisle. It passes models displaying outfits in fluid posed movements and an attentive staff of young women waiting on stylish customers. The store's break room is also depicted as a space of musicality and energetic femininity. When Midge is shown the ropes on her first day, she tours the space in swirling long shots, surrounded by young women whose joyful performance of daily routine borders on dance; they swirl in petticoated skirts as they sit to change shoes, or line up to rhythmically punch in and make final adjustments to their appearances. Like *The Paradise* (BBC One, 2012–13) and *Mr Selfridge* (ITV, 2013–16), the sumptuous pleasures offered by the shopping experience of an earlier era are presented as a lost art.

C. S. Tashiro suggests that historical films 'rely heavily on stylisation' but rarely become as openly stylised as the musical genre (1998: xvi). *Mrs. Maisel*'s construction of a fantasy New York pushes into the musical's stylisation, presenting a city experienced through physical freedom and movement. This musicality and theatricality are showcased in the pas de deux between characters' dynamic, rhythmic physical movement and fast-paced speech, and the lengthy steadicam long shots that capture them. The programme's shooting style favours wide and medium shots to capture performances, filming interactions in two shots rather than close-ups, and it uses dancers as extras for their sense of movement and energy (Seitz 2018b). These looser frames and the moving camera require larger sets and wider stretches of location space to be dressed. Unlike *Mad Men* (AMC, 2007–15), which filmed its largely interior version of mid-century New York in Los Angeles, the deep pockets of streaming service Amazon Prime Video allowed *Mrs. Maisel* to combine studio sets with location shooting in the streets and buildings of New York. In a city as dense and crowded as New York space comes at a price, thus *Mrs. Maisel*'s creation of a heightened 1950s image of the city on location serves as a spectacle of Amazon's financial investment. This investment is relayed through promotional paratexts, with interviews and behind-the-scenes press coverage highlighting the 'richness' of production design that leads to 'maximum impact' (Tashiro 1998: xiv). Through this discourse, the research and attention to detail of highly skilled production personnel and the scale of *Mrs. Maisel*'s world-building position the programme's vision of mid-century New York as 'authentic'. This is not a period drama of constrained frames necessitated by minimal set dressing on a small budget; here the programme's swirling visual dynamics and domination of space signify it as prestige TV.

This press and promotional discourse foregrounds the blend of verisimilitude and fantasy characteristic of period drama. *Mrs. Maisel*'s stylised late 1950s New York is presented as an exactingly constructed yet playful world, a self-aware reconstruction of the past. To draw on Richard Dyer's discussion of pastiche, this is 'an imitation you are meant to know is an imitation' (2007: 11). Rather than present a realist image of the city, its colourful, kinetic New York is built from the city's filmic representations. This is a heightened, 1950s classic Hollywood studio vision of Manhattan, evoking musicals such as *The Band Wagon* (dir. Vincente Minnelli; 1953), *Guys and Dolls* (dir. Joseph L. Mankiewicz; 1955) and *Funny Face* (dir. Stanley Donen; 1957), career girl movies like *Designing Woman* (dir. Vincente Minnelli; 1957) and *The Best of Everything* (dir. Jean Negulesco; 1959), and Doris Day romantic comedies like *Pillow Talk* (dir. Michael Gordon; 1959). Production designer Bill Groom drew from cinema for the programme's interiors, including copying the kitchen of Midge's married home from a Doris Day film (Hernandez 2018). *Mrs. Maisel*'s colour scheme and cinematography blend the heightened naturalism of a 'romantic realism' lighting style with an 'aggressively pastel' colour scheme drawn from 1950s cinema and advertising, echoing the period's use of strong colour accents against neutral backgrounds (Anonymous n.d.; K. H. Martin 2018).

In the promotional discourse Groom frames his reconstruction of a period New York in terms of layering, as 'a process of elimination, imagination and transformation' (Rorke 2018). This aligns with Christine Geraghty's characterisation of period film's layered city, with an 'imaginative version of one past city' layered onto 'the physical remnants of another' (2008: 179). New York is a city of layers, with its buildings and neighbourhoods preserved or torn down and replaced. Tamar Katz argues the perpetual change of the New York landscape turns 'individual structures into relics, precious for their scarcity'. These bear the aura of the past (2010: 820–1). Period drama's location filming peels back the layers of time from the contemporary city, uncovering spaces that still embody its chosen period. *Mrs. Maisel*'s production design also physically layers the past onto the present, building fake shop fronts, windows and signage onto New York streets. Production design and visual effects also disguise the contemporary city, the former concealing air conditioners, lamp posts and locks, and the latter constructing a moving digital 'matte' of a garment district street and erasing skyscrapers from skylines.

Groom highlighted the need to reflect layered New York in his production design, noting that 1950s New York was as layered with the past as the city is now (Hernandez 2018). The post-war suburbia that dominates the cultural memory of 1950s America is fresh and new, but *Mrs. Maisel*'s New York is a mixture of time periods. It features gleaming post-war skyscrapers, and older neighbourhoods like the Upper West Side and the Village. It also showcases 'heritage' spaces of upper-middle-class Jewish New York, from the cavernous, majestic space of the family's synagogue to the upstate Catskills resorts to the local butcher shop. The layered city allows *Mrs. Maisel*'s mid-century New York to feel both distant and familiar, using apartment blocks and city streets recognisable from decades of Hollywood's location filmmaking. In *Mrs. Maisel* period drama's play between distance and closeness constructs a fantasy, playful vision of New York, one that naturalises its heroine's outsized personality together with the musicality and dynamism of her world. If *Mrs. Maisel*'s Hollywood-derived 1950s New York is coded as fantasy, by contrast *The Deuce*'s vision of New York in the 1970s and 1980s is coded as realism.

Lost New York: *The Deuce*

The late 2010s produced a number of 1970s-set US period dramas produced by cable channels and streaming outlets that focused on the entertainment industries and subcultures of American cities, particularly New York. HBO's *Vinyl* (2016) showcased the excesses of Manhattan's recording industry. FX's *Fosse/Verdon* (2019) moved between the Broadway theatre community and Hollywood filmmaking. *The Get Down* (Netflix, 2016–17) put a somewhat fantastical spin on the emergence of hip-hop in the South Bronx. *I'm Dying Up Here* (Showtime, 2017–18) explored the dingy clubs of the 'alternative' LA stand-up comedy scene. Linked to these was *Pose* (FX, 2018–), set in the late 1980s and early 1990s queer Black and Latinx ball culture. Like *The Get Down* and parts of *The Deuce*, *Pose* explores the struggle to carve out city space and a creative life. (I discuss *Pose* further in Chapter 5.) I focus here on *The Deuce*, which charted the 1970s and 1980s sex trade and pornography industry centred on Manhattan's Times Square neighbourhood, particularly 42nd Street. The programme spanned three seasons set in 1971–2, 1977 and 1984–5, which charted the changes impacting this community at a transformative point in New York's history. Charlotte Brunsdon views the televisual city as characterised by repetition and familiarity (2018: 61), and *The Deuce* uses serialised television's repeated returns, along with each season's time jump, to chart changing city space through period drama's combination of intimacy and spectacle.

Produced as part of David Simon's long-term working relationship with US subscription cable channel HBO, *The Deuce* is positioned as realist, 'authored' prestige drama. The drama continues Simon's previous use of sprawling ensemble storytelling to chart cities as social and economic systems in *The Wire* (2002–9), *Treme* (2010–13) and *Show Me a Hero* (2015). Both Simon and co-creator George Pelecanos (a crime novelist who was a long-time writer on Simon's projects) are invested in the interrelationship of city space, economic systems and labour, explored through realist, socially conscious serialised storytelling. *The Deuce*'s sprawling narrative presents a '360-degree view of New York's sex economy' (Grant 2018: 15). Its ensemble weaves together the sex workers and their pimps; the porn producers and the former sex workers who transition into the safer space of porn acting; the diners and bartenders who serve the Deuce's community; the police who monitor the district and skim its profits; the mobsters who take their cut and finance the district's bars, discos, brothels, sex shows and porn films; and the government workers attempting to redevelop the neighbourhood.

The Deuce is centred on one of the city's iconic spaces in Times Square. Named after the police slang term for the stretch of 42nd Street (Forty-Deuce) between 8th and 9th Avenues, the Deuce was the city's de facto red-light district in the second half of the twentieth century, lined with exploitation cinemas, amusement arcades, sex shops, peep shows and bars. The Deuce rubbed elbows with the Theatre District, as is illustrated by a season one scene where bar-owner Vince and his mobster bosses watch an upscale couple fearfully navigate an afternoon street dotted with sex workers after a theatre matinee (01: 04). The neighbourhood embodies the city's declining economic fortunes across the late 1960s and 1970s, along with the changes in the regulation of pornography during the 1970s and 1980s. Across the fifteen years the programme spans, the Deuce holds on as the city begins to change around it. But by *The Deuce*'s final season, set in 1985, its derelict, crime-ridden streets symbolise 'a past that is marked as precarious or lost' (Katz 2010: 121). The neighbourhood and the pornography industry have mutated into a harsher space, on the precipice of redevelopment and cultural change.

The Deuce's first two seasons depict one of pop culture's most mythologised spaces, 1970s New York city. It depicts a 'lost' New York, now erased by Manhattan's redevelopment and the gentrification of Times Square. The city moved from bankruptcy in 1975 to extreme wealth in the new millennium, built around globalised capitalism and financial services. The programme illustrates how period drama enables viewers to 'inhabit a world by definition gone' to 'see a city that is no longer there' (Katz 2010: 811). It exhibits urban nostalgia's desire for less traditional communities, ones imagined 'through conflict rather than consensus' (Katz 2010: 814). The sex, violence and seedy glamour of the Times Square neighbourhood serves as a spatial marker of the city's 1970s gritty authenticity. This blends with the industry reputation of Simon and Pelecanos to position the programme as a realist representation of the city's past.

The Deuce's spatial imaginary is built from the cultural memory of 1970s New York as a violent city in crisis, possessing a dark, gritty glamour. This is an image fed by the music – disco, punk, hip-hop – and art scenes the city birthed, as well as its cinematic representations. Across the 1960s and 1970s New York underwent a decline in its manufacturing industries and housing stock, which contributed to 'white flight' to the suburbs and left the city's government in dire financial straits by the mid-1970s. At the same time the city was substantially opened up to location filmmaking. This resulted in a proliferation of 'films with images of urban despair and immorality' that blended the mythic construct of 'movie New York' with the realism coded through location filming (Sanders 2002: 346). Films such as *Midnight Cowboy* (dir. John Schlesinger; 1969), *Klute* (dir. Alan J. Pakula; 1971), *The French Connection* (dir. William Friedkin; 1971), *Superfly* (dir. Gordon Parks Jr.; 1972) and *Taxi Driver* (dir. Martin Scorsese; 1976) drew on yet also contributed to popular understandings of New York as a space of urban decline (Corkin 2011), with the sleaze of the Times Square neighbourhood a key spatial marker.

The Deuce draws on these cinematic images of 1970s New York as a 'distinctive and largely degraded locale' populated by people on the margins (Corkin 2011: 9). It presents 'the city as a nexus of commerce, desire, and despair' (Corkin 2011: 7). Yet it works to centralise women's perspective much more fully than the crime and blaxploitation film cycles of the 1970s. *The Deuce* articulates 42nd Street as a space of labour, spatially charting the sex trade and its surrounding industries as an intersecting ecosystem. In season one the large sidewalks of 42nd Street are the programme's defining spaces, bustling with visitors and traders, patrolled by a shambolic and corrupt police force. The wide, dirty sidewalks are layered with trash and lined with garbage bags. Sex workers and their pimps hover underneath the glowing lights of the cinema marquees and slump against shop window advertisements for food and sex. The air is filled with drunk arguments, searing car horns, the shouts of sex workers and hawkers plying their trade, and an undertow of violence. The programme tracks the mob's 'investment' in local businesses, including the massage parlours that move the sex workers from the streets and New York's emerging pornography industry. The latter is charted through Harvey's scrappy yet slowly professionalising film studio. In season two this expands into a space of escape and potential creative fulfilment for some of the show's sex workers, particularly Lori's ascendant porn star and Candy's aspiring director.

Unlike *Mrs. Maisel*'s New York, which could draw on the preserved building stock of Manhattan's wealthy enclaves, *The Deuce*'s New York was viewed as a 'blight'. It was wiped out as the Times Square neighbourhood was redeveloped into a corporate tourist mecca across the late 1990s and 2000s. The programme's production team struggled to find an undeveloped space left in the city that could double for the distinct geography of 42nd Street. Press coverage highlights the production team's sourcing of Harlem's undeveloped Amsterdam Avenue, between 164th and 166th Streets. Their transformation of a stretch of the street into the 'exposed and decrepit' 1971 Times Square neighbourhood is presented as period drama spectacle. As with *Mrs. Maisel*, production design is positioned as a marker of spatial authenticity (Cheslaw 2019; Russell 2017). To reproduce the phenomenal scale of 42nd Street with its iconic row of cinema marquees, six lanes of traffic and twenty-two-feet-wide sidewalks, the production team had to build canopies to fit onto the Amsterdam Avenue buildings. The block was fitted with a 'huge marquee piece' that was hung from buildings' fire escapes, topped with light boxes (Cheslaw 2019). These were augmented by visual effects to feature film titles that transitioned from exploitation, underground and imported art house cinema titles in season one to American pornography in season two. This signalled the rise of the local porn industry and the mainstreaming of 'porn chic' in the mid-1970s. David Simon's 'auteur' brand codes the programme as realist drama. Rather than transforming New York through visual effects, this physical reconstruction of lost New York space asserts its commitment to verisimilitude through the layering of practical elements onto contemporary New York. Here the spectacle of skilled labour and practical elements constructs a textured and tactile past, an immersive space for actors and viewers alike.

The Deuce's view of New York is ground level and intimate, centring the trade of bodies and conflicts over public space. However, its recreation of 42nd Street is also treated as visual spectacle. After keeping its focus relatively small for its first fifteen minutes, episode

01: 01 introduces gambler Frankie (the twin of barman Vince) and the geography of the Deuce in a sequence that culminates in the spectacular reveal of 42nd Street. The soundscape asserts the sequence's realist tone, crowded with the diegetic sounds of traffic and crowds with only snatches of muted diegetic music. As Frankie confidently strides through under-lit night-time streets, the camera tracks behind then in front of him. We cut to a side view to track him along a pavement lined with garbage bags as he passes the large, white, glittering sign of Playland, a neon sign touting 'Girls Girls Girls' glowing in its window. The brightness is startling against the brown and dark shades of the city street. An overhead shot sees Frankie pick his way across multiple lanes of traffic before an extreme long shot opens up the space and places him in the middle of a huge city street. His silhouette is tiny against a glowing but uncannily unadorned and traffic-filled Times Square, with six lanes of traffic and the iconic Winston cigarette billboard in left of frame. Frankie continues down a side street, casually greeting a transgender sex worker giving oral sex in a phone booth, setting out the Deuce as a grimy community. The sequence then moves to a high-angle crane shot at the corner of a street, which draws back and pans left to reveal one side of 42nd Street in a spectacular wide shot of glowing light. Its crowded sidewalks are lined with huge cinema marquees displaying titles including *Thar She Blows* (dir. Richard Kanter; 1968), *The Wizard of Gore* (dir. Herschell Gordon Lewis; 1970) and *He and She* (dir. Matt Cimber; 1970). An edit takes us down to the sidewalk, where Frankie walks below and is framed against light bulb-bordered marquees advertising *Mondo Trasho* (dir. John Waters; 1969) and *The Conformist* (dir. Bernardo Bertolucci; 1970) before he finds his bookie. The sequence crosses the road to introduce independent sex worker Candy kerbside looking for customers and resisting the sales pitch of Rodney, one of the programme's swaggering pimps. One of season one's most visually spectacular sequences, it sets out the geography and vibrant culture of the Deuce, created by computer-generated imagery in Times Square and a blend of practical and visual effects on 42nd Street. These wide shots of city landscapes showcase the programme's reconstruction of the dynamic, tawdry, run-down glamour of a lost New York. This sequence draws on cultural memories of and urban nostalgia for a 1970s New York imagined 'through conflict rather than consensus' (Katz 2010: 814) to set out a space starkly different from the Disneyfied tourist mecca of contemporary Times Square. Frankie's journey makes a spectacle of the neighbourhood's uncanny difference as it sets out the stark, ground-level ecology of its street life.

Figure 4.4 The sex workers set against the 42nd Street cinema awnings in
The Deuce (HBO, 2017–19)

Across season one this street is the stage for the women's nightly
ritual of attracting customers. We repeatedly track or pick them out
– primarily Candy, Lori, Ruby and Shay in this patch – in long shots
down or along the sidewalk, posed underneath the glowing bulbs of
the awnings. The faded glamour of the structures feeds the performance of searching for a 'date'. The programme spatially marks out
a dichotomy between the neighbourhood's public and private spaces.
On the street, in Vince's bar and in the local diner the camera has a
fluidity that tracks the energy of these spaces and the interwoven lives
of the neighbourhood's sex workers, pimps, police and bartenders.
But once the women move indoors with their customers the camera
becomes static. The seedy $10 hotel rooms, with their faded wallpaper
and stained bed linen, are spaces of bored routine laced with danger.
These are sonically porous spaces; the aggressive, irritable soundscape
of the street filters in as the women dutifully perform their false
attraction and desire, and on occasion suffer violent beatings. Their
repetitive spatial movement from the street to hotel room conveys
the mundane routine of sex work behind the women's performance of
empty fantasy, as well as the detachment needed to survive this labour.
    The women's commodification is made even more routine in the
semi-private space of the massage parlour. The pink-walled staging
lounge with a bar and armed guard presents the parlour as a safer space
than the street, its French-ish name constructing a facade of glamour.
Here the girls slump on sofas or line up in floaty negligees ready for

a customer to select them. Yet with the women's street-based performance of picking up 'dates' removed, they become silent, dehumanised
products, illustrated by the row of cell-like rooms with rickety plastic
folding doors. Episode 01: 06 sees Darlene work her first shift in the
parlour, and we see a room for the first time in a sequence that uses
intimacy to figure entrapment. Sparsely furnished with a wash basin
and small bed, its thin walls vibrate from a neighbouring assignation.
The camera closes down Darlene in a tight shot that highlights the
cell-like space. This is even smaller than the strip's grotty hotel rooms
and distinct from the wide-open space of its sidewalk. The women's
illusion of agency is removed by a space that formalises their role as
commodity.

Through period drama's blend of intimacy and the spectacular,
The Deuce immerses itself in the worlds and lives of the women that
usually serve as spatial set dressing for a 'broken' 1970s New York.
Layering the city's 'lost' past onto its present, it reconstructs its grimy
1970s glamour to explore the capitalist ecosystem that sold fantasies
of desire, a world bounded by violence, oppression and struggles
for freedom. Television's serialised returns allow the series to chart
shifting city space and characters' relationship with it, together with
the changes in its power structures that led to the demise of the
Deuce.

Conclusion

Exploring period drama's rendering of space and place showcases the
genre's blend of the 'visual (and aural) spectacle of pastness' (Vidal
2012a: 9) with television's intimate experience. *Underground* shapes
its encounter with the house through the perspectives of its enslaved
workers, using dynamic camerawork to signal its disruption of a 'heritage' vision of the antebellum South. *To Walk Invisible*'s and *Outlander*'s
framing of regional British wild landscapes foregrounds a sensual
experience of the past. *The Deuce*'s and *Mrs. Maisel*'s visions of New
York demonstrate how a frame of space and place can show period
drama's divergent encounters with a city. These two case studies
illustrate the genre's increasing investment in the twentieth-century
city, joining the grand house, rural space and Dickensian London as
the recurring iconography of the genre. Both programmes are shaped
by cultural memories of New York, and their respective engagement
with realism and fantasy demonstrates the breadth and complexity of
the genre's encounters with its past, along with its continuing investment in women's experience. The layered nature of a city such as New

York brings new ways of thinking about the genre's reconstructions and reimaginings.

Note

1. I use the term 'big house' here as this is how the enslaved characters refer to the plantation house and so it maintains the programme's privileging of their perspective.

5 Gender and Sexuality

In the summer of 2019 US television executive Jeffrey Hirsch set out the new direction of subscription cable channel Starz, whose programming had up until then been relatively male-focused. Based on the awkwardly worded concept 'premium female', this new strategy targeted women aged twenty-four to fifty-four who liked 'high scripted drama' and 'great women in history' (in Goldberg 2019). The foundation of Starz's women in history theme was the highly successful *Outlander* (2014–) along with the channel's adaptations of Philippa Gregory's historical novels *The White Queen* (2013) (co-produced with BBC One), *The White Princess* (2017) and *The Spanish Princess* (2019–). Hirsch claimed of *Outlander*'s appeal that 'you can say that it's great because women like it because she's a surgeon who goes back in time, but there's also another side of that, which is there's some eye candy for that audience' (in Goldberg 2019). Hirsch's reductive characterisation was not well received by *Outlander*'s creative team or its fans. His comments illustrate Jorie Lagerway's (2017) assertion that the generically hybrid *Outlander* has been framed as female-targeted romance. This aligned the series with the lower cultural status of melodrama rather than the higher-status prestige TV linked to similar masculine-focused narratives.

Hirsch's comments illustrate how period drama is frequently perceived as a 'quintessentially "feminine" genre' (Pidduck 2004: 16), one whose investment in fantasy and melodrama creates 'a special critical relationship with women and feminine culture that revolves around identity, taste and consumption' (Vidal 2012a: 24). The 'feminine' nature of period drama is not necessarily tied to a gendered body, as we can understand both femininity and masculinity as but 'one form of gender expression – a trait that a range of sexed bodies may possess or perform' (Levine 2015: 5). Although period drama frequently engages with 'masculine' topics of war, action and crime, these topics often lead a programme to be positioned as 'historical drama' to avoid the genre's feminised connotations. For example, Andrew Higson's discussion of early twenty-first-century trends in period film divides the masculine, action-focused 'dirty realist' historical epic from 'the middlebrow, middle-aged and feminine' intimate 'costume dramas' set in the nineteenth and early twentieth centuries (2010: 194–5). *Outlander* illustrates how period drama can blend both these aspects, drawing power and affective pleasures from both sweeping action and intimate bodies. (I explore *Outlander*'s bodies further in Chapter 6.)

This chapter explores period drama through the frame of gender and sexuality. The control of or resistance to social and cultural norms of gender and sexuality are central structuring forces of period drama, as it explores historical periods shaped by distinctly different perspectives on gender and sexuality than those of contemporary society. It first tracks this through stories of women at work, a genre trend across the 2000s and 2010s. I highlight two British dramas' depiction of women's war work and a strand of US dramas focused on mid-century working women. The violent masculinities of action-adventures and crime thrillers and the genre's interest in the trauma of war are developed in a case study of Birmingham gangster drama *Peaky Blinders* (BBC Two/ BBC One, 2013–). A case study of queer Victorian worlds looks at biographical dramas of Yorkshire diarist Anne Lister and adaptations of Sarah Waters's neo-Victorian novels. The chapter closes with a case study of New York ballroom drama *Pose* (FX, 2018–), which inserts trans and queer communities of colour into period drama. These case studies show that gender and sexuality exist in conversation with race and class, offering an intersectional approach to genre study. These are not binary but stretchy, expansive concepts (Moseley et al. 2017: 5).

Period drama exhibits an interest in historical manifestations of masculinity, particularly the impact of patriarchal culture, power and violence on individual men. However, it has a particular investment in the lived experience of women throughout history. This is because masculinity is conventionally (and falsely) understood as stable, whereas 'femininity is understood as historically variable and contingent, making period drama a rich site for exploring popular understandings of womanhood while effectively parsing its relationship to the present' (Luckett 2017: 17). It has long been one of the few television genres (alongside soap opera) to consistently centre female characters, including older women. Period drama foregrounds women's struggles against the 'constraints of conventions, sexual representation and economic disadvantage' (Pidduck 2004: 1), as well as exploring the play of power and desire. It can also exhibit playfulness and fantasy, offering self-conscious reworkings of the past that can open up space for ambiguous interpretations of gender identity and a queering of desire.

Exploring period drama through a frame of gender and sexuality highlights the genre's foundational strand of melodrama. Both this and the following chapter emphasise the genre's 'emotional landscape' (Pribram 2018: 759), its desire to draw the past close whilst showcasing its distance from the present day. Period drama uses melodrama's 'emphasis on what it *feels* like to have your fate determined by remote, external forces beyond your control' (Geraghty 2008: 10) to shape an emotion-centred experience of history. Melodrama explores the material conditions of lives that are shaped by the contradictory social forces of history, particularly women and the queer community. Thus it frequently shapes period drama's visions of the past.

Period drama's readings of the past are shaped by the perspective of the present and this is particularly the case with gender and sexuality. Chapter 3's discussion of *Shoulder to Shoulder* (BBC Two, 1974) illustrated how the genre draws the past close. The programme's story of first-wave feminism's battle for the vote is shaped by the 1970s women's liberation movement and its investment in women's social roles, sexuality and identity. Period drama shows a preference for literary heroines that can be read as proto-feminist, emergent modern women. In search of this, certain brand-name authors of the literary canon – notably the Brontës and Jane Austen – are returned to again and again. Austen's 'memorable heroines, incisive wit and complex interplay of social convention, individual choice and romance' make them ripe for reworking through contemporary feminist perspectives (Pidduck 2004: 28). Casting and performance help to draw out the 'ambition and sensibility' that position her heroines as modern women. Although as Charlotte Brunsdon notes, female characters see the most reworking in literary adaptations (2018: 80). Anachronistic adjustment is often required to align them more comfortably with contemporary expectations of active, independent-thinking women who desire love and equality. Charles Dickens makes reworking a particular struggle, as his tendency towards child-women offers limited opportunities for contemporary preferences for layered femininities.

Julianne Pidduck argues that period drama frames the past through a perspective of liberal feminism, and that this risks collapsing historical difference by shaping women's experiences into familiar white, middle-class, Western quests for self (2004: 28). Stories of royal women exhibit period drama's search for stories of powerful women within patriarchally constructed society. They offer compelling negotiations of gendered power in historical contexts where women otherwise had little, combined with ample opportunities for glamour and spectacle. For example, medieval queens are a consistent fascination, from 1970s BBC blockbuster *Elizabeth R* tracking the life of Queen Elizabeth I of England and Ireland (BBC Two, 1971), to Spanish series *Isabel* (La 1, 2012–14) chronicling the reign of Queen Isabella I of Castile, to The CW's *Reign* (2013–17) reimagining the early life of Mary, Queen of Scots as a teen melodrama. These dramas read contemporary feminist investments in ambition, agency and sexual liberation onto historic queens' struggle for power (Woodacre 2018). Period drama's search for an emergent feminist consciousness in the pre-feminist past can risk privileging 'easy identification' over discomfiting distance and a sense of the past as a 'foreign country' (Agnew 2007: 300). In its desire to bring the past close and prompt affective pleasures, period drama can risk producing representations that reshape the past in the image of the present.

Women at work

This desire for identification and the search for an emergent feminist consciousness is seen in the focus on women at work in period dramas of the 2000s and 2010s. Work allows the genre to explore women's lives beyond the domestic space, contributing to a more complex vision of women's history. Narratives of work present independent, active and resistant women within historical worlds otherwise marked by gendered constraint, offering fantasies of achievement and expertise. Moya Luckett notes that period drama frequently links women's work to agency and glamour, although these dramas 'may belie the reality of many mundane, poorly paid, low-prestige and boring jobs' by 'setting up horizons that are often too utopian' (2017: 30).

To sketch out some of the tendencies of this genre trend, some programmes isolate female characters in largely male workspaces, positioning them as transgressing patriarchal boundaries. We see this in Midge's position as a female comedian in *The Marvelous Mrs. Maisel* (Amazon Prime Video, 2017–). In *The Deuce* (HBO, 2017–19) Candy transitions from sex work to carve out a career in the male-dominated realm of porn directing. *The Alienist* (TNT, 2018–) models its aspiring detective heroine Sara Howard on the first woman employed by the New York Police Department. Other dramas immerse the viewer in largely female working communities, ensembles focused on 'a cross-section of feminine types' (Ball 2013: 246) such as the midwives of *Call the Midwife* (BBC One, 2012–) and the telephonists of *Cable Girls* (Netflix, 2017–20). Work-set dramas frequently offer aspirational narratives of ambitious working-class women's advancement in neoliberal fantasies of meritocracy, although success on the department store floors of *The Paradise* (BBC One, 2012–13) and *Mr Selfridge* (ITV, 2013–16) and in the advertising offices of *Mad Men* (AMC, 2007–15) is not without struggle and disillusionment. By tracing connections and continuities, these dramas use the 'recent past to uncover more complex and potentially progressive histories that variously ground, rationalise, inspire and justify contemporary women's professional lives' (Luckett 2017: 15). However, in positioning their heroines as novelties and pioneers (Luckett 2017: 18), these programmes rely on and contribute to the cultural amnesia present in popular beliefs about the histories of working women. This ignores the presence of women in the workplace previous to the changing opportunities for white middle-class women in the 1970s, in particular the necessity of labour for working-class women and women of colour.

Narratives of women's work allow period drama to play out many of the struggles of contemporary womanhood in the historical body. The genre's working woman is frequently presented as a transgressive modern thinker in a period setting, an illustration of the inevitable progress to follow. For example, Lynn Spigel (2013) suggests that 1960s-set US dramas position their female protagonists on the cusp of social change, offering the promise of a hopeful future. For Spigel, cable drama *Mad Men* and its short-lived network imitators—*Pan Am* (ABC, 2011–12), *The Playboy Club* (NBC, 2011) and *Vegas* (CBS, 2012–13)—offer a compelling fantasy for young viewers who are aware they may no longer access such a hopeful future, as millennials are 'repeatedly reminded they have no future, or at least no future as good as the one their baby-boomer parents planned' (2013: 278). Period drama here offers a nostalgia for a better future that may never be. Period drama's working women also illustrate a *lack* of progress; characters struggle to balance relationships, family and career, and come up against sexism, harassment and inequality. Whilst more stark than contemporary women's experiences, these remain familiar from viewers' lives. Through the working woman, period drama finds the present in the past.

Land Girls (BBC One, 2009–11) and *The Bletchley Circle* (ITV, 2012–14) use narratives of work to insert women's history into the dominant masculine-centred narratives of the Second World War. These dramas enabled the exploration and preservation of 'marginalised and largely untold histories' of wartime (Mahoney 2015: 4). This countered women's largely incidental presence in military dramas such as *Band of Brothers* (HBO, 2001) and *The Pacific* (HBO, 2010), and expanded period drama's depictions of women's war work beyond nursing. Their precursor in constructing 'a rich "herstory"' (Jennings 2017: 182) of women marginalised by dominant historical accounts of the conflict was *Tenko* (BBC One, 1981–4). This female ensemble drama was set in a women's prisoner-of-war camp in Second World War Japan. Like *Tenko*'s prison camp, a focus on women's war work presents 'a liminal space that disrupts the usual everyday negotiations of female identity within a patriarchal society' (Jennings 2017: 185).

Commissioned as part of the BBC's commemoration of the seventieth anniversary of the outbreak of the Second World War, *Land Girls* was part of a strand of daytime television largely targeted at retired audiences, which illuminated everyday life on the British home front. The programme follows a group of women working in agricultural labour as part of the Women's Land Army, exploring the mundane pleasures of manual labour along with romantic pursuits and class conflict. Bonnie White (2019) points out the series used war work to tell little-known stories of life on the home front, including conscientious objectors, prisoners of war and segregation in the US Army.

The prime-time ITV prestige drama *The Bletchley Circle* followed the post-war lives of a quartet of women who had been engaged in a much more glamorous form of war service. Their war work at the secret Bletchley Park codebreaking base appears in flashback in the 1952-set narrative. The women use their cryptography skills to track a serial killer, with their skills exceeding those of the police. E. Deidre Pribram suggests the women's amateur detective work compensates for their 'discontent, anger and frustration' at their post-war lives and the lack of recognition of their secret war service (2018: 766). Within its crime drama frame *The Bletchley Circle* deals with the lived contradictions of the post-war return of highly intelligent female workers to the unchallenging spheres of domesticity and low-wage work (Mahoney 2015; Pribram 2018). The women's investigation enables them to recapture their value, energy and exuberance, offering space for an alternate vision of women's post-war history.

Both *Land Girls* and *The Bletchley Circle* depict the matriarchal communities of war work as spaces that enable transgressions of 1940s gender norms; work physically, intellectually and at times sexually liberates their female ensembles. Work widens world views, enables self-discovery and offers escape from constrained home lives. Yet Cat Mahoney (2015) argues that their characters' 'traditional performances of femininity' and the programmes' serialised structure work to restore cultural norms. Ultimately these women are to return to the domestic sphere (Mahoney 2015: 10). For Mahoney, their transgressions are rendered comfortingly conservative by the historical knowledge that the wartime upheaval is finite and will not radically challenge gender roles. Thus both programmes present a 'safe version of female empowerment and emancipation' in the knowledge that hegemonic norms will be reasserted (Mahoney 2015: 5).

The cultural changes of the 1960s presented a stronger challenge to these hegemonic norms. Women at work is a central focus of the mid-century period dramas that proliferated in the 2010s after the success of AMC cable drama *Mad Men*. In contrast, the 1960s cultural changes related to race and sexuality received markedly less attention and are relegated to supporting storylines in these dramas. *Mad Men* is, alongside *Downton Abbey* (ITV, 2010–15), perhaps the most discussed programme of contemporary television's period drama boom, with considerable academic attention paid to its gender dynamics. A prime example of prestige cable drama's investment in the 'difficult man' (Martin 2013), the programme follows Don Draper and his fellow Madison Avenue advertising executives' struggles with the structures of mid-century masculinity. Its trio of female characters – housewife Betty, office manager Joan and the programme's co-lead copywriter Peggy – embody the frustrations of mid-century femininity as the programme tracks its way through the 1960s. Through Joan and Peggy, the programme repeatedly sets out the parameters and constraints of white-collar working women. It dramatises the personal costs of ambition by showing 'not only women's limited possibilities but also the conflicted positions in which they find themselves' (Landsberg 2015: 94). Lynn Spigel argues that these career and family struggles embody a nascent feminist consciousness that never coalesces into a politicised vision. Instead, *Mad Men* draws on traditions of melodrama to focus on individual struggle as a means to explore social problems. Women's progress is rendered in terms of personal triumph and failure rather than directly referencing feminism's collective action (Spigel 2013: 273).

Spigel argues that *Mad Men* and the network television imitators that followed it refocused the cultural memory of the late 1950s and early 1960s. These dramas moved away from American suburbia, instead presenting urban cosmopolitan lifestyles as a space of glamour and possibility; worlds 'where women have a certain amount of power and mobility, and men must meet their challenge' (Spigel 2013: 271). The (mostly) single white middle-class working woman in the city is a particular feature of mid-century period dramas. Work is tied to independence, self-fulfilment and freedom. Work can be an urban adventure, the playful 'great reprieve' of the young single city girl experimenting with freedoms before marriage (Robertson Wojcik 2010). Or it can be an aspirational career carved out from patriarchally structured businesses. The first two seasons of *The Marvelous Mrs. Maisel* blends the two. Midge's comedy ambitions present her as the transgressive career woman in a man's world. Her department store job and her friendship with her young female colleagues allows her to enjoy the lifestyle of a young single girl in the city by proxy. However, this liminal, transitive world of sexual and social exploration and shared apartment living is never depicted as a potential new life for Midge. She maintains a secure position in her upper-middle-class childhood home and sleeps with her husband despite their separation. Instead, her colleagues' house parties become another stage to refine her act on her journey to stand-up comedy success.

In US network dramas *Pan Am* and *The Playboy Club* work is cast as a glamorous adventure for young single women, offering 'a vision of the past in which women of the 1960s were already hoping to be post-feminists: independent, career-focused, yet hyperbolically "feminine" in their embrace of fashion, shopping and dating' (Spigel 2013: 273). US cable and streaming dramas *Mad Men*, *Masters of Sex* (Showtime, 2013–16) and *Good Girls Revolt* (Amazon Prime Video, 2016), as well as UK drama *The Hour* (BBC Two, 2011–12) present aspiring and 'liberated' 1960s career girls with more complicated struggles. Across these programmes middle-class working women chafe at the patriarchal restrictions in their pursuit of advertising, sex research, journalism and television production. These women exhibit ambivalence about 'the contradictory pleasures and pressures of female labour' (Luckett 2017: 17). Here period dramas foreground the contemporary resonance of an 'only supposedly expired past' (Pribram 2018: 746). Throughout the late 2010s, fights against workplace harassment and for equal pay and recognition consistently made headline news as part of a renewed feminist consciousness across Western culture (Ryan and Keller 2018; Banet-Weiser 2018).

These programmes' serialised storytelling illustrates the slow progress and setbacks of cultural change, the less utopian experience of 'cycles of return, stasis and retreat' (Luckett 2017: 21). Peggy's and Joan's success is achieved incrementally across seven seasons and a decade of work in *Mad Men*. The single season of *Good Girls Revolt* fictionalises the real-life labour organisation of the female workforce at *Newsweek* magazine. The season tracks the slow and nuanced process of convincing the newsroom's female 'researchers' (who did the work of journalists) to join a gender discrimination lawsuit. The women give notice of their legal action only at the finale's climax, and the series was cancelled before it could further dramatise what would become a land-mark piece of legal action for news media and the women's movement (Del Barco 2016). *Good Girls Revolt*'s 1969 setting and predominantly female creative team results in a stronger focus on feminism as a larger collective political movement than any of its fellow mid-century dramas. Yet this is still framed around a young, glamorous, white middle-class ensemble.

In both British war work and the more glamorous worlds of mid-century media, white, largely middle-class female protagonists are presented as transgressive and resistant, pushing against the restricted opportunities for women within their historical moments. Rather than their work being depicted as a mundane necessity, these are the 'super girl achievers' (Spigel 2013: 277). Work is glamorous, despite and at times because of its struggles. Across period drama, working women offer opportunities to draw the past close by recognising contemporary struggles in the women of the past. These spaces offer active femininities within worlds controlled by restrictive patriarchal structures. Set on the cusp of seismic social change, mid-century dramas draw on melodrama to chart the emotional landscapes of frustration and resistance, reading the era's emerging political battles through individual struggle.

Masculine action and dirty realism

Period drama's exploration of women at work reads women's history through small-scale battles and mid-century glamour. The 'dirty realist' action epic and crime drama present a larger landscape for interrogating historical masculinity. Through its exploration of individual men's struggles with patriarchal power, period drama has the 'capacity to disrupt conceptualisation of "hegemonic masculinity"' (Byrne et al. 2018: 3). As I discuss period drama's romantic heroes in Chapter 6, I focus here on action-adventure and crime thrillers. These programmes combine a visceral physicality with elements of male melodrama to explore themes of duty, power and trauma. They celebrate a muscular image of patriarchy and masculinity, exhibiting an ambiguous relationship with violence.

A 2010s strand of pre-modern action-adventures in the US and UK was arguably inspired by the blockbusting success of HBO's epic fantasy series *Game of Thrones* (HBO, 2011–19).[1] Blending political intrigue with viscerally bloody battle scenes, these programmes tell a 'conventionally masculine version of history for boys' (Higson 2010: 203). *Vikings* (History Channel, 2013–19), *The Last Kingdom* (BBC

One/Netflix, 2015–), *The Bastard Executioner* (FX, 2015) and *Knightfall* (History Channel, 2017–19) centre at times reluctant warriors in epic stories of male-dominated communities of knights and Vikings. These dramas combine what Andrew Higson (2010) terms 'dirty realism' with blood-soaked fantasies of at times brutal gory violence. They paint a vision of pre-modern Europe as a strange, dangerous, raw space of unrestrained passions and primitive society, where broadswords and battle privilege a muscular, violent masculinity.

Bettina Bildhauer suggests that medieval narratives can foreground the pre-modern past's 'backwardness', presenting it as a time 'of barbarism and ignorance, brutality and superstition, dungeons, disease and dirt' (2013: 8). Yet in these 'dirty realist' action-centred period dramas this backwardness is privileged as a fantasy space of unrestrained hyper-masculinity. Their vision of the past plays out 'modes of behaviour that are considered unrespectable or decadent, outmoded or primitive' in contemporary society (Higson 2010: 126). Here masculinity is depicted as dangerous, wild and uncultivated, unrestricted by the 'veneer of refinement, respectability and safeness' that Higson suggests characterises the 'modern past' (2010: 208). The mud and blood of 'dirty realism' codes the violence of this masculine history as demythologised and 'authentic', yet these dramas are at their heart fantasies of male dominance, patriarchal power and *Boy's Own* adventure.

Precursors to this 2010s 'dirty realist' trend can be found in 1990s British period dramas *Sharpe* (ITV, 1993–7, 2006, 2008) and *Hornblower* (ITV, 1998–2003). These were part of the 1990s British period drama boom but positioned themselves as counterpoints to the dominant trend of female-centred classic serials. The dramas offer swashbuckling military and maritime *Boy's Own* adventures set against the backdrop of the French Revolutionary and Napoleonic Wars. Their protagonists model a 'tough, decent martial Britishness', whose steadfast masculinity Jerome de Groot contrasts with the refined, constrained gentlemen of country house-set period dramas (2009: 196). Both Hornblower and Sharpe offer heroic ideals of masculinity shaped by an aggressive patriotism that operates through 'duty, respect and honour' (de Groot 2009: 197). De Groot suggests these 'sit at an angle to the more conservative presentations of Britishness represented by the BBC's classic serials', whose 'witty withdrawn manner' codes them as feminine (2009: 196). Yet both programmes centralise a strongly conservative image of 'tough' masculinity through their romantic vision of masculine action and assertion of patriotic duty. The 'dirty realist' action of the pre-modern 2010s strand is shaded with contemporary ideologies of a more complex masculinity. These programmes' vision of unreconstructed masculinity is frequently staged around a protagonist that embodies a conflicted masculinity. These men seek to balance violent duty with a quest for understanding of self and a fulfilling family life.

Swashbuckling seafaring thrills of the pirate kind are the focus of Starz's *Black Sails* (2014–17). The US subscription cable drama draws on the pirate's status as mythical figure whose 'bluff derring-do and proclivity toward personal violence are allied with martial, heroic ideals of masculinity' (Erin Mackie quoted in Swaminathan 2017: 144). This is constructed within the Starz model of historical action-adventures (previous to its 2019 'premium female' shift) that were pre-cursors to the 2010s medieval strand. Starz offered up male-targeted macho, bloody historical action-adventures with a tinge of fantasy in sword-and-sandals epic *Spartacus* (2010–13) and *Camelot* (2011), set in King Arthur's court. *Black Sails* is positioned as a prequel to *Treasure Island*, centred on James Flint's daring pirate adventures around the early eighteenth-century Caribbean. In its second season the drama skews its vision of gruff, leather-clad adventure by revealing an origin story that queers its enigmatic pirate hero. The programme's queer-ness is otherwise largely the preserve of its female characters, whose same-sex love scenes are framed primarily for the male gaze. However, season two reveals Flint's hidden past to be a forbidden love affair with his best friend Thomas Hamilton. The relationship is the catalyst for Flint's exile from the British Navy, with his shame, anger and grief over this love and Hamilton's death driving him to choose a pirate's life. Srividhya Swaminathan argues that pirate culture draws from a fluidity of race and nationality (2017: 143). The positioning of *Black Sails*'s gruff, hyper-masculine pirate anti-hero as bisexual – and his hidden past one of tender romance – draws sexuality into the fluidity of pirate masculinity.

Trauma and gangster masculinity: *Peaky Blinders*

As period drama's medieval and seafaring action-adventures illustrate, war is a space where myths of masculinity are built and reworked. Television has been one of the primary cultural spaces for explora-tions of the First World War, shaping popular perceptions of the conflict as one of disillusionment and wasted young lives (Hanna 2009). Julie Anne Taddeo (2018a) argues that twenty-first-century period drama expands the perspective on war beyond the previously dominant stories of the upper-class officers in series such as *Upstairs, Downstairs* (ITV, 1971–5) and *Testament of Youth* (BBC One, 1979).

Working-class experience is incorporated, producing a 'bottom up' cultural memory of the conflict (Taddeo 2018a: 169). The vogue for British Edwardian period drama in the 2000s and 2010s saw the First World War incorporated into *Downton Abbey*, *Mr Selfridge* and *The Village* (BBC One, 2013–14). These dramas primarily explored the home front and returning veterans, highlighting the physical and emotional costs of the war on their male characters.

The centenary of the First World War prompted a proliferation of programming across a range of genres, led by the BBC's four-year centenary project stretching from 2014 to 2018. Two dramas targeting younger audiences depicted the experiences of working-class teenagers in the trenches. BBC Three's hybrid docudrama series *Our World War* (2014) told three stories of young British soldiers at different points in the war. It drew on the first-person filmmaking style of the channel's BAFTA-winning documentary series *Our War* (2011–14), which told squaddie-centred stories of the Afghanistan and Iraq conflicts (Woods 2016: 170–3). This technique – which incorporated shots from cameras attached to performers' bodies – communicated the visceral experience of close combat and connected the experiences of two generations of young men. Taddeo cautions against a 'romanticising and universalising of the "ordinary soldier"' in programmes such as British–Polish co-production *The Passing Bells* (BBC One, 2014) (2018a: 182). This drama crossed national boundaries to map the parallel experiences of two working-class teenagers, one British, one German, across the entire conflict.

In 2014–15 Australian television produced a similar breadth of centenary programming to commemorate the Gallipoli conflict. The battle in Turkey was the source of 'the nation's favourite legend' of the Anzac soldier. Channel 9's $15 million drama *Gallipoli* presented a young protagonist who Carolyn Holbrook (2016) suggests was 'far from the larrikin digger of national folklore'. The programme troubled the myth of the Anzac's brave sacrifice by constructing an anti-war narrative focused on the brutality and horror of the campaign, centred on a protagonist whose youth was 'a metaphor for the young Australian nation' (Holbrook 2016).

The brutality of the First World War is embodied by the traumatised veteran, a recurring trope in 1920s-set period drama. The conflict is used to bring psychological complexity to male protagonists, drawing on contemporary understandings of the psychological impact of war that had been given renewed focus by the long-running Iraq and Afghanistan conflicts of the 2000s. German drama *Babylon Berlin*'s (Sky One/ARD, 2017–) protagonist Inspector Gereon Rath attempts to hide the near-catatonic fits caused by his PTSD by self-medicating with morphine. This suffering contributes to Rath's characterisation as a haunted noir hero. His sensitive, fragile masculinity facilitates the development of his unofficial investigatory partnership with aspiring female detective, the street-savvy Charlotte Ritter. She frequently takes the more dominant, adventurous role in their pairing. Where this fragility makes Rath a suitably sensitive twenty-first-century hero, his boorish colleague Bruno Wolter's scornful attitude towards shell-shocked veterans illustrates how post-war society perceived the psychological wounds of combat as emasculating. The Prohibition-era US gangster drama *Boardwalk Empire* (HBO, 2010–14) features traumatised American veterans of the First World War. These men find a sense of worth and outlet for their war-honed violence in the brutal organised crime culture of Atlantic City. The disfigured Richard Harrow sports an eerie tin mask to cover his facial disfigurement and uses his sniper skills to become an assassin for aspiring mob boss Nucky Thompson's bootlegging business. The disillusioned Jimmy Darmody sees organised crime as the only outlet for the psychological numbness of shell shock, his belief being that the war has left him a broken murderer beyond redemption (White 2017).

Jimmy's bleak numbness is echoed in Tommy Shelby, patriarch of the Shelby gangster family in *Peaky Blinders*. The series was created by Steven Knight, who felt that his home town of Birmingham was underrepresented in British drama and that the city's importance as a dynamic manufacturing base post-industrial revolution was an untapped source of storytelling. With an eye towards representing the city's working-class community, he drew on local legends of violent crime gangs to inspire the Shelby family. First broadcast on BBC Two as part of the BBC's commemoration of the centenary of the First World War, *Peaky Blinders* aired in a mid-week slot that signalled it as a more challenging genre iteration. The programme developed into a valuable brand for the BBC and was promoted to the BBC One Sunday 9 p.m. prestige slot for its fifth season. *Peaky Blinders* uses the weight of the war on its veterans as a structuring device; the First World War 'inflects the fine grain of its psychic landscape' (Long 2017: 174). War trauma contributes to the programme's ambivalent model of masculinity as the Shelby brothers exploit the bonds built in wartime conflict to strengthen their control over the post-war working-class Birmingham neighbourhood of Small Heath. The brothers use their war-honed violence and fearsome reputation to climb their way from racketeering petty criminals to feared and wealthy crime lords, and by season five Tommy has won a seat in the House of Commons as a Labour politician.

As Paul Long argues, the programme offers a rare and complex interiority to working-class men, in part through its recognition of them as
marked by the mental scars of war (2017: 174). Yet the damage war has
wrought is still a cause of personal shame – particularly for Tommy's
brother Arthur who has been rendered dangerously unstable – as this
'is a milieu in which nobody is willing or able to deal emotionally with
this legacy' (Long 2017: 174). The ambivalent address of *Peaky Blinders*
combines an examination of the fractured masculinity of working-
class veterans with a stylised, sensual treatment of the Shelby brothers' violent actions. It blends attraction and repulsion (Long 2017:
170), intimacy and spectacle through its presentation of post-war
Birmingham as a space of visceral violence and mythic masculinities.

Peaky Blinders presents the Shelby family's neighbourhood of Small
Heath as a resolutely working-class space of violent spectacle. Physical
labour, vulgar speech and muscular masculinity define its community. Semi-naked labourers toil amidst sparks and fire, smeared with
dirt and soot, composed in sensual tableaux of heroic labour under
permanently grey skies. At night men drink, fight and fornicate in
the streets in 'visceral portraits of physical encounters' (2017: 172).
The programme's mise-en-scène and mannered visual style and the
angular rasp of its soundtrack contribute to its blend of attraction
and repulsion. *Peaky Blinders*'s heightened aesthetic uses extreme slow
motion and chiaroscuro lighting to capture gunfire and hand-to-hand
combat in iconographic imagery. Blood is rendered as scars of crimson
against its desaturated colour palette. The anachronistic soundtrack
uses guitar-driven contemporary rock, blues and folk to assert the
programme's difference from the wealth of Edwardian and post-war
period dramas on 2010s British television. Electric guitars and driving
rhythms weave with the sounds of clanging factory machinery and
chaotic streets whilst haunting folk refrains speak for men characterised by their silence (Shine 2017).

The Shelby family style themselves as glamorous, sharply dressed
outlaws, their gypsy ethnicity positioning them as outsiders to the
Small Heath community. Tommy is introduced riding a horse through
the streets of soot-blackened industrial 1919 Birmingham. He is a
vision of masculine power seemingly transported from the American
Old West, a black hat exchanged for a flat cap. Tommy is clearly
modelled on the 'difficult men' anti-heroes of US prestige TV, and the
programme's use of anachronistic contemporary rock music and stylised aesthetics saw it received as an Americanised image of working-
class British masculinity. Like *Deadwood* (HBO, 2004–6) and *Boardwalk
Empire*, the series draws on the classic romantic masculine archetypes

Figure 5.1 Tommy rides his horse through industrial Birmingham in *Peaky Blinders* (BBC Two/BBC One, 2013–)

of the outlaw and the gangster, whilst laying claim to realism through a depiction of these lifestyles' casual brutality. However, Paul Long identifies a British period drama antecedent in Jack Ford, the working-class war-veteran hero of 1970s period drama *When the Boat Comes In* (BBC One, 1976–81). Set amidst the shifting post-war social and political contexts of 1920s and 1930s North-East England, *When the Boat Comes In* centred its protagonist in narratives of working-class labour, union politics and criminality that are echoed in *Peaky Blinders*. Both Tommy and Ford are 'a kind of working-class individualist' with 'class bravado' and a drive for success (Long 2017: 175).

Like the medieval action-adventure's 'history for boys', the imagery of *Peaky Blinders* fetishises the violence that its narrative and emotional landscape exhibits more ambivalence over. The imagery lingers on the men's thirst for violence, a lust the war has let loose, in slow motion and visceral tableaux. However, we see the personal and emotional catalysts for and costs of these acts. The programme illustrates how the war's disruption of social order fractured Victorian-informed ideals of masculine restraint and patriotic duty as well as the class structures of Edwardian society. The war has broken both Tommy and Arthur, unleashing the Shelby brothers' rage and violence (Taddeo 2018a: 180). It has liberated them from the structures of society and trained them to kill in cold blood. It has also hardened and strengthened their sister and aunt, who ran the family's gambling and protection business in their absence.

Tommy exhibits a cold detachment and suppression of his emotions; Cillian Murphy's internal, minimal and frequently silent performance makes Tommy's explosions of violent rage even more fearsome. The camera lingers in elongated slow-motion close-ups of Tommy in contemplation or cold, unreadable blankness. He is the iconographic portrait of gangster coolness and control, making his moments of violence all the more fearsome. Drawing on Richard Dyer's (1994) discussions of Englishness and emotional reticence in period drama, Julianne Pidduck maps a 'text of muteness' across the genre's masculinities. She suggests romantic heroes struggle with emotional expression, which produces an 'exquisite anguish' (2004: 52). An 'old-fashioned, unbending masculinity' becomes 'an object of desire and sympathy' (Pidduck 2004: 52). However, Tommy's 'text of muteness' is not the result of a class-based emotional reticence; it is the manifestation of the trauma caused by his war service, spent digging oppressive tunnels underneath enemy lines. His post-war silence is a signal of his threat. PTSD has transformed him into a man emptied out and self-medicating with opium. Period drama's romanticism of the masochistic 'suffering men' is here blended with a nihilistic brutality; Tommy's 'hidden emotional world' (Pidduck 2004: 52) is a soullessness that enables his criminal rise.

Through this portrayal of a tortured yet cool gangster masculinity, *Peaky Blinders* constructs a threatening yet seductive masculine community. Its stylised aesthetics and soundtrack emphasise the presentness of this image of the past, drawing connections between this post-war period and today. Yet at the same time its stylisation makes a spectacle of its hyper-masculine working-class community. Its strange otherworldliness illustrates period drama's play between an affective closeness and foreign distance.

Queer Victoriana: Sarah Waters and Miss Ann Lister

The past's affective closeness and foreign distance shapes period drama's queer narratives. Cultural perceptions of the genre's inherent conservatism, whilst reductive, allow programmes that reach beyond heterosexual romance to present themselves as offering counter-histories. For example, perceptions of the genre's accepted eroticism and conservative heteronormativity shaped the promotion of the 'transgressive' and titillating lesbian sex scenes in BBC Two's 2002 adaptation of Sarah Waters's neo-Victorian novel *Tipping the Velvet*. In countering the genre's limited address to queer experience, queer period dramas fill in the gaps in official histories and cultural memory. Adaptations of the trio of neo-Victorian novels by Sarah Waters – *Tipping the Velvet, Fingersmith* (BBC One, 2005) and *Affinity* (ITV, 2008) – 'peeked under the stiff skirts of Victoriana and found an unspoken lesbian subculture nestling there' (Bidisha 2008). Queer desire is also centred in biographical dramas *The Secret Diaries of Miss Anne Lister* (BBC Two, 2010) and *Gentleman Jack* (HBO/BBC One, 2019), which chronicle the life of nineteenth-century Yorkshire land-owner and diarist Ann Lister.

I use 'queer' in this chapter to encompass lesbian, gay and bisexual identities, and trans and gender-nonconforming characters. This recognises the fluid nature of sexual and gender identity, particularly in historical contexts absent the understanding or availability of con-temporary languages of identification.[2] Here queer functions 'not just as a question of representation but as a broader structure of feeling', a sensibility (Shacklock 2019: 513). Period drama can use queerness as part of its play with closeness and distance, to signal the past as a strange, fantastical space. In the royal court of *Versailles* (Canal+, 2015–18) or the Weimar Berlin of *Babylon Berlin*, the construction of the past as a familiar yet foreign place is signalled by a fluidity of iden-tity and sexuality. The genre's affective dynamics, its intimate atten-tion to touch and texture in both the body and mise-en-scène, opens up space for queer eroticism in its 'complex choreography of desires' (Pidduck 2004: 139). Period drama explores unspoken or hidden desire through the 'gaze' (discussed further in the following chapter), exhibits a fascination with the cultures of constraint and a pleasure in moments of transgression. This lends itself to explorations of queer desire and expression that are circumscribed by social barriers of invis-ibility and oppression. However, as with racism and sexism, period drama can situate homophobic prejudice as a 'regrettable historical fact' (Hennessee 2017: 215), signalled as something safely situated in the past and moved beyond in neoliberal accounts of social progress. Here 'the plight of the queer subject during a period less tolerant of homosexuality is used to prove the narrative's commitment to histori-cal accuracy' (Kies and West III 2017: 161).

Queer desire and struggle flickers through the ensembles of largely hetero-focused 2010s period drama in the UK and US, from *Victoria* (ITV, 2016–) to *Black Sails, Downton Abbey* to *Mad Men*. A limited number of programmes centre themselves explicitly on queer experi-ence. Biographical dramas and literary adaptations seek to 'reclaim a queer heritage' (Harper 2014: 118) by unearthing queer stories and inserting them into the national imaginary. Yet these programmes frequently shape complicated desires and the complexity of queer identities into the genre's familiar heteronormative structures. Until relatively recently perceptions of the genre's conservatism and the tastes and views of sections of its audience have influenced period drama's representations of historically situated queer experience. *Portrait of a Marriage*, the 1990 BBC Two biographical drama about Vita Sackville-West's relationship with Violet Trefusis, was broadcast at a time of political repression. Amber K. Regis notes that the programme aired two years after Margaret Thatcher's Conservative government implemented the 'section 28' legislation which prohibited the 'promotion' of homosexuality in public institutions (2012: 148). Regis argues the programme's limited sex scenes and its use of butch/femme dynamics produced a 'careful screening of sex [that] was intended to appease traditional audiences of costume drama, burying lesbianism within a heterosexual framework to protect the series' appeal to middle-class audiences' (2012: 150). US broadcaster PBS produced an edited version of the serial for its *Masterpiece Theatre* strand, claiming the edits were for pacing purposes, cutting thirty-four minutes of content. Whilst this was a regular practice with its British acquisitions, the broadcaster offered an optional 'softer' version for local PBS stations 'in accordance with the public's "concerns and sensibilities"' (Ben Macintyre quoted in Regis 2012: 150). This signalled an expectation that representations of queer desire would prove a problem for period drama's US audience.

Less tentativeness was evident twelve years later in BBC Two's 2002 adaptation of Sarah Waters's *Tipping the Velvet*, which did not shy away from depicting lesbian sex in Nan's coming-of-age adventures in queer Victorian London. Heather Emmens suggests the programme 'marked a milestone for the mainstream portrayal of lesbian characters' (2009: 134). In contrast to the tentative *Portrait of a Marriage*, *Tipping the Velvet* spectacularised queer desire and was shaped by a promotional discourse of scandal and titillation. Adaptor Andrew Davis promised the programme would appeal to male audiences and be 'absolutely filthy' (Claire Cozens quoted in Regis 2012: 154), leading the tabloid press to hype its anticipated explicitness. Regis argues the programme was positioned as a 'spectacle adapted for, and consumed by the heterosexual male gaze' (2012: 155). Davis and the programme's male director made lesbian desire safe and unthreatening by moulding it into heteronormative frames. The novel's butch and androgynous characters were given femme styling, which together with bawdy sex scenes evoked 'the pseudo-lesbian imagery of heterosexual pornography' (Emmens 2009: 137). Period drama's realist conventions were disrupted by the programme's camp, stylised aesthetic that disrupted time and action through slow and fast motion. This playful artifice showed the influence of the recent hit musical *Moulin Rouge* (dir. Baz Luhrmann; 2001) and communicates the novel's centralising of performativity in Nan's role as a music hall male impersonator and as an object of desire in London's bohemian party scene. Yet Regis asserts that this stylisation made safe *Tipping the Velvet*'s depiction of lesbian desire and exploration of gender identity as it was 'contained by unreality' (2012: 155). The past was pulled close through a highly contemporary aesthetic, yet this stylisation simultaneously forced a distance. The more radical elements of the novel's gender politics – its cross-dressing, gender play and lesbian desire – were neutralised, held at a distance and structured for the male gaze.

The 2005 adaptation of Waters's *Fingersmith* was received without *Tipping the Velvet*'s frame of curiosity and titillation. Whereas the 2002 serial was scheduled in the midweek BBC Two slot used for riskier period dramas, *Fingersmith* took the prestige drama slot of Sunday 9 p.m. on BBC One. This indicated the increased presence of lesbian representation in British and US television across the 2000s, as well as the programmes' tonal differences. Adapted by Peter Ransley and directed by Aisling Walsh, *Fingersmith*'s darker, gothic-toned melo-drama deploys false identities, doubles and multiple perspectives. Its twisting plot pastiches the Victorian sensation novel. London thief Sue is enlisted in the plot of con artist Rivers, who plans to seduce and marry gentlewoman Maud. Maud is isolated from society, living with and working for her austere uncle on his country estate, and Sue is installed as her maid. She works with Rivers to free Maud from her uncle's clutches, with the pair plotting to steal Maud's fortune by having her committed to a madhouse. Sue falls in love with Maud but in a mid-narrative twist she ends up duped by Maud and Rivers and imprisoned in her place. The serial's perspective suddenly switches to Maud, revealing her as more than an innocent victim.

In contrast to *Tipping the Velvet*'s detached, bawdy tone and lesbian sex read through the male gaze, *Fingersmith*'s female director attends to female intimacy and desire. The programme's sole sex scene is seen twice, from first Sue's and later Maud's perspective. It is depicted through soft light and music, intimate close-ups, tentative, delicate touch, and mingling textures of hair, night-clothes and bed linen. The first half of the three-part adaptation is told through Sue's per-spective, with her narration communicating her confused desire and guilt at her role in Rivers's plot. Throughout Sue's time with Maud, the intimate bond between the lady's maid and her employer is given erotic charge. The camera's close attention to the texture of clothing

Figure 5.2 The intimacy of a lady's maid's duties becomes erotic in
Fingersmith (BBC One, 2005)

and touch of hands in this section gives Sue's daily labour an intimacy
that becomes sensual. The programme lingers on Sue's dressing and
undressing of Maud's complicated layers of clothing with hooped
petticoats, delicate buttons and her ever-present gloves. Both women
are dark-haired, pale-skinned and petite, allowing Sue and Maud to
switch places at the narrative's first twist. Before this Maud dresses
Sue in her own clothes as gifts and as part of the pair's role play,
producing a doubling that is both gothic and erotic. When the plot
is retold from Maud's perspective, events that initially communicated the women's naive intimate bond are re-viewed through the
detached, dark charge of Maud's self-loathing. Yet these scenes retain
an element of intimate sensuality as Maud's manipulation blends
with her desire for Sue and her guilt over the imminent betrayal.
Fingersmith presents a gothic queering of the homosocial spaces
of Victorian society familiar from period drama, both the intimate
dynamics of the servant–mistress hierarchy and the platonic bonds of
female companionship.

The queering of the intimate bonds of female companionship is
the focus of two BBC period dramas based on the life of nineteenth-
century Yorkshire landowner and prolific diarist Anne Lister. Lister's
hidden and coded diaries 'have been variously termed the "Rosetta
Stone" and the "Dead Sea Scrolls" of lesbianism for the light they
shed on explicit same-sex practices among women decades before the
identity category of the lesbian came into being' (Joyce 2019: 601).
Written by Jane English and accompanied by a documentary about

Lister, the 2010 single drama *The Secret Diaries of Miss Anne Lister* was scheduled on BBC Two, typically home of more challenging or contentious period dramas. This signalled Lister's acquisitive queer desire as a counter-history, and the programme depicts her as a domineering serial seductress.

Gentleman Jack is a 2019 HBO/BBC co-production,[3] scheduled in the prestige drama slot of Sunday 9 p.m. on BBC One. This signalled a mainstreaming of queer period drama. The drama was the product of writer/producer/director Sally Wainwright's star power; one of the reigning 'auteurs' of 2010s British television, she wrote all and directed six of the first eight-episode season. Anne Lister (and occasionally her sister) breaks the fourth wall to glance at the camera like the transgressive twenty-first-century protagonist of *Fleabag* (BBC Three, 2016–19), an affectation also shared by Becky Sharpe in ITV's 2018 adaptation of *Vanity Fair*. The device is used to signal Becky Sharpe's and Ann Lister's self-awareness and connection with the twenty-first-century viewer, positioning them as evolved beyond the constraints of the historical world they inhabit. Anne Lister can 'move through the world like Mr. Darcy' (Hogan 2019) and is presented as both a transgressive, proto-feminist period heroine and a soft butch iteration of period masculinity's 'exquisite anguish' (Pidduck 2004: 52).

Gentleman Jack focuses on the period of Lister's life when she courted neighbouring landowner Anne Walker, which Simon Joyce suggests downplays Lister's gender nonconformity. Instead, the relationship is presented in terms familiar to a twenty-first-century mainstream audience, 'as a prototypical example of marriage equality' (Joyce 2019: 601). The programme draws the past close by rendering the foreign concept of the nineteenth-century 'female husband' in recognisable frames. *Gentleman Jack* structures Lister's promiscuous seductions and her unstable sense of her identity and desires (Clark 1996; Joyce 2019: 604–5) into a narrative of committed same-sex romance. This shapes the fluidity and confusion of her biographical narrative into a story familiar from period drama's conventions of heterosexual romance.

I discuss both *Secret Diaries* and *Gentleman Jack*'s deployment of 'the gaze' and patterns of looking in the following chapter. The Sarah Waters adaptations and Ann Lister dramas illustrate period drama's shifting presentations of Victorian queer female desire. Shaped as a bawdy spectacle for the male gaze or more intimate romances, these programmes build counter-histories of Victorian life, queering the intimate bonds of female companionship. Yet they can also exhibit period drama's tension between distance and closeness, softening the distanced experience of the past as a 'foreign country' by reading its social practices and a queer fluidity of identity and desire within contemporary heteronormative frames.

Queer New York: *Pose*

Pose builds a counter-history of 1980s New York, telling the story of the city's underground ball culture and its Black and Latinx queer and trans community. A US cable drama from FX, *Pose* is part of the wider 2010s televisual trend for 1980s-set period drama. Set in 1987–8 and jumping to 1990–1 in its second season, the programme rewrites the cultural memory of the decade, reframing recent history to tell the ignored or forgotten histories of New York's queer and trans people of colour. *Pose* asserts the cultural impact of the city's ball culture beyond Madonna's hit song 'Vogue' and inserts trans women and queer people of colour into the cultural and historical narrative of the AIDS epidemic. The latter has largely been told through the experiences of cis-gender white men, as seen in *The Deuce*'s third season. Within this representational landscape *Pose*'s intersectional approach to queer experience is rare, particularly in period drama's glimpses at queer history. Alfred L. Martin notes that 'black queerness has bubbled up within television discourse, although not in the same ways afforded white gay men', with the media industries continuing 'to treat identity categories as discrete rather than intersectional' (2018b). *Pose* explores New York's ball culture through a focus on two competing 'houses', families of choice formed by queer youth who have been abandoned by their own. Queer family melodrama is interwoven with the spectacle of the balls. Winning a category brings cultural capital within the community, and characters dance and 'walk', competing for judges and a raucous crowd. *Pose*'s narrative blends the hierarchies and interpersonal conflicts of the ball scene, the matriarchal challenges of the house 'mothers', and the creative and emotional coming of age of the younger family members.

Pose was created by Steven Canals with Brad Falchuk and superproducer Ryan Murphy, who had a long-standing relationship with FX. With its cast of trans and queer people of colour, *Pose* is frequently described as revolutionary by the mere fact of its existence (McFarland 2018; Seid 2019), as well as for its attention to the hierarchies and spectrum of lived experience within the community (Kumari Upadhyaya 2019). The press promotion of this diversity – which included trans voices in its writers room and a racially diverse crew – serves as a calling card for FX. For a channel whose programming and key creative talent remained largely white (and largely male) until quite recently, *Pose*'s diversity supports FX's reputation for risk-taking prestige TV and distinct creative voices. This diversity and 'risk' help it target a white, affluent, liberal audience (Warner 2016; A. L. Martin 2018b). These viewers' entry into the unfamiliar world of the ball scene is facilitated by the inclusion of an ostensibly sympathetic cis white couple as supporting members of season one's ensemble – businessman Stan, who works at Donald Trump's company, and his suburban wife. Eva Pensis argues Stan's 'relationship' with trans sex worker Angel performs respectability politics by blurring narratives of romantic love and survival sex work in a way that makes 'black and trans life presentable and non-threatening to a global audience' (2019: 16).

Beyond Stan's presence, which doesn't continue into season two, *Pose*'s large ensemble is focalised through Latinx trans woman Blanca and queer Black runaway and aspiring dancer Damon. Blanca takes Damon under her wing in her newly formed House of Evangelista, a 'found family' which also includes sex worker and aspiring model Angel and grifter Lil' Papi. Blanca establishes the house after being diagnosed with HIV, to fulfil her dream of becoming a house mother. With the support of Pray Tell, her friend and ball MC, she houses her scrappy found family in a run-down Bronx apartment. By centralising ideals of family and the mentorship of surrogate parents, *Pose* preaches a message of acceptance and self-love for those taught their lives are dirty, expendable and insignificant (McDonald 2019).

In her discussion of 'queer kinaesthesia' Zoe Shacklock asserts that 'queer identity is first and foremost a question of collaborative, communal existence, rather than an atomised, singular mode of subjectivity' (2019: 516). In *Pose* queer identity is communal rather than singular. Both the performance space of the ballroom and the emotional support and safe homes of the found families are presented as key to queer survival. Blanca provides the security and support needed for her children to express their true queer selves both on the ball's catwalk and in New York's creative industries. Critic Matt Zoller Seitz (2018a) aligns the surrogate family's warmth and Blanca's unconditional love and drive for her children's success with proudly sentimental family-focused period dramas *The Waltons* (CBS, 1971–81) and *Little House on the Prairie* (NBC, 1974–82). Seitz (2018a) argues *Pose* serves as a balm of sweetness and affirmation for a contemporary US culture shaped by President Trump's displays of cruelty. Where the 1970s period dramas offered conservative visions of the American past centred on large white families in small rural communities – Depression-era and wartime Virginia, and late nineteenth-century Minnesota, respectively – *Pose* functions through Gilad Padva's conception of 'queer nostalgia' (2014).

Padva links queerness and nostalgia, suggesting that 'their vitality, colourfulness, and somewhat unruly and utopian nature, can be useful resources for self and communal growth and development' (2014: 7). They assert that the 'importance of nostalgia in queer imagination' complicates readings of nostalgia as a conservative longing for a 'return' to an idealised home, particularly for a community with historically fraught links with biological families (2014: 7). Instead, Padva suggests the possibility of queer nostalgia to serve as 'a sort of therapeutic process of coming to terms with who we are, what we want to be, and what we can be' (2014: 11). *Pose* looks back to 1980s New York as period of queer crisis, due to the AIDS epidemic and the everyday struggles against the city's marginalisation of its queer and trans communities of colour. The programme can be read as queer nostalgia through its shaping of this crisis and struggle into a narrative of survival and coming to self-love. This is achieved through the embrace of the collective – the found family and ball culture. Here *Pose*'s optimism and sentimentality does not hide a painful history but 'plays its own part in mediating and modifying the past in order to make it more bearable' (Padva 2014: 228). Its blend of familial warmth and creative nourishment offers 'ways of imaginatively fulfilling desired authenticities, particularly for those who find themselves marginalized' (Padva 2014: 229). This has particular resonance for a programme that debuted at a time of heightened violence against transgender people of colour (Pensis 2019: 16).

The 2010s saw increased cultural awareness of queer and transgender identity in the US and UK. This cultural visibility and the tentative shifts in late 2010s US television towards an increased diversity of representation facilitated *Pose*'s inclusion of queer and trans voices in its creative team. These voices helped the programme assert the 'authenticity' of its representations. Yet this narrative of 'progress' exists alongside a severe right-wing backlash against trans rights and the persistence of a structural violence that disproportionately impacts trans women of colour (Pensis 2019: 16). *Pose* illustrates the everyday dangers of presenting as trans in a hostile late twentieth-century New York. It highlights sex work as one of the limited means of economic support for trans women of colour, with an underlying awareness of its violence and danger brought to the foreground in Candy's off-screen death in season two. However, this starkness sits in tension with the programme's inherent romanticism, sentimentality and tendency towards aspirational storytelling, which results in a perpetually unbalanced tone.

This tension is present in season one's depiction of Angel's sex work, which somewhat contrasts with *The Deuce*'s exploration of the bleak everyday of the sex trade. Eva Pensis argues *Pose* maps a romanticised vision of sex work through Angel's 'relationship' with her cis white customer Stan, who keeps her as his lover and mistress in her own apartment (2019: 18–19). Yet the eventual failure of Angel's aspirational dreams of a heteronormative life with Stan works to cement *Pose*'s focus on its queer community. Come the close of season one she affirms her place within the House of Evangelista and reclaims her starring role on the ball's runway. Season two continues this unstable blend of aspirational New York fantasy and the stark challenges of everyday struggles for trans people of colour. It offers an intensified focus on the deathly impact of AIDS sweeping the ball's community. We see the impact of the numbing parade of funerals and follow the direct action of activist group Act Up![4] This is blended with aspirational storylines that see several of Blanca's children achieve success in New York's creative industries. *Pose* attempts to resolve this messy instability through an intense emotionality and sentimentality, rendering both strands through a melodrama-drenched storytelling that seeks to draw the audience close. In *Pose* period drama's melodrama 'translate[s] the past into an idiom of melancholy and loss' (Vidal 2012a: 22). Yet the series channels the pain of AIDS-related illness and loss, together with the violence connected to survival sex work, through the uplifting sensory experience of queer New York's ball culture, rendered as visual and aural spectacle.

Belén Vidal separates period dramas that defamiliarise the past through pastiche, which is used 'as a strategy for progressive politics', from those that use the 'unironic emotional intensity' of melodrama to 'express an attachment with the past' and resist 'explicitly political readings' (2012a: 35). In its charting of the impact of AIDS on the Black and Latinx queer community *Pose* attempts to build a progressively politicised melodrama, one that presents a counter-history to the cultural amnesia present in dominant narratives of the crisis. The programme repeatedly highlights the impact of government neglect and limited access to healthcare, teaching compassion for the disease's feared victims dying in neglected hospital wings and buried in unmarked mass graves on New York's Hart Island. Season two's time jump to 1990 places it near the peak of the epidemic and the programme becomes more explicit in its role as didactic educator. This is presented through Pray Tell's and Blanca's experiences of living with

HIV. As community elders they repeatedly frame their experiences as educational for their young family members and by extension contemporary viewers, whose experience and knowledge of the disease has been lessened by medical advances.

Pose's melodrama offers an 'appeal to intense feeling through historically situated styles' (Vidal 2012a: 35). Here the messy instability of its blend of reality and romanticism extends to its relatively loose period recreation. In Chapter 4 I discussed *The Deuce*'s and *Mrs. Maisel*'s reconstructions of a detailed vision of period New York shaped by verisimilitude and fantasy. In contrast, *Pose* (in part due to budgetary restraints) more loosely evokes the late 1980s and early 1990s through mise-en-scène and soundtrack. The programme builds an affective experience of the past driven by the emotional realism and catharsis of its melodrama-informed storytelling, together with the fantasy-tinged visual spectacle of the ball's runway. The ball scenes present creative life as a defiant expression of queer identity and community. Its runway is depicted as a utopian space for the characters to escape to beyond their day-to-day lives of struggle and fear. Staged with visual dynamism and driven by the alternately celebratory and cutting commentary of Pray Tell as MC, these sequences are akin to musical numbers. Discussing the musical, Richard Dyer argues entertainment offers 'the image of "something better" to escape into, or something we want deeply that our day-to-day lives don't provide' (2002: 20). In

Figure 5.3 Performing a spectacle of glamorous femininity at *Pose*'s (FX, 2018–) ball

Pose the ball offers the image of 'something better' for New York's queer and trans communities of colour, offering 'temporary answers to the inadequacies of . . . society' (Dyer 2002: 25), moments of affective excess and freedom for the programme's characters.

Pose's competitive ball culture presents a queering of period drama's set piece, the society ball. In period drama's stories of pre-twentieth-century society the ball embodies 'the tension between social regulation and renegade desire [which] is played out in a spectacle of costume, music and dance' (Pidduck 2004: 58). *Pose*'s ballroom plays out the social regulation of the community's complex social dynamics. This intersects with characters' use of performance to express their true selves. This focus on creative expression 'presents identity as a function of embodied performance' (Shacklock 2019: 509). Success in characters' chosen categories provides validation of queer men's dance skill and trans women's aspirations to perform a flawless image of glamorous femininity, asserting a 'defiant sense of self' (Shacklock 2019: 510). Successful performance is rewarded with cultural capital and visibility, rather than the society ball's courtship and romance. In *Pose* costume, music and dance are modes of queer expressions of self, presenting queer self-love as 'renegade desire' in the straight white New York beyond the space of the ballroom.

Pose shows that period drama's move into the 1980s can still uncover marginalised histories, rewriting narratives of the recent past shaped by cultural memory. Its Black and Latinx queer and trans ensemble counters television's default to white, cis-gendered queer narratives. *Pose* employs period drama's melodrama-informed exploration of historical events through their impact on individuals. It focuses on found family and interpersonal conflict as a way to explore queer identity and the AIDS crisis. The programme's showcasing of ball culture highlights period drama's investment in the affective dynamics of period spectacle, dance and performance. This centres its experience of the past through the affective bodies of 'queer kinaesthesia' (Shacklock 2019).

Conclusion

This chapter's theme of gender and sexuality illustrates period drama's affective engagement with the past, together with its tracing of connections and continuities between the past and the present. It has also highlighted the tensions and play between closeness and distance that are central to the genre. Period drama's increasing interest in women at work contributes to a more complex vision of women's history. At the same time these programmes illustrate how a desire for identification and drawing the past close can cloud its foreignness and specificity. The muscular violence of 'dirty realist' action epics and crime dramas offer the pleasures of unconstrained masculinities. Yet they shade this with ambivalence through the incorporation of protagonists with contemporary-informed conflicted masculinities. Queer Victoriana dramas build counter-histories that write lesbian desire into dominant narratives of the era, queering the intimate bonds of female companionship. Yet they also shape the complexities of historical queer identity into the genre's accepted heteronormative romance narratives. *Pose* similarly writes the Black and Latinx, queer and trans community back into period drama's vision of the 1980s. It uses melodrama and queer nostalgia to shape an at times unstable, affect-driven narrative of queer community. Some of these themes continue in Chapter 6's focus on bodies and costume.

Notes

1. Andrew Higson groups the medieval, Elizabethan, English Civil War and Restoration periods into the 'pre-modern'.
2. This was illustrated in the conflict over the wording of the 'rainbow plaque' unveiled in York in 2019 to commemorate Anne Lister as an LGBTQ+ pioneer of marriage equality. Simon Joyce highlights how the plaque's description of Lister as 'gender-nonconforming entrepreneur' and the absence of the word 'lesbian' proved 'extraordinarily divisive, setting parts of the LGBTQ+ coalition at odds with each other' (2019: 601).
3. In the 2010s BBC and ITV expanded their period drama co-production partners beyond PBS and *Masterpiece*. As a channel whose brand blends prestige TV with risk-taking and challenging content, HBO is a less conservative partner than PBS's *Masterpiece*, whose viewership may not be as welcoming of *Gentleman Jack*'s queer romance.
4. Here the programme ventures into alt-history, writing Black, Latinx and trans characters into a largely cis white activist group that had a complicated relationship with and largely excluded trans women (Greer 2018).

6 Bodies and Costume

The spectacle of costume is frequently touted as one of period drama's primary pleasures. Costume tells a story; it is encoded with meanings. Its silhouette and tailoring places a body in a particular moment in time through the curve of a corset, the cut of a suit jacket, the volume of a skirt's petticoats. Costumes and bodies illustrate period drama's blend of realism and fantasy, spectacle and intimacy. Costume can present the body as spectacle, signalling the verisimilitude of a programme's exacting period reconstruction or its flights of fantasy. Period drama's intimate address can also offer a close, at times sensual attention to bodies and textures. Exploring period drama through the frame of bodies and costume draws out the genre's 'preference for affective rather than intellectual histories' and its redramatising of 'the past as an emotionally charged space' (Vidal 2012a: 21).

Bodies and costume chart period drama's 'nuanced relations of desire, power and agency that emerge through subtle economies of gesture, costume, mise-en-scène and performance' (Pidduck 2004: 17). The genre derives pleasure from constraint and release. It delights in setting boundaries and breaking them, whether through snatched moments – a glance, a touch, a kiss, a confession – or a break from society's constraints. Period drama's fantasy is frequently manifest in heroines (and heroes) who exhibit a desire for power and release. Yet it also has an 'ambivalent fascination' with the constraining patriarchal, social and class barriers they push against (Pidduck 2004: 72). Period drama frequently draws its affective power from melodrama, the tension between what is felt and what can be said, the 'actions not taken' in these rigorously controlled worlds (Pidduck 2004: 50). The increased eroticism of period drama in the 2000s and 2010s presents a much more direct 'representation of (particularly female) sexuality and desire' (Goodman and Moseley 2018: 53). These are figuring as acts of resistance against social controls. Across period drama resistance is rewarded with the freedom of romantic fantasy – a love match that also provides financial security – or melodrama's more tragic ends, the result of the reassertion of control.

Exploring period drama through bodies and costume highlights romance, desire and eroticism as some of the genre's key structuring forces. The genre's romantic and erotic investments have been viewed with the same suspicion as the seductive pleasures of its period imagery. Identification and investment challenge the 'formal distance and historical particularity' that John Caughie argues are needed to understand difference and change in period narratives (2000: 216). Similarly, Alison Landsberg suggests that immersion and identification need to be broken to produce a critical understanding of the past as a 'foreign place' (2015: 91). Romance, desire and their related pleasures are frequently read as producing uncritical or conservative encounters with the past. This is seen in Esther Sonnet's assertion that the popularity of Jane Austen's marriage plots exhibits a post-feminist longing for a return to a 'specifically pre-feminist past' (1999: 58). However, Belén Vidal recognises period drama's complexity, asserting that the genre does not forget or reject feminism's lessons; instead it filters women's struggle for self-expression through the politics of romance (2012a: 128).

The first section of this chapter draws on a range of programmes to chart period drama's investment in 'the gaze', bodies and costume. It then delves into case studies that illustrate affective encounters with the past. These draw out how costume and the body contribute to storytelling and characterisation, as well as the genre's visual pleasures and its play with constraint and release. The social-climbing sex worker protagonist of *The Crimson Petal and the White* (BBC Two, 2011) inhabits a neo-Victorian London shaped by sex and the abject. *Outlander* (Starz, 2014–) attends to female pleasure and sexual desire, offering a tactile, sensual encounter with bodies, costumes and Scottish landscapes. *Dickinson* (Apple TV+, 2019–) uses tonal instability, anachronisms and transgressive bodies to communicate the surreal, queer world view of its teenage poet protagonist.

The gaze

Period drama's play of constraint and release produces narrative, romantic and erotic tension. The genre's patterns of looking – 'the look' or 'the gaze' – frequently produce pleasurable tension within frames of social constraint. Esther Sonnet suggests period drama's articulation of desire is conservative and regressive, arguing that pleasure is derived from the *'performance* of repression' (1999: 58).

For Sonnet this over-investment in 'the look' aligns with a form of 'genteel' spectatorship that derives cultural capital from a restrained performance of desire, which exists in opposition to the vulgar, 'carnal sexuality' of mainstream cinema (1999: 58). She connects this 'genteel' desire with the 'Darcy effect' of BBC One's 1995 adaptation of *Pride and Prejudice*. Sonnet figures Darcy's romantic form of masculinity as 'the ideological staple of popular cultural genres from Gainsborough costume-pictures to historical romance sagas and the formula fictions of Mills and Boon', suggesting this illustrates a longing for a return to a pre-feminist past (1999: 58–9). Yet period drama's patterns of looking offer a more complex relationship with desire than Sonnet's reading of regression.

Period drama's patterns of looking centre the active female gaze. Julianne Pidduck (2004) identifies a recurring image of the woman at the window in 1990s film and television adaptations of Jane Austen novels. The watching woman 'suggests a polite, yet coyly lascivi-ous, desiring female gaze' (Pidduck 2004: 26). This reading echoes Lisa Hopkins's influential discussion of the 1995 *Pride and Prejudice*, which positions the programme as a defining moment in television's engagement with female desire. Hopkins argues that the 1990s Austen adaptations gave women 'every opportunity and encourage-ment to exercise the pleasures of looking' (2001: 120). In adapting Austen's novel Andrew Davies sought to write Darcy's perspective into the narrative, including a much-parodied 'sexing up' of his hero through bathing scenes in bathtubs and lakes. Hopkins suggests the programme is unashamed in its appeal to women, 'fetishizing and framing Darcy and offering him up to the female gaze' (2001: 112). Darcy is the site of *Pride and Prejudice*'s visual pleasure, as much as and perhaps more so than his grand Pemberley estate. Importantly Hopkins combines the camera's gaze with the hero's own gaze upon the heroine, a look that embodies his romantic desire and longing. We watch as Elizabeth Bennet becomes the focus of Darcy's gaze and at the same time he is presented as the object of the camera and audience's gaze. '[H]e looks at her, we look at him', developing a 'powerful erotic charge, of which he is clearly the centre' (Hopkins 2001: 114). A defining pleasure of period drama is a romantic hero who we might say 'gives good gaze', able to build erotic tension through a wordless performance of – often conflicted – desire. This desire is framed and controlled by social conventions and codes of masculinity. It is arguably informed by the repression that Sonnet identifies, but rather than exhibiting 'genteel' restraint, this gaze is eroticised.

Discussing John Thornton, the romantic hero of *North & South* (BBC One, 2004), Sarah Fanning suggests that period dramas 'allow for historical men to be reinterpreted as objects of the female gaze, but also to become emotionally expressive, vulnerable, self-aware, and sensitive to women' (2018: 95). Fanning suggests that the serial's prioritising of emotional display marks a shift in the genre's gaze upon the romantic hero (2018: 102). Rather than eroticising Thornton's body, the camera's lingering attention to his face foregrounds his emotional state, evoking sympathy for his conflicted desires for Margaret and his 'sense of loss and impotence' (Fanning 2018: 102). Richard Armitage's performance blends Thornton's gruff, plain-speaking Northern masculinity with silence and deep thought. *North & South* produces an intense erotic charge through the camera's gaze on Thornton; as 'he looks at her, we look at him' (Hopkins 2001: 114). His desire for Margaret shapes him into a sensitive object of desire for the audience. This desire is communicated through period drama's constraint and release. Thornton's longing gazes at Margaret communicate both desire and emotional suffering, exhibited in his quietly uttered yet desperate plea for Margaret to 'look back at me' as he watches her carriage drive away and leave Milton. Thornton's gazes are combined with outbursts of passionate emotion, such as his introduction beating a mill-hand over a safety breach (episode one) and his failed proposal to Margaret (episode two). Here he declares in anguish and frustration at Margaret's shocked rejection, 'I don't wanna to possess you! I wish to marry you because I love you!' For Fanning the serial's 'prioritising of the emotional display of Thornton's deep interior subjectivity and wounded masculinity' is central to its reworking of him into a model of post-feminist masculinity (2018: 103). Across the serial he transforms into an emotionally expressive and equal partner for Margaret and her progressive ambitions.

Biographic dramas *The Secret Diaries of Miss Anne Lister* (BBC Two, 2010) and *Gentleman Jack* (HBO/BBC One, 2019) queer the period drama gaze, positioning nineteenth-century Yorkshire landowner and diarist Anne Lister as the dashing seducer of local women. Anne is given the narrative centrality and emotional access of the female protagonists of *Pride and Prejudice* and *North & South*. Yet her confident stride and dominant social position, together with her masculine-styled clothing, also align her with romantic heroes Darcy and Thornton. Bex Harper highlights how *The Secret Diaries* aligns the viewer with Anne's desirous queer gaze in its opening sequence and a later church service, using close-ups, point of view shots and narration to foreground her 'act of looking' at women (2014: 120–1). Rather than gazing *at* the romantic hero whilst he gazes at the heroine, the camera here interpolates the viewer *into* Anne's desirous, promiscuous gaze at local women and her lingering gaze upon her love object Mariana. Harper suggests that the programme presents Anne's queer desire as conforming to rather than challenging the established patriarchal system. In her seductions and subjugations of women in her social circle and her eventual relationship with Ann Walker, she performs a dominant, forceful model of nineteenth-century masculinity (Harper 2014: 122–3). *Gentleman Jack* both conforms to and complicates the romantic patterns mobilised by period drama's gaze by centring its narrative on Anne's romance with the emotionally unstable Walker. Their romance is mapped onto the genre's familiar heteronormative romantic arcs. Anne moves through the world like Mr Darcy (Hogan 2019) and the camera watches her gaze longingly and desirously at Walker. However, rather than being the strong, silent object of the camera's desirous gaze, Anne looks back at the viewer in direct address and opens her heart in her diary entries. She takes a dominant role in her seduction of and relationship with the wavering and psychologically vulnerable Walker, but like Darcy and Thornton, she must embrace emotional vulnerability to make herself worthy of the woman she loves. Both *The Secret Diaries* and *Gentleman Jack* use non-naturalistic devices of point of view and direct address to disrupt period drama's eroticised gaze, queering the established visual dynamics of the genre's heterosexual romances.

Bodies

Beyond the gaze, bodies are a primary site of period drama's visual pleasures and its play between constraint and release. Bodies enact, are controlled by or rebel against the social codes of the past, whose restrictiveness can be imprisoning. They are also frequently the centre of period drama's at times ambivalent eroticisation of constraint. The genre often uses casting and physicality to trace connections between the present and the past. John Caughie argues that period drama's bodies can complicate the assertion of verisimilitude produced by its mise-en-scène since 'the furniture may be authentic nineteenth-century, but the body of the actor and its gestures are our contemporary' (2000: 224). A body that exhibits presentness in the past is increasingly central to many post-1990s period dramas, influenced by post-heritage shifts and Andrew Davies's 'sexed up' Austen adaptations. Whether sexualised, dynamic or grubbily 'realist', bodies are used to counter cultural perceptions of the genre as stuffy or 'buttoned up'. Period drama's promotional discourses frequently signal a

protagonist's modernity by highlighting their physicality and movement, asserting connections between the past and present. Female
protagonists' freedom of movement in rural and city spaces indicates
their lack of interest in social boundaries, particularly when contrasted
with the restraint of other women in the narrative. From Elizabeth
Bennet's running down the hillside in the opening scene of *Pride and
Prejudice*, to Emily Brontë's sturdy traversing of moorland in *To Walk
Invisible* (BBC One, 2016), to the confident swift stride of Ann Lister
and *Howards End*'s (BBC One/Starz, 2017) Margaret Schlegel: here
female protagonists' physical freedom within worlds structured by
gendered constraint signals their renegade natures or desires.

Dance offers a blend of constraint and release, particularly within
the highly controlled social codes of eighteenth- and nineteenth-
century elite society. In dramas set during these periods the ball is
a site of courting rituals, a space that plays out 'the tension between
social regulation and renegade desire' (Pidduck 2004: 58). The dance
floor is depicted as a heavily observed space of social ritual, spectacle and display, where bodies create precise patterns and dynamic
movement. Within period drama's controlled and gender-regulated
societies dance also provides the opportunities for private conversations with the opposite sex. Even when overlooked by observers it is a
space of snatched intimacies and moments of touch that are otherwise
socially precluded. Katharina Lindner explains that dance acts as an
'embodied encounter, in which relations of reciprocity, alignment,
tension, proximity, desire and conflict are enacted via the coming
together of . . . bodies in motion' (2017: 46). The dance floor's socially
sanctioned body contact and dynamic movement with the opposite sex
produces erotic charge; within long shots of spectacular mise-en-scène
and ritualised group movement intimate close-ups will accentuate
gazes and clasped hands. In *Poldark* (BBC One, 2015–19) episode 01:
02 Ross Poldark dances with Elizabeth, his first love who married his
cousin Francis when Ross was away at war. As Ross and Elizabeth
dance together, the diegetic courtly strings fade out and are replaced
by a delicate non-diegetic piano melody that signals the pair's connection. The camera isolates them from the other dancers in a tight mid-
shot and mirroring close-ups as they share sustained gazes and smile
in intense pleasure at their proximity. A progressive slowing down of
the image communicates the pair's savouring of this moment and their
heedless disregard for social convention. Their dance is intercut with
Francis's anguished stare and as the dance comes to a close, the scandalised whispers of observers. Ross and Elizabeth's dance is an eroti-
cally charged moment of intimacy produced by gazes and moments of

touch. In this public event, the pair's 'renegade desire' is on display. Dance is imbued with erotic charge as characters are frequently unable to express their desires in period drama's constrained worlds.

Julianne Pidduck suggests that infusing the period drama with sexuality counters perceptions that the genre reproduces a 'dead' past, as it 'implies an immediacy and intensity' (2004: 40). A programme will use the presence of sex and eroticised bodies to signal its challenge to constraint and its 'modern' intervention in history: the titillating transgressive peek under the skirts of a genre conventionally understood as conservative and chaste. Basil Glynn (2012) suggests that in the 2000s US subscription cable channel Showtime used sex to signal its period dramas' difference from previous British iterations. This instead aligned them with the permissive sexuality of US cable drama. Showtime's flagship royal 'romp' *The Tudors* (2007–10) showcases a youthful, handsome, sexually voracious Henry VIII. The programme's investment in 'male power, male beauty and male heterosexual desire' (Glynn 2012: 164) was displayed through relatively explicit sex scenes and a display of the female body strongly centred around the male gaze. However, recent genre shifts towards increased eroticism are not without precedent. Claire Monk identifies 'sexuality and sensation' as part of period drama's British lineage, particularly during the 1970s when it reflected a country grappling with an increasingly sexualised society (2015: 39). Helen Wheatley highlights the presence of erotic spectacles in period drama since the 1970s, including 'long scenes of Sheila White's barely concealed nudity marking Messalina's sexual conquests in *I, Claudius*' (BBC Two, 1976) as well as the display of 'open desire and sexual freedom' (2016: 192) in the 1993 adaptation of *Lady Chatterley's Lover* (BBC One).

Wheatley's examples were fleeting erotic spectacles within a late twentieth-century period drama landscape dominated by eroticised constraint. The twenty-first century has seen sensuality and erotic spectacle permeate the genre, with Katherine Byrne et al. noting that 'quite graphic sexuality and nudity have become an inevitable part of all but the cosiest Sunday night television' (Byrne et al. 2018: 8). The increasing sensuality of Sunday night British period drama can be charted through three Andrew Davies Austen adaptations that span the mid-1990s through to the late 2010s. One of British period drama's most prominent 'auteurs', Davies is notorious for 'sexing up' his interpretations of classic literature. His 1995 *Pride and Prejudice* inserted scenes of Darcy bathing, swimming and fencing to assert his virility. The sequence depicting a frustrated Darcy passionately writing a pivotal letter to Elizabeth employs 'visual imagery . . . structured by

a heady mingling of two *leitmotifs*: heat and sex' (Hopkins 2001: 116).
By 2008 Davies's adaptation of *Sense & Sensibility* moves beyond
metaphor, adding a prologue that dramatises Willoughby's seduction
of Eliza Williams by candlelight, in a pre-narrative event recounted
only through inference in the novel. This brings an erotic frisson to
the drama and courted controversy from the conservative parts of the
British press. Claire Cheverall (2018) suggests the sequence positions
Willoughby as a 'peddler of dangerous sexual desire' and constructs a
'sense of sexual exploitation or violation' that foregrounds the danger
of sex for unmarried women in this period.

    Sanditon (ITV, 2019) is a largely original drama from Andrew
Davies that is built out from the few existing chapters of Austen's
final, unfinished novel. The resulting Austen–Davies hybrid offers
a blend of society satire, romance and romp. Its kidnappings and
action sequences – including a carriage chase – are a departure from
the reserved, witty romances of earlier Austen adaptations. *Sanditon*
attempts to blend the Austen 'brand' with the swashbuckling sensuality
of recent US period dramas like *Outlander*. Pre-broadcast press coverage hyped the serial as 'risqué' (Singh 2019b), and *Sanditon* presents
more sexually explicit scenes than ITV Sunday evening period dramas
such as *Downton Abbey* (2010–15) and *Victoria* (2016–) typically offer.
The seductions of villainous rake Sir Edward Denham threaten to ruin
both his sister Esther Denham – whom he holds in an incestuous thrall
– and his aunt's companion, the seemingly innocent Clara Brereton.
Denham and Clara are revealed to be bound in a web of seductions,
blackmail and double-crosses and early in the serial are glimpsed in a
secret sexual assignation in the woods. In episode six they plot to gain
control of the dying Lady Denham's inheritance, cementing their
deal with sexual intercourse on the floor of her austere and cavernous
receiving room. Filmed from overhead, the shock of the act's deviation
from the social conventions of previous Austen adaptations signals the
pair's villainous contempt for their benefactor.

    Sanditon also features a scene that now seems de rigueur for British
Sunday night period drama, the eroticised display of the romantic
hero's body. *Outlander* and BBC One's *Poldark* present a 'knowing
display of the male body' that indicates a 'significant shift to a privileging of an openly desiring female gaze' (Goodman and Moseley 2018:
55). Helen Wheatley suggests both programmes' aesthetics and patterns of looking encourage a 'brazen gaze, an unashamed looking'
at their heroes' eroticised bodies (2016: 213). In *Sanditon* episode
two, protagonist Charlotte Heywood accidentally comes upon the
arrogant anti-hero Sidney Parker striding naked from the sea after a

bracing swim, with actor Theo James filmed from behind in long shot. Charlotte quickly turns away embarrassed whilst Parker is unashamed, his nudity signalling his rakish disregard for social decorum. This investment in the spectacle of the male form makes period drama 'likely sites of anxiety for straight male spectators' (Monk 2001: 9), whereas sequences such as *Sanditon*'s nude bathing playfully hail the genre's female and queer audiences through an attention to their 'brazen gaze' (Wheatley 2016: 213). However Georgian rules of decorum mean the young and innocent Charlotte is unable to share this gaze.

In the 2010s period drama frequently presents the male body as spectacle, but the genre also features scarred and damaged men. This damage can be physical – *Poldark*, *Outlander*, *Downton Abbey* – or mental – *Peaky Blinders* (BBC Two/BBC One, 2013–), *The Village* (BBC One, 2013–14), *Mr Selfridge* (ITV, 2013–16). Byrne et al. position these scarred male bodies as period drama's challenge to traditional models of patriarchal masculinity; their scars signal these men's complex relationship with masculine ideals of strength, virility and power (2018: 8). Precursors to this trend are found in the brutalised male bodies of Catherine Cookson's popular historical romances, which were adapted in eighteen ITV dramas across the 1990s. These Cookson adaptations largely focused on female experience; however, James Leggott (2016) notes that the male-centred stories invariable saw a fetishistic lingering on the attack or disfigurement of their handsome protagonists. Punished for their pride or aspiration, these emasculated, wounded men became the chosen suitors of female characters, suggesting their damage produced a gentler, more sympathetic masculinity (Leggott 2016: 185).

Underground (WGN, 2016–17) looks beyond these romance-tinged, scarred white heroes, instead presenting the scarred bodies of enslaved Black men and women as embodiments of slavery's violence and trauma. Here '[t]he story of black resistance is written on the black body' (Dubek 2018: 71). Both Noah and Pearl have backs crisscrossed with scars from the lash, Cato has a facial burn and Moses the minister has an eye stitched shut. In episode one the soft forearms of light-skinned house slave Rosalee are whipped by the overseer as the plantation master's family watches. This catalyses her decision to join the escape mission, and throughout her arduous journey the resulting raw-edged scars are a constant reminder of what she has fled. Both Noah and Cato take ownership of their scars. Noah has each new scar on his back tattooed as a reminder of his enduring strength. The untrustworthy overseer Cato reveals he burned his own face to conceal the brands burned into his skin after multiple escape attempts. Rosalee and Noah's romance blends *Underground*'s scarred Black bodies as symbols of trauma with period drama's eroticised gaze on the male body. The camera aligns with Rosalee as she gazes at Noah's scarred, muscled body when he asks her to tend his wounds, and she frequently snatches glances at it during their journey North.

Underground repeatedly draws attention to the use of sexual assault by white masters and mistresses, along with other white plantation staff, as a tool of control in the system of slavery. This forms part of period drama's long history with sexual violence, with rape plots stretching from BBC Two's 1967 blockbuster adaptation of *The Forsythe Saga* to recent dramas *Harlots* (ITV/Hulu, 2017–) and *Jamestown* (Sky One, 2017–19). The pervasiveness of rape and threats of sexual violence are part of the genre's investment in women's experience of history, illustrating the structuring force of gendered control within patriarchal societies. However, Katherine Byrne and Julie Anne Taddeo argue that period drama's presentation of sexual violence can be 'gratuitous, problematic or sensationalised' (2019: 380). The presence of sexual violence is frequently used to code a 'dirty realist' period drama as grittily historically 'authentic'. A sexual assault serves this purpose in the opening episode of *Jamestown*, with the act presented as an inevitability for the women who arrive in a dirty, violent, majority-male colonial settlement in 1607 America. The threat of sexual violence is used to showcase the women's limited access to power in a colony presented as wild and 'lawless', emphasising their status as possessions, as their passage was paid for by husbands they had never met. Byrne and Taddeo (2019) highlight *Outlander*'s and *Banished*'s (BBC Two, 2015) use of rape plots to signal women's lack of power within the wild and 'lawless' male-dominated eighteenth-century societies of the Scottish Highlands and an Australian penal colony. They argue *Outlander*, *Banished* and *Poldark* continue the genre's ambivalent treatment of sexual assault, blurring it with romanticism and eroticisation (2019: 380). However, they also suggest these representations open up conservations about 'consent, rape myths and rape fantasy and thus form part of the dialogue and increasing public awareness around sexual violence' (2019: 380). Period drama can offer space for viewers to explore illicit and taboo desires, safely contained in the past, whilst at the same time presenting a politicised commentary on gendered power, consent and trauma.

Costume

Period drama's bodies play out the genre's investment in constraint and release; they are objects of spectacle yet also symbols of damage and oppressive horror. Many of these elements extend to the clothing they wear. Renee Baert describes clothing as 'never natural' but readable, a 'semiotically dense and complex social form' (1994: 355, 359). The bonnet-clad head and particularly the corset-encased body are part of the iconography of period drama. They contribute to cultural perceptions of the genre as feminine, conservative and restrained. Costume acts as one of period drama's primary signifiers of tone and historical interpretation. For example, costume markers were used by novelist and screenwriter Deborah Moggach to highlight the representation of the Bennet family's poverty in her 2005 film adaptation of *Pride & Prejudice*, directed by Joe Wright. By describing her adaptation as a 'muddy-hem version' of Austen, Moggach coded the film as a 'realist' interpretation, in contrast to the pristine clothing and picturesque mise-en-scène of the 1990s Austen cycle (Cartmell 2010: 86). Moggach's framing conveniently ignored the post-walk, muddy-hemmed Elizabeth of the 1995 adaptation, who scandalises the women of Netherfield with her appearance. Yet the phrase has achieved permanence as a costume marker of 'dirty realist' influences in recent period drama (Higson 2010: 225). In *The Devil's Whore* (Channel 4, 2008), *Outlander*, *Poldark* and *To Walk Invisible*, amongst others, muddy hems are used to signal their heroines' transgressive or classed physicality, and their comfort in traversing rural landscapes.

In period drama, costume can act as 'the agent of subversion, parody, adventure, fantasy, exploration, play' (Baert 1994: 372), at times exacting in its reconstruction, at others self-conscious. It is in conversation with the viewer and signals a programme's tone. Distinguishing between the 'look through' and 'look at' costume, Stella Bruzzi argues that 'clothing exists as a discourse not wholly dependent on the structures of narrative and character for signification' (1997: xvi). The 'look through' relates to costumes that serve primarily to signal a project's historical authenticity, that do not draw attention away from its narrative, whereas playful or eroticised costume prompts a 'look at' it, serving as arresting or sensual spectacle (Bruzzi 1997: 36). The 'look at' costume is central to discussions of period drama. The heritage debate positioned mise-en-scène and costume as a kind of spiderweb, whose fetishised period detail captures audiences and produces a 'political suspicious nostalgia' that is 'disconnected from the (historical) past by an aesthetic of surfaces' (Vidal 2012a: 18). However, Pam Cook offers a more nuanced approach to costume's storytelling potential, highlighting its pleasurable disruption 'of the concerns of narrative and dialogue' (1996: 67). Costume as spectacle can disrupt the codes of realism tied to period drama's historical or literary authenticity (Vidal

2012a: 10–11), signalling the role of fantasy in the genre's engagement with the past.

Costume functions as a historical and cultural marker that helps period drama quickly denote time and place. The three seasons of *The Deuce* (HBO, 2017–19) use clothing and music to signify the time jumps between each season. Candy moves from the tube top and blonde curly wig of her street-based sex worker in 1971, to a lux silver jumpsuit at a trendy disco as her porn star status rises in 1977, to power-dressing shoulder pads and short hair as she struggles to maintain power as a porn director in 1985. As costume is so 'semiotically dense' and loaded with historical signifiers, it signals a programme's attention to research and verisimilitude in its period reconstruction. Promotional and press discourse will foreground a programme's costumes as objects of pleasurable spectacle and as a marker of its authenticity and prestige. In the 'Mad Style' blogs, fashion blog *Tom + Lorenzo* presented painstakingly detailed analysis of the costumes of *Mad Men* (AMC, 2007–15) and the work of its costume designer Janie Bryant (Fitzgerald and Marquez 2010). Tom Fitzgerald and Lorenzo Marquez provided deep dives into the costumes of major female characters and from season four onwards broke down each episode outfit by outfit. These blogs explored each costume's historical accuracy, storytelling role and contribution to the shifts in characterisation across the programme's long-form serialised narrative. Fitzgerald and Marquez's analysis illustrates Sarah Cardwell's assertion that an 'authentic' representation of the past is key for audiences' acceptance of period drama's fictional narrative, allowing them to forge 'imaginative links with the past' (2002: 115). *Mad Men*'s representations of the past were judged as accurate due to the intensive research and knowledge displayed through its 'authentic' costumes.

Alison Landsberg suggests that 'authentic' props and costumes can 'transport the modern viewer into the past', but can also foreground the past's difference (2015: 93). We see again period drama's tension between distance and closeness. Clothing can help construct the past as an alienating and foreign place, accentuating strangeness and exoticism by producing silhouettes and bodies that are distant from contemporary experience. Spectacular clothing that draws attention through its strangeness can also be comic, be it the extravagant outfits and wigs of the Georgian elite in *The Fortunes and Misfortunes of Moll Flanders* (ITV, 1996), *Harlots* and *Outlander*, or the garish polyester fashions of 1980s-set dramas *Brief Encounters* (ITV, 2016), *Glow* (Netflix, 2017–) and *Pose* (FX, 2018–). The latter set of dramas play on audience memory to make a pleasurable spectacle of the decade's fashion crimes.

Period drama can produce a 'double-edged discourse' that depicts clothing as sensuous pleasure, empowerment and self-expression for female characters, whilst at the same time illustrating its role as a tool of gendered control (Vidal 2012b: 106). This is particularly embodied in the corseted female body. Corsets characterise the past as a less liberated age, but also repeatedly eroticise this constraint. The corset's tight laces can rigidly and painfully constrain, but the garment can also produce an unruly body, a heaving bosom that threatens (or promises) to spill out of its binds (Gilligan 2011: 9). The corset's complicated structure and bodily manipulation creates an 'othered' female form that can possess fetishistic sexual allure. The garment illustrates Stella Bruzzi's assertion that period costumes can signify the 'presence of an active sexual discourse' that draws transgressive eroticism from society's 'ostensible moral restrictiveness' (1997: 37).

By drawing attention – producing the 'look at' – costumes can play a role in period drama's 'erotic language' (Bruzzi 1997: 39). Across *Fingersmith* (BBC One, 2005) the camera pays repeated attention to Maud's gloves, which she never removes, even in bed. They signify her entrapment by her controlling uncle, as they protect his prized archive of erotic literature that Maud labours over. Their removal is figured as transgressive. This is performed aggressively by the villainous Rivers when he pulls down Maud's glove to kiss her palm, whereas the gloves are removed slowly and delicately in the women's love scene. The gloves are part of *Fingersmith*'s erotic language yet also signal gendered control. Bruzzi's Freudian-informed analysis frames this 'active sexual discourse' as a 'fetishistic attraction' that 'is the basis for a covert dialogue between character and character and character and spectator' (1997: 37). But perhaps a more open framing is to consider costume's production of an affective encounter with the past, derived from sensuousness and texture. Discussing queer period drama, Richard Dyer notes that 'one of the defining pleasures of the films is looking at men wearing nice clothes' and imagining yourself touching or wearing those clothes (2001: 46). Period drama's clothing can offer sensuous spectacle and an intimate encounter. Attention is paid to its intricacy; the caress of a character's hand or the camera's gaze showcases woven, knitted and embroidered textures. The workmanship is displayed through this attention to the folds, layers and sweeps of fabric that are layered onto the body in complicated configurations.

For example, the opening credits of *Gentleman Jack* present Anne Lister's masculine-attired body as visual spectacle, rendered in segments as she is dressed. Fragmented stylised close-ups and an attention to layers and textures queer the gendered costume iconography of period drama. The sequence accentuates details through short, sharp shots that include moments of slow motion, highlighting the buttoning of undershorts, the corset staves pulled tight and a rigid busk inserted into its front, a pocket watch tucked in, Anne's hand shooting through the cuff of a black suit jacket, a greatcoat shrugged onto her sharply tailored shoulders, black leather gloves grasped in her hand and top hat placed at a rakish angle. The sequence constructs Anne's body as transgressive through the progressive layering of the corseted female form with sharply tailored masculine clothing. It foregrounds Anne's use of clothing to assert her masculinised identity, signifying her dashing figure as a form of battle armour.

The attention paid to dressing and undressing in period drama showcases the genre's use of costume 'to bring out an element of fantasy and escapist spectacle while raising attention [to] conflicting discourses on femininity' (Vidal 2012b: 93). The complexity of the task accentuates the labour of femininity, particularly through the need for extra hands to enclose or free the female body from its casements and construct clothing's complicated layers. In this way costume helps to signal class. Characters are divided between those who work or those at permanent leisure through clothing that is functional or ornamental and bordering on entrapment. Historically, the display of unwieldly and elaborate clothing served as 'a sign of the freedoms of women of [the] leisure class from the physical requirements even of household labour' (Baert 1994: 355). Across period drama classed privilege is signified by fashions, hairstyles and bodily ornamentation that require the labour of servants to achieve. The need for extra hands to undress can be mundane routine, as in *Upstairs, Downstairs*'s frequent depiction of 'characters dressing and undressing, stressing the everydayness of period detail' (Wheatley 2005: 147), or it can be a sensual act, as in *Fingersmith*'s eroticising of the servant–mistress relationship or in *Outlander* episode 01: 07 where Jamie unlaces Claire's layers on their wedding night.

The act of undressing can highlight period drama's attention to the affective experience of women through history. At times the mundane routine of removing constraining foundation garments foregrounds their impact on women's bodies. In *Mad Men* episode 02: 08, the statuesque Joan sits on her bed at the end of a long day and massages the deep grooves cut into her shoulder by her 1960s long-line bra and girdle. In *The Marvelous Mrs. Maisel* (Amazon Prime Video, 2017–) episode 01: 08, Midge lies in her childhood bed with her estranged husband Joel after the pair briefly reconcile. Joel traces with surprise the unfamiliar red marks on her back left by her girdle. She explains they have always been there, but she used to powder over them every evening before they went to bed. This act was just a part of her ritual concealment of the labour needed to construct mid-century feminine perfection. In the opening episode of *The Alienist* (TNT, 2018–), Sara Howard ponders the social expectation for women to reshape their bodies to fit male ideals as her maid peels her corset painfully from her skin, revealing the lattice of deep marks it has imprinted on her body. From the mundane to the grotesque these marked bodies physicalise the labour of femininity. These wounding foundation garments are essential to the outfits and silhouettes that elsewhere in these episodes are presented as visual pleasures. This illustrates period drama's production of contradicting, conflicting images (Landsberg 2015: 94), with costume frequently serving to highlight women's lived contradictions.

Bodies and costume blend realism and fantasy, constraint and release, playing key roles in period drama's affective experience of the past. They serve as arresting spectacle and support storytelling and historical specificity; they produce moments of erotic contemplation and highlight the mundane everyday. I now move to explore in more detail the role of bodies and costumes in three programmes. I begin with *The Crimson Petal and the White*'s construction of a neo-Victorian counter-history of nineteenth-century London, which is depicted as a place of sex and the abject.

The Crimson Petal and the White

The Crimson Petal and the White is a gothic melodrama of sex work, social climbing and female confinement adapted from Michael Faber's 2002 neo-Victorian novel. Adapted by Lucinda Coxon and directed by Marc Munden, the drama aired in a midweek 9 p.m. slot on BBC Two, signalling it as a more challenging and darker encounter with the past than those scheduled in the BBC One Sunday evening slot. It follows Sugar, a sex worker and aspiring author of macabre and sensationalist fiction, through London's squalid, threatening under-belly. Sugar performs a model of intelligent, refined and seductively submissive femininity for her clients. She channels her rage at her exploitation into the violent revenge fantasies of her novel. She savvily manipulates her besotted client, weak-willed businessman William Rackham. She makes herself indispensable as an unofficial advisor to his toiletries business then gets herself installed as his mistress with her own Marylebone flat. Eventually she manoeuvres herself into his family home, taking on the role of governess to his neglected daughter.

Sugar journeys from freedom to containment as she climbs out of the filth and exploitation of the St Giles neighbourhood only to find new horrors in Rackham's haunted house. Costume and the body serve as sensuous spectacle across the programme, marking Sugar's shifting identity and contributing to the gothic melodrama's play of freedom and constraint.

Like more recent period dramas featuring sex workers, including *Ripper Street* (BBC One/Amazon Prime Video, 2012–16), *Harlots* and *Taboo* (BBC One, 2017–), *Crimson Petal* blends transgressive frankness and playful spectacle in its approach to bodies and costume. These dramas position sex work as performance, depicting the world of transactional sex as a blend of eroticised and grotesque bodies. The sex economy is part of these programmes' depiction of society's seedy yet glamorous underbelly, setting themselves out as counter-narratives to established histories. The period drama of the 2010s saw an increase in sex worker protagonists and ensemble members, particularly in violent, male-centred 'dirty realist' dramas like *Ripper Street* and *Taboo*. When period dramas are set in historical periods and masculine milieus where patriarchal social codes largely constrain the movement of women of higher social standing, the figure of the sex worker enables these programmes to incorporate a glamorous, active and transgressive female character. In the Victorian London of *Crimson Petal*, Sugar's trade enables her to be physically active and spatially transgressive, in contrast to Rackham's sheltered, childlike wife. Sugar strides unconstrained through city streets and parks, with her sexual labour a blend of titillation, performance and the mundane. The programme is notably ambivalent about the 'freedoms' Sugar achieves, whether labouring in her mother's brothel or Rackham's home.

Neo-Victorian narratives like *Crimson Petal* make 'visible the underside of Victorian Britain' (Whelehan 2012: 273). They read the era through contemporary investments in class, gender and sexuality, as well as 'wider disquisitions on empire, social freedom, and individual choice' (Whelehan 2012: 275). The BBC's promotional discourse claimed that *Crimson Petal*'s gothic and highly stylised vision of Victorian London was 'period drama but not as you know it' (Mendes 2017: 916). However, Imelda Whelehan notes that neo-Victorian sensibilities have increasingly filtered into the aesthetics, narrative and representations of twenty-first-century adaptations of Victorian literature (2012: 277). Risqué content and counter-narratives have made neo-Victorian a period drama norm.

Crimson Petal's critical re-reading of Victorian London employs non-naturalistic and at times surreal camerawork and editing to present an unstable world of 'sex and the abject' (Whelehan 2012: 275). Its neo-Victorian perspective is embodied in bodies and costumes, pushing the 'muddy hem' 'dirty realist' mode of period drama into grotesquery and blending this with sensuous gothic melodrama. Sugar swiftly traverses the cramped, dark St Giles streets, her boots squelching into the filthy mud that cakes the hem of her elaborate dresses. She subjects her body to violent scrubbing and harsh douches after sex with Rackham and late in the serial administers an internal dose of borax in an attempt at a home abortion. The programme's attention to texture draws the past close into an affective encounter that revels in discomfort. It draws attention to what is normally hidden: the squelch of the St Giles mud, faces caked in layers of powder, Sugar's patchwork of blistered, scaly skin and the pale, flaky lips caused by her dry skin condition, her hairy armpits and ink-stained fingers, the blood of her violent revenge fantasies and later the blood of a miscarriage on her thighs.

The opening sequence of episode one aligns Sugar with the gloomy London streets, presented as fearful spaces of poverty, desperation and the trade of sex, yet also sets her apart from this world, using bodies and costume to assert her difference. Introduced in fragmented shots during the credits, Sugar sits at her writing desk, scratching out her 'macabre and sensationalist' novel (Whelehan 2012: 277). She is dressed only in her undergarments, and the boned skeleton of her bustle hangs on her chair, revealing the base layers of the sex worker's performance of femininity. Sugar's 'menacing and cautionary' (Mendes 2017: 918) voice-over introduces herself as the all-knowing guide to this unfamiliar, fearful London. The adaptation shifts the novel's omniscient narrator into the narrative voice of Sugar's in-progress novel. This voice-over addresses the upper-class Victorian slumming sexual tourist or philanthropist. But it also speaks to viewers' expectations of Victorian period drama: 'Keep your wits about you. This city is vast and intricate, and you do not know your way around. You imagine from other stories you've read that you know it well – but those stories flattered you. You are an alien from another time and place altogether'.

As the voice-over unfolds, the camera chases behind a now dressed Sugar as she flows down the stairs of the brothel and out into the gloomy, cramped streets of St Giles. In juddering quick edits, the camera's unbalanced frames alternate between embodying her point of view in disorientating warped wide-angles and following behind as she swiftly strides through these 'vast and intricate' streets. She is captured in fragmented glimpses and moments of slow motion, a dynamic,

Figure 6.1 Sugar as visual spectacle set against the grey London streets of *The Crimson Petal and the White* (BBC Two, 2011)

elusive presence. The back of her jacket is intricately embroidered with wings, positioning her 'as an uncaged bird, a free agent crossing class borders' (Primorac 2018: 124). The green tones of her outfit connect her to but also separate her from the neighbourhood's murky grey-blue colour palette. The outfit's tailored form, sensuous satin texture and the flow of her long sweeping shawl position her as a visual spectacle, set against the neighbourhood's deep blue and grey light, dark corners, poverty and grotesque abjection.

Ana Cristina Mendes positions Sugar as a flâneuse, a tour guide to 1874 London (2017: 919). She traverses the streets of St Giles and wider London with ease, following Rackham to spy on him in the wide white streets of his upper-class neighbourhood, admiring the majestic facade of his family home. Across episode one Sugar stalks the St Giles neighbourhood, expertly manoeuvring her extravagantly bustled, intricately layered outfit through its crowded, muddy streets. This physical mobility presents her as a modern woman, connected to both the physical freedoms of Victorian modernity and those of the twenty-first-century woman. Late Victorian modernity was signified by working- and middle-class women's increasing physical mobility through walking and public transport (Mendes 2017: 919). Sugar's active body figures her as 'a mediator between and across times and spaces' (Mendes 2017: 919). As a sex worker she has connection to and mastery of the street, although she is separated from it through her exclusive work in her mother's red-velvet-draped brothel, where Rackham is the only customer that we see.

Sugar is an autodidact and a writer, actively attempting to shape her own narrative. Her acumen and advice help the passive, bumbling Rackham develop into a successful businessman. In contrast, his wife Agnes is withdrawn and unstable; she is constrained, a prisoner of her mind and home. A space of high ceilings, dark, oppressive wood and the blood-red walls of its central staircase, this is progressively rendered as a gothic space as she – and later Sugar – feels increasingly trapped. *Crimson Petal* initially builds on the established tropes of Victorian femininity to set up contrasts between Rackham's two women, the seductive whore and the angel of the house. At first Agnes seems to embody the Victorian feminine ideal of dainty child-like innocence, but this innocence is quickly repositioned as disturbed. Her mental illness is in part due to her extreme naivety over her body; she does not understand her monthly period and it its revealed that she rejected the existence of her pregnancy and the daughter she bore. This instability is compounded by the sexual abuse she suffers at the hands of her doctor, which he disguises as treatment. She is unable to participate in the society of her class, and with her frailness and religious mania she comes to embody the gothic trope of the madwoman in the attic, the abused and imprisoned wife.

Agnes's dresses are white and cream, over-intricate and delicate, signalling her child-like delicacy and innocence. Yet their lace and frills hang rumpled, musty and limp, as do the long curls of her golden hair. This communicates her arrested development, her lack of control over her own body and her household staff. Agnes's delicate yet bedraggled whiteness contrasts with the sumptuous textures of Sugar's tailored, form-fitting outfits in rich fabrics and jewel tones. These are part of her professional performance of an elite, refined yet seductive femininity, one marketed to potential clients with a promise of submission. She is constructed as an object of spectacle, whose structured outfits (with long sleeves that help to conceal her skin condition) set her apart from the exaggerated, unruly femininity of the neighbourhood's other sex workers with their exposed skin, draping fabrics, frills and feathers.

Sugar escapes the St Giles dirt and poverty by manipulating herself into a position of exclusivity with Rackham. In her new garden flat the shouts and screams of the city's underbelly are replaced with soft light and the gentle sound of birdsong. Yet this social ascension is accompanied by increasing isolation and constraint. When she joins Rackham's house as a governess she transforms herself from sex worker to caregiver. She winds her long red tumbling curls into a restricted hair style and cuts a fringe, with the camera holding close to the touch and sound of the rasping scissors. She is clothed in simple, high-necked dresses in dark fabrics, with a white bow at her neck, the refined, invisible body of the household staff. When she transitions from Rackham's mistress to his employee, she is installed in a cramped bedroom in the house's servants' quarters with a small single bed. Neglected by her lover and kept hidden from Agnes, Sugar is no longer able to shape her own narrative. She instead devotes herself to the education of Rackham's daughter. Where Sugar had previously dominated the frame, she is now presented in unbalanced compositions; in the cold white space of the nursery she is marooned in corners of the frame. In her religious mania Agnes constructs Sugar as an angel come to rescue her. But Agnes's sanity has deteriorated and she haunts the house like a still-living ghost in sequences of increasingly horror-tinged imagery. Sugar eventually helps free Agnes from the patriarchal prison of the Rackham house, before escaping herself with Rackham's daughter, fulfilling the symbolism of her jacket's embroidered wings.

Crimson Petal uses bodies and costume to figure Sugar as spectacle whilst also exposing her abjection and progressively constraining her. It depicts Victorian London's underworld and its privileged society as gothic spaces shaped by sex and the abject. These elements draw out period drama's tension between closeness and distance. The camera's close attention to texture draws the viewer at times uncomfortably close to abject bodies and acts. At the same time the programme's non-naturalistic camerawork and editing create distance, playing 'with the grammatical elements of different genres' (Munden 2011) to present a defamiliarised, distanced neo-Victorian world that is unsettlingly strange. *Crimson Petal* produces a gothic-toned, affect-driven encounter with the past that documents the progressive constraining of its active, dynamic heroine, with her loss of control signalled by the increasing restraint of her body and costume. *Outlander* also features an active heroine and presents the past through a sensorial investment in bodies and their costumes, as well as the surrounding Scottish landscape. A sweeping romantic adventure, it blends spectacle and intimacy in a narrative that centres bodies and erotic desire.

Outlander

Outlander is a fantasy adventure series adapted from Diane Gabaldon's best-selling series of historical novels. Created by Ronald D. Moore, a long-time 'auteur' of US television telefantasy, and broadcast on US premium cable channel Starz, it follows Claire Randall, a former Army combat nurse. In 1945 on a second honeymoon with her husband Frank in the Scottish Highlands Claire visits an ancient stone circle.

When she touches a standing stone she is mystically drawn 200 years back in time to Culloden-era Scotland, then under occupation by the British Army. She falls into the clutches of sadistic British Army officer Captain Jack Randall and is rescued by a group of Scottish highlanders, including strapping redhead Jamie Fraser. Claire and Jamie develop a combative friendship and after they are forced to marry to evade Captain Randall, they fall deeply in love. The programme's epic narrative sprawls across the Scottish Highlands, France and the Caribbean, before relocating to America in season four. I focus here on the Scotland-set season one along with season two's move to Paris. As a romantic adventure with strong roots in melodrama, *Outlander*'s sensorial experience of the past blends epic spectacle, a dynamic physicality and moments of bloody violence with a visual language invested in texture, tactility and intimacy. It embeds female pleasure in its storytelling through its attention to romance, the sexual desires of its combative, time-travelling heroine, and the visual pleasure of bodies and costume.

Jorie Lagerway notes that *Outlander*'s generic hybridity defies easy classification, as the series blends epic battles and visceral violence, time-travel fantasy, melodrama and erotic romance (2017: 198). Its time-travel conceit distinguishes it from other period dramas discussed in this book and it has some links with *Lost in Austen* (ITV, 2008). The ITV serial has a twenty-first-century woman drawn into the *Pride and Prejudice* novel and influences its storytelling. *Outlander* lacks that programme's postmodern self-reflexivity and contemporary heroine, instead presenting a doubled period identity through the 1940s and the 1740s. However, Claire's cosmopolitan upbringing, wartime service and medical skills shape her into a 'modern woman' even for her 1940s origins. This modernity marks her out as period drama's proto-feminist heroine, and when marooned in 1740s Scotland she struggles against a society where 'patriarchy was absolute, unlabelled, and unquestionable' (Lagerway 2017: 209). Claire is a physically and narratively active heroine. Presented as a mature woman, she is skilled and knowledgeable in both her role as a healer (and later a surgeon) and her sexual interactions.

Outlander's romantic-adventure narrative blends the two gendered forms of historical storytelling that Julianne Pidduck takes from Deleuze: the large masculine epic narrative and its broader tales of heroic muscular action, and the smaller feminine narrative, the restricted movement of the intimate, interior costume drama (2004: 5–6). In combining these narrative forms *Outlander* casts Claire as both romantic and action heroine in her own epic adventure across the landscapes and bodies of the Highlands. Despite the constraints of her corseted clothes, she runs through woods and tramps over hills. She scraps, shouts and fights off the near constant threat of sexual violence. The pilot introduces Claire through duality. At first she is a woman contemplating the image of domesticity figured by a vase in a shop window. The sequence then shifts to a flashback to her war service, immersing the viewer in a blood-soaked field hospital to present her as a woman of action and skill. She is established from the outset as a woman with conflicted desires for action and domesticity, freedom and restraint.

Claire's costumes help shape her conflicted identity, positioning her as a labouring practical body and as an object of visual spectacle. *Outlander* uses costume as a storytelling tool, blending Stella Bruzzi's distinction between costume designed to be 'looked through' and that designed to be 'looked at' (1997: 36). Claire traverses the Highlands on foot and horseback so her hardwearing, everyday clothing is made to withstand physical labour and the Scottish weather. Whilst mundane and everyday, this clothing is still visually compelling, with its folds and gathers, tactile textures and layers. However, other costumes are designed as visual spectacles, exhibited in moments of display that are accentuated through aesthetics and feature in publicity and fan discourse. These moments illustrate Pam Cook's point that costume, hair and decor are 'intertextual sign systems with their own logic which constantly threatens to disrupt the concerns of narrative and dialogue' (1996: 67). The narrative pauses for these spectacular costume moments, yet they are also affectively tied to storytelling. In episode 01: 07, Claire's wedding dress is given a dazzling slow-motion reveal as her cloak is removed and the gown's delicate lace, grey satin, silver threads and pearls shimmer in the sunlight. This moment is relayed in flashback from Jamie's perspective, illustrating how he was dazzled by her beauty. The arresting spectacle of the dress shifts what had up to then been presented as a hastily convened, comic-tinged marriage of convenience into a sweepingly romantic moment.

For part of season two the action relocates from the spectacular landscapes of the Scottish Highlands to the extravagant French royal court and Paris high society. Jorie Lagerway argues that in this locational shift 'Claire's dresses replace labouring male bodies as a central visual spectacle of the mise-en-scène' (2017: 207). The narrative pauses for just a moment to display each gown Claire wears in Paris, with the most spectacular being the red gown she wears as a strategic political gambit in episode 02: 02. This features a scandalously deep plunging bodice and a wide, heavily petticoated skirt whose dense, intricate folds of fabric bloom out from her corseted waist. Its sleek red satin glows as it is backlit by a shaft of sunlight in a breath-taking staircase reveal to Jamie and the audience. In this moment the narrative pauses to gaze upon this gown just as Jamie does. Yet this gown's captivating spectacle has narrative purpose, as Claire deploys it as a piece of political strategy in her appearance at the French royal court. She shapes herself as a sensuous, erotic object to be 'looked at' in order to dominate the mise-en-scène and gain the attention of the king, enabling the couple to plead their political cause.

Whether period drama's costume is 'looked at' or 'looked through', it requires significant production labour, and *Outlander*'s costume department is one of the production's largest. As the period and Scottish region is not heavily represented in rentable costume stores, the department needs to make the majority of its costume by hand. Costume designer Terry Dresbach chronicled this labour across her time on the project, before her retirement after completing season four. She used her blog and personal Twitter account to showcase her team's detailed research and skilled craftsmanship. Here she took pride in documenting the minute detail involved in the programme's spectacular, labour-intensive gowns, whilst also showcasing the storytelling of more everyday outfits. In season four the Fraser family start a new life as subsistence farmers on the rural American frontier. Dresbach's tweets highlighted how she designed outfits that used mending, repurposing and patchwork. Costume built a shadow narrative of the family's reworking of handed-down and worn-out clothing to make the most of what little they owned.[1] This illustrates how Dresbach repeatedly connected discourses of production labour to storytelling and characters' lived experience. Through these paratexts, she set out her team's skill and research, highlighting and explaining the craftsmanship in elements only glimpsed on camera.

In part Dresbach used these spaces to assert her skill as a highly experienced costume designer. At times her tweets were deployed as evidence to counter some vocal fan critiques that questioned the authenticity of her historical reconstructions. Social media can amplify the audience practice of patrolling period drama's historical reconstruction for its 'realism' and 'authenticity', which is particularly focused at elements of costume and mise-en-scène. Sarah Cardwell suggests that an 'authentic' representation of the past is key to an audience's acceptance of the validity of a fictional narrative. Mise-en-scène, costumes, hairstyles and locations, as well as performative and social elements of behaviour and speech help audiences to forge 'imaginative links with the past' (Cardwell 2002: 115). *Outlander*'s time-travel frame and its links to romance and melodrama (both genres with lower cultural status) could potentially trouble its claims to period drama's verisimilitude and attendant prestige. Stella Bruzzi notes that unlike male-focused period narratives, historical romances are frequently charged with sidelining history in favour of 'far more trivial interests in desire, sex and clothes' (1997: 35). By displaying the research, attention to detail and skill of her costume department, Dresbach asserts that her costumes – and by extension the programme – embody historical 'authenticity'. This allows viewers to 'forge imaginative links' and accept the validity of *Outlander*'s construction of the past, despite its elements of fantasy.

Outlander centres an affective experience of the past, presented through an intimate, tactile gaze, a focus on touch and the textures of clothing and skin. Close-ups draw attention to the pleasurable textures of clothing that communicate place, climate and social situation. Claire is clothed in layers of cotton, tweed and wool that protect her from the elements, whose heather colours and nubbled, woven textures link her to the land. The sweeping folds of Jamie's voluminous tartan kilt serve as both clothing and protection. The camera draws in close to moments of visceral violence and sensual touch, and across the series we hold close to Claire's intimate repairs on Jamie's damaged warrior body. Touch and texture play a role in the programme's eroticised, 'brazen gaze' (Wheatley 2016: 213) at his body, its central visual spectacle.

Shifting my attention from *Outlander*'s costumes to its bodies and sensuality, Jamie's heather-shaded clothing and russet hair connect his body to the Scottish land that he is shown to be innately comfortable traversing and working within. His masculinity draws from his Scottish identity and the Highlands' legend as a wild, primal place (Goodman and Moseley 2018: 56). His muscular yet heavily scarred body signals his sensitive masculinity through a blend of vulnerability and victimhood, strength and resilience. Jamie's scarred back is the result of a series of brutal flayings by Captain Randall. He embodies a Scotland violently oppressed by the British Army, entwining desire and nationhood, bodies and landscapes. His back's hardened, rope-like texture 'resembles a relief map of a territory, with ridges, rivers and trails etched upon it. His body has literally become a landscape' (Goodman and Moseley 2018: 67). In episode 01: 07, as Claire circles a naked Jamie, the camera follows her hand as it traces his muscular body, presented as an erotic spectacle. As she reaches his back the firelight highlights the contrast in textures of the scars and his smooth, muscled buttocks. Richard Dyer suggests that muscularity is the sign

Figure 6.2 The camera follows Claire's hand as she circles Jamie in *Outlander* (Starz, 2014–)

of power: natural, achieved and phallic, and that the taut buttock maintains its masculinity even as the object of the gaze (2002: 132). Thus, Jamie's smooth, powerful, eroticised buttocks counteract the vulnerability and horror of his scarred flesh.

This moment illustrates the close attention given to the intensity of touch in *Outlander*'s erotic encounters. The programme's early seasons centre sex and female pleasure, the erotic contemplation of its camera bringing 'female desire "up close" as never before' (Wheatley 2016: 218). It positions Claire as a sexually active and desiring woman, 'a key proponent of the brazen gaze as she regards Jamie' (Wheatley 2016: 217) as she tends his wounds, and more explicitly during their wedding night. This desiring gaze blends with an eroticism expressed through touch and texture. Claire and Jamie's long wedding night of conversation and sexual discovery progresses through the removal of layers of clothing. In sensual, hesitant close-ups Jamie delicately disassembles the layers of Claire's wedding outfit to leave the soft, skin-like textures of the couple's white underclothes. As the night progresses the camera and lighting draw attention to delicate linen shifts and cotton shirts glancing over bodies, fingers tracing over bodies and mouths meeting flesh, the hard softness of pearls against Claire's skin and Jamie's curls entangling in the fur bedding. This attention to and eroticisation of tactility and texture serves to aestheticise female desire.

Sex plays a central role in Claire and Jamie's relationship and the programme uses sex to develop characterisation and storytelling. Across *Outlander* sex serves as exploration, as a sign of ownership, and as an act of dedication. After spending the war apart, sex as exploration is part of Claire and her husband Frank's attempts to rebuild their connection during their Scottish honeymoon. Most importantly it forms part of Claire and Jamie's wedding night, where their conversations are blended with a trio of sex scenes that show the progression of their bond through increasing intimacy and intensity. Sex as ownership occurs later in season one, where the couple negotiate the power dynamics of their new marriage in part through an extended sex scene (01: 09). Here Claire challenges Jamie's assumption of his patriarchal 'ownership' of her, using their passionate sexual bond to assert their equality in both desire and possession. Ownership is also articulated in Captain Randall's sadomasochistic desire to possess Jamie – describing him as 'a magnificent creature' – with Jamie's to-be-looked-at-ness here reworked into victimhood through Randall's torture and rape (01: 16).

Outlander positions marriage as a partnership, and at its foundation is sex as dedication, expressed through both husbands' attention to Claire's sexual pleasure and their seeking of her enthusiastic consent. This focus on her sexual pleasure and equality serves to differentiate her marriages from the near constant threat of sexual violence in 1740s Scotland, a culture where she and other women are viewed as property. Jorie Lagerway notes that Jamie's appeal and heroism are drawn not just from his strapping physique and traditional masculinity, but 'the fundamental (feminist) *equality* between him and Claire' (2017: 204). Jamie is the active, hard-bodied hero, but he is ultimately rendered as the broken victim whom Claire must save from Randall's clutches at the end of season one, illustrating the programme's complication of eighteenth-century models of masculinity.

Jamie's vulnerability shows how *Outlander*'s affective pleasures are drawn from relationships and systems of looking that challenge historical and patriarchal gender norms. By centring period drama's structuring forces of romance, desire and eroticism, *Outlander* embraces the genre's elements of fantasy, blending a romantic narrative with the epic sweep of its adventure and political drama. It presents bodies and costumes as visual spectacle and objects of desire, drawing the audience close by investing them in the sexual desires of its central couple and their transformations through romantic love's suffering and intensity of feeling (Pidduck 2004: 17). *Dickinson* continues *Outlander*'s focus on female desire and challenging patriarchal norms, pushing period drama's blend of realism and fantasy to an at times surreal edge. The drama depicts poet Emily Dickinson as a teenager pushing against the constraints of 1850s America, whose transgressive body signals her as a woman out of time.

Dickinson

A teenage Emily Dickinson rushes out of a house party into her sister's bedroom, high on opium. She claws at the skirts of her bright blue party dress, pulling up layer after layer of white petticoat before revealing bloomers soaked red with blood. She screams 'nooooo' before collapsing dramatically to the floor and dragging herself over to her friend and lover Sue to complain about getting her period. *Dickinson* reimagines the nineteenth-century American poet as a transgressive teenage body, 'a rebellious queer, goth goofball' (VanArendonk 2019). Countering the myth of Dickinson as a constrained, reclusive spinster, the programme paints a revisionist, at times surreal, portrait of the poet as a passionate young woman.

Created by Alena Smith, *Dickinson* was part of the initial 2019 launch of programming from new streaming platform Apple TV+. It illustrates how period drama is used as a marker of prestige to help new television outlets establish their brand identity. The programme's playful revisionism and genre hybridity sought to make Apple TV+ stand out in Peak TV's crowded marketplace. *Dickinson* drew from a late 2010s trend in playfully ahistorical or anachronistic reimaginings of historical figures. This included Broadway musical *Hamilton* (written and composed by Lin-Manuel Miranda; 2015), sketch comedy *Drunk History* (Comedy Central, 2013–), sitcom *Another Period* (Comedy Central, 2015–18) and period film *The Favourite* (dir. Yorgos Lanthimos; 2019). *LA Times* writer Emily Zemler described this trend as comic 'historical remix' (2019), which is used to highlight the perspectives of previously marginalised figures. *Dickinson*'s historical remix blends period drama with the late 2010s trend for hyper-stylised teen dramas that included *Riverdale* (The CW, 2016–), *Stranger Things* (Netflix, 2017–) and *The End of the F***ing World* (Channel 4/Netflix, 2017–19).

The programme heightens the connections period drama traces between the contemporary audience and the past, blurring the 1850s and the present to suggest Emily was a woman out of time, 'best understood as a contemporary millennial' (McHenry 2019). Emily's world blends the verisimilitude of its exacting period reconstruction with playful anachronism and fantasy, soundtracked with contemporary hip-hop, pop and electronica. Johanna Winant connects the programme's tonal instability and anachronisms to the experience of Dickinson's poetry, which is 'full of overlapping and contradictory tones and moments that are difficult to interpret' (2019). *Dickinson* reconstructs 'the past as an emotionally charged space, and shows a preference for affective rather than intellectual histories' (Vidal 2012a:

21) in order to communicate its protagonist's queer desires and the strange, surreal world view of her poetry.

Emily's ahistorical physicality communicates her outspoken frustration at and resistance to the social constraints of her privileged life in 1850s Amherst, Massachusetts. She wears the era's corseted full skirts and intricately coiled hairstyles, yet her body and language are frequently those of a twenty-first-century teen. These anachronisms express her 'transgressive desires [that] erupt within highly regulated societies' (Pidduck 2004: 45). Emily fist bumps in greeting, throws devil horns in excitement, slouches and slumps onto sofas. She lapses into the slang of a contemporary American teen, a 'bitch, please' moment here, a 'dude!' exclamation there. As I have highlighted, period dramas can use freedom of movement to signal a female protagonist's modernity, indicating a lack of interest in social boundaries. In *Dickinson*, Emily's moments of twenty-first-century speech and physicality communicate her youthful resistance to attempts to form her into a vision of refined feminine decorum. Through her transgressive body, she rebels against her mother's plans for marriage and motherhood, fearing they will rob her of time to write and stifle her creativity.

Emily's freedom of movement is at times at odds with the rigid constraint produced by the era's corseted outfits. She moves as if unencumbered by their form. This contemporary-feeling physicality occurs within costumes and sets that are constructed as studied recreations. Within the mise-en-scène of the past her physical and verbal presentness sets her apart from her community. This is accentuated by her outspoken disinterest in the marriage track, her obsessive creativity and her fascination with death. Her siblings and friends present more conventional models of nineteenth-century privileged youth. However, they share some of her loose, transgressive physicality and language, particularly when frustrated at the social rules and patriarchal power of mid-nineteenth-century America. Outbursts of twenty-first-century speech and physicality distinguish the town's youth from the parental generation, depicting the generation gap as one of centuries.

Like *Underground* and *Peaky Blinders*, *Dickinson* uses a contemporary soundtrack to draw connections between the present and the past. As with those programmes, even when characters' physicality is accurate to their historical setting, the music makes their bodies *seem* modern. *Dickinson*'s anachronistic soundtrack disrupts the historical authenticity signalled by its costume and set design, accentuating characters' bodily and sexual transgressions. Episode 01: 02 focuses on the love affair between Emily and her best friend (and brother's girlfriend) Sue.

When the pair dress up as male students to gain access to a college lecture their queer desire is blended with Emily's frustration at the social controls on young women. In a dressing-up montage the pair flirtatiously cavort in various stages of undress and perform strutting parodies of masculinity, accompanied by Lizzo's raucously swaggering pop/R&B anthem 'Boys'. Lizzo's joyful, confident and unruly star persona is layered onto the girls' giggling, queerly transgressive bodies as they stage various dandily androgynous looks for each other and the camera.

Anachronistic music and transgressive bodies feature at the house party the Dickinson siblings throw when their parents leave town in episode 01: 03. The evening begins as a social event familiar from period drama, before devolving into a raucous debauched party more familiar from contemporary teen drama. Soundtracked by swooping electronica and rattling hip-hop, it features girls twerking in frilly ball gowns. These sequences are the most playfully dissonant of *Dickinson*'s blending of the 1850s and the 2010s, asserting the programme's youthful energy and difference. A dance sequence transitions the party from nineteenth- to twenty-first-century physicality, beginning with the partygoers dancing in conventional formal patterns accompanied by diegetic string music. This music fades out and is replaced by Carnage's trap dance track 'I Like Tuh', with the restrained nineteenth-century bodies performing formal circular and paired dance movements in time with the track's complicated rhythms. The

Figure 6.3 A *Dickinson* (Apple TV+, 2019–) nineteenth-century formal dance transitions into twenty-first-century dance styles

dancers line up face to face and at the track's breakdown they move in pairs down the line, transitioning into twenty-first-century dance movements. The dance's formal patterns dissemble into dancing pairs who grind and twerk. Slow motion accentuates the comic spectacle of the refined, polite dancers breaking free, the juxtaposition of anachronistic dance within an otherwise realist mise-en-scène. Later in the evening the partygoers are blissed out on opium. They loosely dance and make out in woozy, crowded mid-shots and close-ups, echoing hard-partying characters in boundary-pushing teen dramas *Skins* (E4, 2007–13) and *Euphoria* (HBO, 2019–). The party's blending of nineteenth-century costumes and bodies with twenty-first-century physicality, and the use of anachronistic music throughout the series, makes explicit *Dickinson*'s connections between past and present. It produces a playful, potentially scandalising dissonance.

This dissonance is embodied by *Dickinson*'s protagonist, with the programme binding itself to Emily's frustrated, poetic and dark world view. It explores period drama's narratives of 'desire, power and agency' (Pidduck 2004: 17) through her body and passions. Johanna Winant (2019) argues that the overtness of the programme's clash of past and present jolts the audience from the comfort provided by historical recreation into an instability that distances them from it. This jolt affectively communicates the style and effect of Dickinson's poetry and way of thinking. '[I]ts pacing is unpredictable; its timing is odd. It makes you gasp, and then laugh. The show embraces the surreal, sometimes in funny ways and sometimes in creepy ones' (Winant 2019). Moments of the surreal are used to express Emily's fascination with death. She initially glamorises death, until she experiences it up close. Her fantasies eroticise its personification, played by Black rapper Wiz Khalifa. Death is cool and dangerously seductive. He appears in a ghostly black horse-drawn carriage, dripping with jewellery, a top hat perched on his long dreads and a bare-chested tattooed torso displayed beneath his tailed jacket. Death's visits transform Emily into his sexy gothic bride, red-lipped and clad in a blood-red ballgown, her hair loosely pinned in tumbling curls. In *Dickinson* costume largely serves the verisimilitude of the programme's period recreation, but these sequences centre the 'look at' sensuous costume, drawing on gothic romance imagery to communicate the 'presence of an active sexual discourse' in Emily's fantasies of Death (Bruzzi 1997: 37).

Dickinson follows period drama's recent shifts towards a much more direct 'representation of (particularly female) sexuality and desire' (Goodman and Moseley 2018: 53). As part of its alignment with twenty-first-century teen drama it presents its young characters as filled with desire and sexual appetites that push against the social codes of 1850s upper-class society. Couples make out in public at house parties, Emily's brother Austin snatches kisses with Sue in hallways and the couple engage in pre-marital sex. Emily's sister Lavinia engages in aggressive flirtations and passionate embraces with the local bad boy and sketches herself naked as a gift for him in an allusion to twenty-first-century nude selfies. Lavinia is presented as a flighty, air-headed romantic who desires the married life Emily rejects. Yet the programme recognises that her sexual appetites and desires are as much stifled by social constraints as is Emily's creativity. Both sisters have transgressive bodies.

Emily overflows with desires. She is as passionately committed to Sue as she is her creative expression. The pair steal a kiss in an orchard, exchange intimate letters and share Emily's bed, where they lie face to face, fingers touching, their nightgowns grazing their shoulders. As in *Fingersmith*'s eroticising of the mistress–servant relationship, *Dickinson* gives queer erotic charge to the whispered intimacies of the romantic friendships common in this period. Episode 01: 02 draws connections between the pair's queer desire and Emily's poem 'I Have Never Seen "Volcanoes"'. Each episode is shaped by the themes of a Dickinson poem, with lines from her fragmented, strangely structured poems appearing on screen in flowing script as she conjures them. The words float over and at times burn into the image in their intensity as the episode brings female desire 'up close' (Wheatley 2016: 218). It culminates in Emily's orgasmic climax at the hand of Sue in a montage that draws out the poem's themes and imagery. As the poem's lines unfold across the screen, the girls' lovemaking is interwoven with imagery of volcanoes from a lecture they had earlier attended, and the rising bread Emily has baked in a fiery oven. Here Emily's creative desires and expression are interwoven with her bodily desires; both are presented through an affective, at times sensual, encounter with the past.

Dickinson uses a play between distance and closeness, past and present, to draw the viewer into an affective experience of Emily's skewed perspective. The programme's queerness, bodily and musical anachronisms and the playful dissonance of its tonal blends offer a heightened version of the blend of fantasy and verisimilitude that are central to period drama's encounter with the past.

Conclusion

This chapter's attention to bodies and costume has highlighted romance, desire and eroticism as some of the genre's structuring forces. The dramas discussed here illustrate period drama's drawing of the audience close; they play with constraint and release to construct affect-driven encounters with the past. *The Crimson Petal and the White*'s gothic melodrama plays on the tensions between distance and closeness in its presentation of a neo-Victorian London built on sex and abjection. *Outlander* centres female desire and visual pleasure, blending intimacy and spectacle in its attention to costume, sensuality and its 'brazen gaze' at its hero's body. *Dickinson* presents its protagonist as a woman out of time. It employs Emily's transgressive body and playful anachronisms to communicate the strangeness of her world view in a heightened version of period drama's tracing of connections between the present and the past.

Note

1. See: https://twitter.com/OutlanderCostum/status/1060719787473399813; https://twitter.com/OutlanderCostum/status/1223309343476465664.

7 Conclusion

Across the last forty years, nostalgia and heritage have played a dominant role in shaping understandings of period drama, in both academic and wider cultural discourses. Despite extensive critiques, the 1980s heritage debate retains a lingering influence on discussions of period drama in film and television. This creates artificial divides between 'heritage' and 'post-heritage' perspectives and fails to account for the genre's hybridity, its 'unruly diversity' (Monk 2015: 36). This book has looked beyond the controlling borders of heritage, nostalgia, 'quality' and 'authenticity' (whether literary or historical), exploring the genre from multiple angles to identify continuities and divergences in its approaches to the past. This has given me space to consider period drama's complex and contradictory critical investments in race and nation, class and politics, space and place, gender and sexuality, and bodies and costumes. I have positioned affect, pleasure and fantasy as equal partners to the established frames of nostalgia and heritage. Looking beyond the 'frozen' house-museum or untouched 'heritage' landscapes, I have incorporated the city into understandings of period drama space and place. This book has connected television period drama to wider genre discourses, drawing on film studies approaches and those from literary and history backgrounds, whilst highlighting the genre's distinctly televisual form. Television's serialised storytelling can offer expansive encounters with the past that can last years, with programmes tracking social and cultural change along with their own shifting perspectives on the past. The industry's institutions, brand identities and funding models can delimit or open up which versions of the past are represented, whose stories get to be told.

Period drama offers affective engagements with the past. Its structuring forces are a series of dualities: realism and fantasy, prestige and pleasure, high and low cultural status, closeness and distance, intimacy and spectacle, control and release. Rather than offering a 'nostalgic' escape from the turmoil of contemporary society, period drama instead

returns to the past to understand the present. It repeatedly traces connections between then and now, and its encounters with the past are
shaped by contemporary society's investments. The past is presented
as both an echo chamber and a foreign place. Programmes frequently
exhibit a tension or play between distance and closeness; this world is
like you but not like you. This ambivalence can encourage identification or produce critiques of historical actions and society, often at
the same time. The past's distance from the present produces visual
and emotional spectacle, where spaces, costumes and bodies dazzle
or disgust in their difference, and characters are trapped by or push
against social and physical containments. Period drama is invested in
both spectacle and intimacy – standing back to admire yet also drawing
in close for tactile or emotive encounters, the textures of the past.

To wrap up my analysis I look at a selection of programmes broadcast in 2020, after I had completed the body of this book. These
programmes illustrate the continuation of investments charted in this
book, as well as hinting at evolutions and expansions. Peak TV's prolific production of period drama continued apace in 2020, serving as a
key weapon in the TV drama arms race. This flow of content was only
halted by the global shutdown in the face of the coronavirus pandemic,
although pockets of production resumed in the second half of 2020.

Period drama's blend of realism and fantasy is exhibited in US
drama *The Great* from SVOD Hulu. Created by Tony McNamara,
screenwriter of *The Favourite* (dir. Yorgos Lanthimos; 2019), the series
shares that film's satirical approach to the egotistical buffoonery of
aristocratic luxury. *The Great* continues the strand of historical remix
and playful hybridity seen in *Dickinson* (Apple TV+, 2019–). It also
continues period drama's investment in royal women as a way to tell
stories of powerful women within patriarchally constructed society,
finding comedy in Catherine's canny attempts to negotiate gendered
power. *The Great* is one of two recent programmes to explore the life
of Russian empress Catherine the Great. The four-part *Catherine
the Great* (HBO/Sky Atlantic, 2019) showcases a mature Catherine,
played by British actress Helen Mirren, in a largely conventional
biopic, albeit one laced with the sex, nudity and swearing that are
now conventions of HBO's prestige period dramas. *The Great* uses
comic flippancy and playful anachronism to depict the struggles of a
young, newlywed Catherine, played by American actress Elle Fanning
amidst a largely British cast. The programme was a flagship drama for
the well-established US SVOD Hulu and debuted during a period of
heightened competition in the US television market when a series of
high-profile streaming platforms launched across 2019–20 (Littleton

and Low 2019). In this crowded market *The Great*'s playful genre hybridity asserted Hulu as a home for risk-taking prestige TV, illustrating how innovation and novelty in period drama is strategically deployed to assert brand identity in the Peak TV era.

The Great charts the young Catherine's journey from naïf to idealist to politically savvy revolutionary. She haphazardly plots to mount a coup to free Russia from the grip of her cruel, childish husband, install herself as empress and carry out her plans for a new era of enlightenment. Billing itself as 'an occasionally true story', the programme takes pleasure in inconsistencies and half-truths, offering a comically loose connection with historical accuracy (including a somewhat racially diverse cast playing Russian aristocracy). In 'a show full of satin and blood and excrement and ornamental feathers, sometimes all at once' (VanArendonk 2020), the glamour of the royal court's opulence is intertwined with the era's dark brutality. The heads of vanquished enemies are stuck on sticks or served at dinner as horrifyingly blasé accompaniment to deserts. The programme offers a playful blend of distance and closeness, blending political satire and comic grotesquery with an emotional investment in Catherine's struggles.

Period drama's interpretation of the past is shaped by the investments of contemporary society. Chapter 3 discussed how *Shoulder to Shoulder* reads Britain's Edwardian suffragettes and their fight for the vote through the investments of the 1970s second-wave feminism. In 2020 a renewed popular interest in feminist politics across the late 2010s – what Jessalyn Keller and Maureen Ryan (2018) term 'emergent feminisms' – created the context for a look back to America's second-wave feminist past. US cable drama *Mrs. America* (FX) retells this history through the investments of the contemporary feminist movement. In doing so it sought to counter cultural memories of this period shaped by the feminist backlash of the 1980s (Faludi 1992), if it was remembered at all. The serial was created by Dahvi Waller, working here with a largely female creative team. Waller was experienced at reconstructing the recent US past for prestige TV, having worked on the 1960s-set *Mad Men* (AMC, 2007–15) and 1980s-set *Halt and Catch Fire* (AMC, 2014–17). *Mrs. America* tells the sprawling and complex story of America's women's liberation movement through the lengthy fight to ratify the Equal Rights Amendment and its opposition by conservative activist Phyllis Schlafly. Dividing its narrative between Schlafly and the feminist activists, *Mrs. America* tracks the battle across the 1970s, presenting this as an epic journey from optimism to tragedy. The programme tracks the emergence of the Religious Right through Schlafly and her campaign strategy,

seeking to understand how America got to where it then was under the
presidency of Donald Trump. Like *Shoulder to Shoulder*, it is a female
ensemble drama 'focus[ed] on a cross-section of feminine types' (Ball
2013: 246) that shapes its episodes around individual stories of significant figures of the movement. These include activist and journalist
Gloria Steinem, lawyer and activist Bella Abzug and politician Shirley
Chisholm. But, much like *Shoulder to Shoulder*, in attempting to tell
the story of an entire political movement in a single serial it ended up
somewhat short-changing the complexities and diverse personalities
of the 1970s feminist movement (St Felix 2020; VanDerWerff et al.
2020).

Mrs. America's return to 1970s second-wave feminism responded to
the renewed embrace of (and neoliberal commodification of) feminist
politics that developed in the US and UK across the 2010s. This
intertwined with a larger reckoning with the 2016 election of Donald
Trump, the aggressions of popular misogyny that were tied to the
rise of right-wing populism, and the #MeToo movement highlighting workplace harassment and assault (Banet-Weiser 2018). *Mrs.
America*'s capturing of the zeitgeist shows how the investments of the
present shape viewers' appetite for a return to and reconsideration of
particular periods of cultural shift. In 2016 workplace drama *Good Girls
Revolt* (Amazon Prime Video) similarly looked back to second-wave
feminism, depicting the development of the 1969 legal action for equal
pay brought by *Newsweek* magazine's female researchers. However, it
was cancelled barely a month after its debut on the streaming service
(Porch 2018). *Mrs. America*'s depiction of the 1970s feminist movement was to some extent shaped by late 2010s conversations around
whose voices get heard in both the feminist movement and television
production. Through brief storytelling moments that recognised
the self-interest of 'white feminism' and the need for intersectional
feminism (Cargle 2018; Hill 2019), *Mrs. America* to some extent
highlighted similar struggles within second-wave feminism and the
wider political climate of the 1970s. It showcased tensions within the
women's movement around differing ideologies and blind spots of
race and sexuality. It also tracked political betrayals and wider shifts
in 1970s culture ahead of the 1980 election of Ronald Reagan (after
whose campaign Trump patterned his own). Here we see how period
drama traces connections between the present and the past, looking
back to and re-presenting the past through contemporary investments,
in a bid to understand how the present came to be.

Mrs. America is part of a strand of period dramas on prestige cable
channel FX that followed on from the success of Russian spy drama

The Americans (FX, 2013–18). These offered new perspectives on late twentieth-century history, rewriting cultural memories. *Pose* (FX, 2018–) explores New York's queer ballroom community, as discussed in Chapter 5. *Fosse/Verdon*'s (FX, 2019) dual biodrama repositions actor and choreographer Gwen Verdon as an essential creative partner to her husband, director and choreographer Bob Fosse, countering the cultural narrative of his singular creative genius. Crime thriller *Snowfall* (FX, 2017–) charts the 1980s drug trade through the impact of the crack epidemic on the Black communities of Los Angeles. This broadening of period drama's perspective on late twentieth-century America shows the impact of incremental diversity gains in the US television industry. In 2016 FX committed to a goal of at least 50 per cent of the writers and directors of its programmes being women or people of colour, which it announced it achieved in 2019, in no small part due to these period dramas (Ryan 2016; Low 2019). As I have highlighted throughout this book, it is the structure of the television industry and period drama's funding models, as much as wider cultural investments, that has shaped whose voices get heard and whose past gets represented.

Across the 2010s the British television industry has been in a protracted reckoning with the long-standing lack of diversity in its ranks and how this impacts whose stories are told (Anonymous 2014; Henry 2017, 2019). As one of the country's most prominent national institutions the BBC has been the focus of much of this discourse. In the second half of 2020 two of its flagship period dramas, *A Suitable Boy* and *Small Axe*, indicated a limited attempt to use its cultural weight as a public service broadcaster to broaden the genre's representations. *A Suitable Boy* adapts Vikram Seth's 1993 novel, a sprawling multi-family narrative in early 1950s post-Independence India, in the run-up to the country's first free elections. Centred on a young woman's coming of age, this was the BBC's first drama with an entirely South Asian cast, looking beyond the Raj revival's exploration of India through the perspectives of white British characters. *A Suitable Boy*'s interlinked middle-class, British-educated families illustrate the continuing impact of centuries of colonial rule on Indian culture. It documents the divisions exacerbated by Partition that continue to shape the country. The adaptation is directed by Indian-born and US-based film director Mira Nair, who has largely worked in US cinema outside of her India-set drama *Monsoon Wedding* (2001). Nair's presence and the South Asian cast were marketed as signalling the drama's 'authenticity', its Indian voice and perspective, yet the drama is adapted by white male writer Andrew Davies.

This continues the UK industry's minimising of risk in prestige drama by repeatedly returning to the same set of white, largely male, writers. Davies is a one-man period drama brand, having adapted the 1995 *Pride and Prejudice* and many other works of classic literature. *A Suitable Boy*'s British press coverage positioned Davies as the interpreter of post-Independence India for a British audience. This discourse also attempted to counter critique by emphasising Vikram Seth's choice of Davies to adapt his novel (Singh 2020; Tomlinson 2020). *A Suitable Boy* presents both a familiar and unfamiliar India for white British audiences, and the promotional foregrounding of Davies's authorship sought to manage the tensions between closeness and distance. Press coverage emphasised his ability to find the 'universal' in this culturally specific story and frequently linked wilful teenage heroine Lata, who resists social conventions in her desire for a love match, to Davies's expertise in Austen adaptation. *A Suitable Boy* shows that despite opening up the stories told, the white British voice still retains a tenacious hold on period drama's representations of India.

The BBC's other late 2020 flagship period drama was the anthology drama *Small Axe* from artist and film director Steve McQueen. Long in development, the project was commissioned in 2014 shortly after McQueen's film *12 Years a Slave* (2013) won Best Picture at the BAFTAs and the Academy Awards. In a British television industry with limited opportunities for Black-created prestige drama, this success gave McQueen the cultural clout to create a period drama that looked beyond the familiar Windrush narrative. A co-production with Amazon Prime Video, *Small Axe* was announced as an 'epic' drama but became an anthology of films co-written with Alastair Siddons and Courttia Newland. These are set in West London's West Indian community and told stories stretching from 1968 to the present, immersing the viewer in Black British family homes and West Indian dialect. Like *Guerrilla*'s (Showtime/Sky Atlantic, 2017) setting within Britain's Black revolutionary movement in the 1970s, *Small Axe* counters the cultural amnesia around political and cultural moments that have shaped Black British lives. Broadcast in the prestige slot of Sunday night at 9 p.m. on BBC One, the individual dramas tell stories of Black life and institutional racism that are both intimate and epic. 'Lovers Rock' unfolds over a single night at a house party and 'Education' explores unofficial school segregation through the experiences of a young Black boy. 'Red, White and Blue' sees a Black man attempt to take on the London police force's racism from the inside. 'Mangrove' follows the trial of the 'Mangrove 9', leaders in the British Black power movement who were charged after clashes at a protest against police harassment and violence in Notting Hill, the targets of an institutional operation that sought to discredit the movement (Bunce and Field 2010).

'Mangrove' and 'Red, White and Blue' were selected for the main competition at the 2020 Cannes film festival (whose line-up was announced despite the festival's cancellation due to the coronavirus pandemic). Following the Cannes announcement, McQueen dedicated the *Small Axe* dramas to 'George Floyd and all the other black people that have been murdered, seen or unseen, because of who they are, in the U.S., U.K. and elsewhere' (Ravindran 2020). McQueen's statement was in response to the Black Lives Matter anti-racism protests that had broken out worldwide across May and June. These had been catalysed by a string of highly publicised deaths of Black Americans at the hands of the police and other white men. These events prompted extensive cultural conversations around racial justice and systemic racism, as well as the impact of historical narratives and representations on understandings of national identity (Campbell 2020). McQueen's statement and his subsequent promotional interviews for *Small Axe* highlighted the connections period drama traces between the past and the present, showing the battles of the 1970s and 1980s are still being fought today. McQueen's interviews and essays also drew attention to how British television had contributed to the cultural amnesia over Black British experience and history that was a key issue for the UK's protestors. *Small Axe* illustrates how period drama reflects the world it is produced in as much as the past it represents, and how the genre has the potential to challenge cultural amnesia and existing narratives of nation. Questions remain whether this will be an isolated challenge or signal a genre shift; whether period drama's economics can allow it to find space to tell untold stories, incorporating the histories of the marginalised into the centre.

Bibliography

Abbiss, Will Stanford (2019), 'Proposing a Post-heritage Critical Framework: The Crown, Ambiguity, and Media Self-consciousness', *Television & New Media* 1 (8): 825–41.

Aftab, Kaleem (2019), 'Gurinder Chadha', *Sight and Sound* (August).

Agnew, Vanessa (2007), 'History's Affective Turn: Historical Reenactment and Its Work in the Present', *Rethinking History* 11 (3): 299–312.

Anonymous (n.d.), 'Making Mrs. Maisel Look Marvelous', *Panavision* (blog), https://uk.panavision.com/making-mrs-maisel-look-marvelous.

Anonymous (2014), 'Letter to BBC and Other Broadcasters: Actors and Writers Call for Action Over Diversity', *The Guardian*, 20 August, www.theguardian.com/media/2014/aug/20/bbc-broadcasters-open-letter-actors-writers-diversity-bame.

Baena, Rosalía and Byker, Christa (2015), 'Dialects of Nostalgia: Downton Abbey and English Identity', *National Identities* 17 (3): 259–69.

Baert, Renee (1994), 'Skirting the Issue', *Screen* 35 (4): 354–73.

Ball, Erica L. and Jackson, Kellie Carter (2017), 'Introduction: Reconsidering Roots', in Erica L. Ball and Kellie Carter Jackson (eds), *Reconsidering Roots: Race, Politics, and Memory*, Athens: University of Georgia Press, pp. 1–21

Ball, Vicky (2013), 'Forgotten Sisters: The British Female Ensemble Drama', *Screen* 54 (2): 244–8.

Banet-Weiser, Sarah (2018), *Empowered: Popular Feminism and Popular Misogyny*, Durham: Duke University Press.

Berghahn, Daniela (2019), '"The Past Is a Foreign Country": Exoticism and Nostalgia in Contemporary Transnational Cinema', *Transnational Screens* 10 (1): 34–52.

Bidisha (2008), 'Hooray for Sarah Waters', *The Guardian*, 27 December, www.theguardian.com/commentisfree/2008/dec/27/sarahwaters-television.

Bildhauer, Bettina (2013), *Filming the Middle Ages*, London: Reaktion Books.

Boone, Lisa (2018), '"The Crown" Production Designer Martin Childs Shares How He Creates those Lavish Sets', *Los Angeles Times*, 5 January, www.latimes.com/home/la-hm-the-crown-qa-20180104-htmlstory.html.

Bourne, Stephen (2002), 'Secrets and Lies: Black Histories and British

Historical Films', in Claire Monk and Amy Sargeant (eds), *British Historical Cinema*, London: Taylor & Francis, pp. 47–65.

Boym, Svetlana (2001), *The Future of Nostalgia*, New York: Basic Books.

Bradley, Regina N. (2016), 'Re-imagining Slavery in the Hip-Hop Imagination', *South: A Scholarly Journal* 49 (1): 3–24.

Brown, Maggie (2015), 'How Downton Abbey Helped to Rescue Highclere Castle from Ruin', *The Guardian*, 19 September, www.theguardian.com/tv-and-radio/2015/sep/19/downton-abbey-highclere-castle-tourist-cash-funds-repairs.

Brunsdon, Charlotte (1990), 'Problems with Quality', *Screen* 31 (1): 67–90.

Brunsdon, Charlotte (2018), *Television Cities: Paris, London, Baltimore*, Durham: Duke University Press.

Bruzzi, Stella (1997), *Undressing Cinema: Clothing and Identity in the Movies*, London: Routledge.

Bunce, Robin and Field, Paul (2010), 'Mangrove Nine: The Court Challenge against Police Racism in Notting Hill', *The Guardian*, 29 November, www.theguardian.com/law/2010/nov/29/mangrove-nine-40th-anniversary.

Burton, James (2017), 'Reframing the 1950s: Race and Representation in Recent British Television', in Sarita Malik and Darrell M. Newton (eds), *Adjusting the Contrast: British Television and Constructs of Race*, Manchester: Manchester University Press, pp. 71–89.

Butt, Richard (2014), 'Melodrama and the Classic Television Serial', in Michael Stewart (ed.), *Melodrama in Contemporary Film and Television*, London: Palgrave Macmillan, pp. 27–41.

Byrne, Katherine (2014), 'Adapting Heritage: Class and Conservatism in Downton Abbey', *Rethinking History* 18 (3): 311–27.

Byrne, Katherine (2015), *Edwardians on Screen: From Downton Abbey to Parade's End*, Basingstoke: Palgrave Macmillan.

Byrne, Katherine, Leggott, James and Taddeo, Julie Anne (eds) (2018), 'Introduction', in Katherine Byrne, Julie Anne Taddeo and James Leggott (eds), *Conflicting Masculinities: Men in Television Period Drama*, London: I.B. Tauris, pp. 1–13.

Byrne, Katherine and Taddeo, Julie Anne (2019), 'Calling #TimesUp on the TV Period Drama Rape Narrative', *Critical Studies in Television* 14 (3): 379–98.

Campbell, Lucy (2020), '"I Was Shielded from My History": The Changes Young Black Britons Are Calling for', *The Guardian*, 30 July, www.theguardian.com/uk-news/2020/jul/30/history-young-black-britons-race-schools-policing.

Cannadine, David (1997), *The Pleasures of the Past* (new edn), London: Penguin.

Cardwell, Sarah (2002), *Adaptation Revisited: Television and the Classic Novel*, Manchester: Manchester University Press.

Cardwell, Sarah (2006), 'Working the Land: Representations of Rural England in Adaptations of Thomas Hardy's Novels', in Catherine Fowler (ed.), *Representing the Rural: Space, Place, and Identity in Films about the Land*, Detroit: Wayne State University Press, pp. 19–34.

Cargle, Rachel Elizabeth (2018), 'When Feminism Is White Supremacy in Heels', *Harper's Bazaar*, 16 August, www.harpersbazaar.com/culture/poli tics/a22717725/what-is-toxic-white-feminism/.

Carroll, Rachel (2019), 'Black Victorians, British Television Drama, and the 1978 Adaptation of David Garnett's The Sailor's Return', *The Journal of Commonwealth Literature* 54 (2): 207–24.

Cartmell, Deborah (2010), *Screen Adaptations: Jane Austen's Pride and Prejudice: A Close Study of the Relationship Between Text and Film*, London: Methuen Drama.

Caughie, John (2000), *Television Drama: Realism, Modernism, and British Culture*, Oxford: Oxford University Press.

Césaire, Aimé (2000), *Discourse on Colonialism*, New York: Monthly Review Press.

Channel 4 (2014), 'The Webisodes for The Mill, Series 2', Channel4.com, 2 July, www.channel4.com/press/news/webisodes-mill-series-2.

Cheslaw, Louis (2019), 'How HBO's "The Deuce" Recreated 1980s Times Square for Its Series Finale', *Condé Nast Traveler* (blog), 25 October, www.cntraveler.com/story/on-location-how-hbos-the-deuce-recreated-1980s-times-square.

Cheverall, Clare (2018), '"The Flutter of Pleasure": Jane Austen Adaptations & Sexual Desire', *MAI: Feminism & Visual Culture* 2 (September), https://maifeminism.com/the-flutter-of-pleasure-jane-austen-adaptations-sex ual-desire/.

Clark, Anna (1996), 'Anne Lister's Construction of Lesbian Identity', *Journal of the History of Sexuality* 7 (1): 23–50.

Cockin, Katherine (2004), 'Inventing the Suffragettes: Anachronism, Gnosticism and Corporeality in Contemporary Fiction', *Critical Survey* 16 (3): 17–32.

Connolly, Kate (2017), 'Babylon Berlin: Lavish German Crime Drama Tipped to Be Global Hit', *The Guardian*, 29 October, www.theguardian. com/world/2017/oct/29/babylon-berlin-lavish-german-tv-drama-tipped-glo bal-hit.

Cook, Pam (1996), *Fashioning the Nation: Costume and Identity in British Cinema*, London: BFI Publishing.

Cooke, Lez (2003), *British Television Drama: A History*, London: BFI Publishing.

Cooke, Rachel (2019), 'ITV's Beecham House Is Desperately Clichéd Period Drama', *The New Stateman*, 26 June, www.newstatesman.com/beecham-house-itv-review.

Corkin, Stanley (2011), *Starring New York: Filming the Grime and the Glamour of the Long 1970s*, New York: Oxford University Press.

Cox, Karen L. (2011), *Dreaming of Dixie: How the South Was Created in American Popular Culture*, Chapel Hill: University of North Carolina Press.

Craig, Cairns (2001), 'Rooms without a View', in Ginette Vincendeau (ed.), *Film/Literature/Heritage: A Sight and Sound Reader*, London: BFI Publishing, pp. 3–6.

Dams, Tim (2013), 'Behind the Scenes: C4's The Mill', *Televisual* (blog), 24 July, www.televisual.com/blog-detail/Behind-the-scenes-C4s-The-Mill-_bid-473.html.

Dams, Tim (2016), 'Producers Get Writer's Block', *Televisual* (blog), 15 December, www.televisual.com/blog-detail/Producers-get-writers-block_bid-946.html.

De Groot, Jerome (2009), *Consuming History: Historians and Heritage in Contemporary Popular Culture*, London: Routledge.

De Groot, Jerome (2016), *Remaking History: The Past in Contemporary Historical Fictions*, London: Routledge.

Del Barco, Mandalit (2016), '"Good Girls Revolt" Takes on Gender Bias in the Newsroom', *NPR* (blog), 27 October, www.npr.org/2016/10/27/499469569/good-girls-revolt-takes-on-gender-bias-in-the-newsroom.

Dempster, Sarah (2013), 'The Mill, Where Misery Is Relentless', *The Guardian*, 27 July, www.theguardian.com/tv-and-radio/2013/jul/27/the-mill-relentless-misery.

Dent, Grace (2013), 'Grace Dent on TV: The Mill, Channel 4', *The Independent*, 2 August, www.independent.co.uk/arts-entertainment/tv/features/grace-dent-on-tv-the-mill-channel-4-8742342.html.

Dirlik, Arif (1996), 'Chinese History and the Question of Orientalism', *History and Theory* 35 (4): 96–118.

Dowell, Ben (2017), 'The Crown Netflix: Series Would Not Have Worked on BBC Says Producer', *Radio Times*, 14 September, www.radiotimes.com/news/tv/2017-09-14/bbc-would-have-struggled-to-make-the-crown/.

Dubek, Laura (2018), '"Fight for It!": The Twenty-First-Century Underground Railroad', *The Journal of American Culture* 41 (1): 68–80.

Dyer, Richard (1994), 'Feeling English', *Sight and Sound* (March).

Dyer, Richard (1996), '"There's Nothing I Can Do! Nothing!": Femininity, Seriality and Whiteness in The Jewel in the Crown', *Screen* 37 (3): 225–39.

Dyer, Richard (2001), 'Nice Young Men Who Sell Antiques: Gay Men in Heritage Cinema', in Ginette Vincendeau (ed.), *Film/Literature/Heritage: A Sight and Sound Reader*, London: BFI Publishing, pp. 43–8.

Dyer, Richard (2002), *Only Entertainment* (2nd edn), London: Routledge.

Dyer, Richard (2007), *Pastiche*, London: Routledge.

Dyson, Michael Eric (2016), 'What Donald Trump Doesn't Know about Black People', *The New York Times*, 17 December, www.nytimes.com/2016/12/17/opinion/sunday/what-donald-trump-doesnt-know-about-black-people.html.

Emmens, Heather (2009), 'Taming the Velvet: Lesbian Identity in Cultural Adaptations of Tipping the Velvet', in Rachel Carroll (ed.), *Adaptation in Contemporary Culture: Textual Infidelities*, London: Continuum, pp. 134–46.

Faludi, Susan (1992), *Backlash: The Undeclared War against Women*, London: Vintage.

Fanning, Sarah E. (2018), 'A Post-feminist Hero: Sandy Welch's North and South', in Katherine Byrne, Julie Anne Taddeo and James Leggott (eds), *Conflicting Masculinities: Men in Television Period Drama*, London: I.B. Tauris, pp. 91–110.

Fitzgerald, Louise (2015), 'Taking a Pregnant Pause: Interrogating the Feminist Potential of Call the Midwife', in James Leggott and Julie Anne Taddeo (eds), *Upstairs and Downstairs: British Costume Drama Television from The Forsyte Saga to Downton Abbey*, Lanham, MD: Rowman & Littlefield, pp. 249–63.

Fitzgerald, Tom and Marquez, Lorenzo (2010), 'Mad Style: S4E1 Public Relations', *Tom + Lorenzo* (blog), 28 July, https://tomandlorenzo.com/2010/07/mad-style-public-relations-2/.

Forrest, David (2011), 'Our Friends in the North and the Instability of the Historical Drama as Archive', *Journal of British Cinema and Television* 8 (2): 218–33.

Geraghty, Christine (2008), *Now a Major Motion Picture: Film Adaptations of Literature and Drama*, Lanham, MD: Rowman & Littlefield.

Giddings, Robert and Selby, Keith (2000), *The Classic Serial on Television and Radio*, Basingstoke: Palgrave Macmillan.

Gilligan, Sarah (2011), 'Heaving Cleavages and Fantastic Frock Coats: Gender Fluidity, Celebrity and Tactile Transmediality in Contemporary Costume Cinema', *Film, Fashion & Consumption* 1 (1): 7–38.

Gilroy, Paul (2004), *After Empire: Melancholia or Convivial Culture?*, London: Routledge.

Glynn, Basil (2012), 'The Conquests of Henry VIII: Masculinity, Sex and the National Past in The Tudors', in Beth Johnson, James Aston and Basil Glynn (eds), *Television, Sex and Society: Analyzing Contemporary Representations*, London: Continuum, pp. 157–73.

Goldberg, Lesley (2019), 'Starz Chief Explains the Cabler's "Premium Female" Push', *The Hollywood Reporter*, 26 July, www.hollywoodreporter.com/live-feed/starz-chief-explains-cablers-premium-female-push-1227421.

Goodman, Gemma and Moseley, Rachel (2018), 'Television Costume Drama and the Eroticised, Regionalised Body: Poldark and Outlander', in Katherine Byrne, Julie Anne Taddeo and James Leggott (eds), *Conflicting Masculinities: Men in Television Period Drama*, London: I.B. Tauris, pp. 52–70.

Gordon, David (2019), 'How Marguerite Derricks Makes The Marvelous Mrs. Maisel Dance', *Theater Mania* (blog), 2 June, www.theatermania.com/new-york-city-theater/news/interview-marguerite-derricks-marvelous-mrs-maisel_88902.html.

Grant, Melissa Gira (2018), 'Working the Deuce', *Dissent* 65 (1): 15–18.

Gray, Herman (2005), 'The Politics of Representation in Network Television', in Darnell M. Hunt (ed.), *Channeling Blackness: Studies on Television and Race in America*, Oxford: Oxford University Press, pp. 155–74.

Greer, Evan (2018), 'Powerful Gay Rights Groups Excluded Trans People for Decades – Leaving Them Vulnerable to Trump's Attack', *Washington Post*, 29 October, www.washingtonpost.com/outlook/2018/10/29/trumps-attack-trans-people-should-be-wake-up-call-mainstream-gay-rights-movement/.

Greig, Hannah (2018), '"The New Downton Abbey"? Poldark and the Presentation and Perception of an Eighteenth-Century Past', *Journal of British Cinema and Television* 16 (1): 94–113.

Hall, Stuart (1989), 'Cultural Identity and Cinematic Representation', *Framework: The Journal of Cinema and Media* 36: 68–81.

Hall, Stuart (2005), 'Whose Heritage? Un-settling "the Heritage", Re-imagining the Post-nation', in Jo Littler and Roshi Naidoo (eds), *The Politics of Heritage: The Legacies of 'Race'*, London: Routledge, pp. 21–31.

Hamad, Hannah (2016), 'Contemporary Medical Television and Crisis in the NHS', *Critical Studies in Television* 11 (2): 136–50.

Hanna, Emma (2009), *The Great War on the Small Screen: Representing the First World War in Contemporary Britain*, Edinburgh: Edinburgh University Press.

Harper, Bex (2014), 'British Heritage Television: Reconstructing Queer Desire in Daphne (2007) and The Secret Diaries of Miss Anne Lister (2010)', in Elizabeth Sarah Lewis, Rodrigo Borba, Branca Falabella Fabrico and Diana de Souza Pinto (eds), *Queering Paradigms IV: South–North Dialogues on Queer Epistemologies, Embodiments and Activisms*, Oxford: Peter Lang, pp. 117–37.

Helsinger, Elizabeth K. (2014), *Rural Scenes and National Representation: Britain, 1815–1850*, Princeton, NJ: Princeton University Press.

Hennessee, David (2017), 'Queer Nostalgia in Mad Men', *Queer Studies in Media & Popular Culture* 2 (2): 213–26.

Henry, Lenny (2017), 'Ofcom, Please Listen. Racial Diversity in TV Means Seeing the Bigger Picture', *The Guardian*, 1 August, www.theguardian.com/commentisfree/2017/aug/01/ofcom-racial-diversity-tv-bbc-targets-lenny-henry.

Henry, Lenny (2019), 'Sir Lenny Henry Delivers His Speech at the RTS Cambridge Convention 2019', *Royal Television Society*, 23 September, https://rts.org.uk/article/sir-lenny-henry-delivers-his-speech-rts-cam-bridge-convention-2019.

Hernandez, Arlyn (2018), 'The Marvelous Mrs. Maisel's Set Designer Shares the Secrets to Creating that Magical World', *Apartment Therapy* (blog), 8 January, www.apartmenttherapy.com/marvelous-mrs-maisel-golden-globe-set-design-254069.

Herzog, Kenny (2016), '"Underground": How a Slave-Revolt Series Made It to Primetime TV', *Rolling Stone* (blog), 7 March, www.rollingstone.com/tv/tv-news/underground-how-a-slave-revolt-series-made-it-to-primetime-tv-237147/.

Hesse, Barnor (2002), 'Forgotten Like a Bad Dream: Atlantic Slavery and the

Ethics of Postcolonial Memory', in David Theo Goldberg and Ato Quayson (eds), *Relocating Postcolonialism*, Oxford: Blackwell, pp. 143–73.

Higson, Andrew (2003), *English Heritage, English Cinema: Costume Drama since 1980*, Oxford: Oxford University Press.

Higson, Andrew (2006 [1993]), 'Re-presenting the National Past: Nostalgia and Pastiche in the Heritage Film', in Lester D. Friedman (ed.), *Fires Were Started: British Cinema and Thatcherism* (2nd edn), London: Wallflower Press, pp. 91–109.

Higson, Andrew (2010), *Film England: Culturally English Filmmaking Since the 1990s*, London: I.B. Tauris.

Hill, Libby (2019), 'With Their White Feminist Bias, TV's Prestige Dramas Continue to Fail', *IndieWire*, 11 July, www.indiewire.com/2019/07/white-feminist-bias-handmaids-tale-big-little-lies-game-of-thrones-1202157104/.

Hilmes, Michele (2019), 'Mainstream Trends and Masterpiece Traditions: ITV's Downton Abbey as a Hit Heritage Drama for Masterpiece in the United States', in Matt Hills, Michele Hilmes and Roberta Pearson (eds), *Transatlantic Television Drama: Industries, Programs, and Fans*, Oxford: Oxford University Press, pp. 131–46.

Hipsky, Martin A. (1994), 'Anglophil(m)ia: Why Does America Watch Merchant-Ivory Movies?', *Journal of Popular Film and Television* 22 (3): 98–107.

Hogan, Heather (2019), 'Gentleman Jack's Finale Was One of the Finest Hours in Lesbian Cinematic History', *Autostraddle* (blog), 14 June, www.autostraddle.com/gentleman-jacks-finale-was-one-of-the-finest-hours-in-les bian-cinematic-history/.

Holbrook, Carolyn (2016), 'Anzac on TV', in Michelle Arrow, Jeannine Baker and Clare Monagle (eds), *Small Screens: Essays on Contemporary Australian Television*, Clayton, VIC: Monash University Publishing, pp. 48–64.

Holmwood, Leigh (2009), 'The Death of the Bonnet: BBC to Overhaul Costume Dramas', *The Guardian*, 9 January, www.theguardian.com/media/2009/jan/09/television.

hooks, bell (1992), *Black Looks: Race and Representation*, London: Turnaround.

Hopkins, Lisa (2001), 'Mr. Darcy's Body: Privileging the Female Gaze', in Linda Troost and Sayre N. Greenfield (eds), *Jane Austen in Hollywood* (2nd edn), Lexington: University Press of Kentucky, pp. 111–21.

Hoskins, Colin and Mirus, Rolf (1988), 'Reasons for the US Dominance of the International Trade in Television Programmes', *Media, Culture & Society* 10 (4): 499–515.

Ivie, Devon (2017), 'How The Crown Re-created Buckingham Palace without Actually Filming There', *Vulture* (blog), 21 December, www.vulture.com/2017/12/how-the-crown-recreated-buckingham-palace.html.

Jameson, Fredric (1991), *Postmodernism, or The Cultural Logic of Late Capitalism*, Durham: Duke University Press.

Jeffries, Stuart (2015), 'The Best Exotic Nostalgia Boom: Why Colonial Style

Is Back', *The Guardian*, 19 March, www.theguardian.com/culture/2015/mar/19/the-best-exotic-nostalgia-boom-why-colonial-style-is-back.

Jeffries, Stuart (2017), 'Secrets, Lies and the New Cold War: How the Americans Became Truly Topical TV', *The Guardian*, 30 May, www.theguardian.com/tv-and-radio/2017/may/30/secrets-lies-new-cold-war-how-the-americans-became-topical.

Jennings, Ros (2017), 'Ageing across Space and Time: Exploring Concepts of Ageing and Identity in the Female Ensemble Dramas Tenko and Call the Midwife', *Journal of British Cinema and Television* 14 (2): 179–95.

Johnson, Beth and Forrest, David (eds) (2017), 'Introduction', in Beth Johnson and David Forrest (eds), *Social Class and Television Drama in Contemporary Britain*, London: Palgrave Macmillan, pp. 1–12.

Johnston, Claire (1974), 'Film Culture', *Screen* 15 (4): 82–5.

Joyce, Simon (2019), 'The Perverse Presentism of Rainbow Plaques: Memorializing Anne Lister', *Nineteenth-Century Contexts* 41 (5): 601–10.

Katz, Tamar (2010), 'City Memory, City History: Urban Nostalgia, The Colossus of New York, and Late-Twentieth-Century Historical Fiction', *Contemporary Literature* 51 (4): 810–51.

Kies, Bridget and West III, Thomas J. (2017), 'Queer Nostalgia and Queer Histories in Uncertain Times', *Queer Studies in Media & Popular Culture* 2 (2): 161–5.

Kilkenny, Katie (2018), '"Howards End": How a 1910 Novel Became a Progressive Miniseries', *The Hollywood Reporter*, 15 April, www.hollywoodreporter.com/live-feed/howards-end-how-a-1910-novel-became-a-progressive-miniseries-1102801.

Kim, Jeongmee (ed.) (2014), *Reading Asian Television Drama: Crossing Borders and Breaking Boundaries*, London: I.B. Tauris.

Kleinecke-Bates, Iris (2014), *Victorians on Screen: The Nineteenth Century on British Television, 1994–2005*, London: Palgrave Macmillan.

Knox, Simone (2012), 'Masterpiece Theatre and British Drama Imports on US Television: Discourses of Tension', *Critical Studies in Television* 7 (1): 29–48.

Kumari Upadhyaya, Kayla (2019), 'Pose's Second Season Finale Serves Romance, Drama, and Spectacle', *TV Club* (blog), 20 August, https://tv.avclub.com/poses-second-season-finale-serves-romance-drama-and-s-1837422469.

Lagerway, Jorie (2017), 'The Feminist Game of Thrones: Outlander and Gendered Discourses of TV Genre', in Mary Harrod and Katarzyna Paszkiewicz (eds), *Women Do Genre in Film and Television*, London: Routledge, pp. 198–212.

Lambert, Raphaël (2017), 'The Conservative Dispositions of Roots', *Transition* 122: 98–112.

Landsberg, Alison (2015), *Engaging the Past: Mass Culture and the Production of Historical Knowledge*, New York: Columbia University Press.

Lawrence, Ben (2013), 'The Village: Episode Six', *The Telegraph*, 5 May, www.telegraph.co.uk/culture/tvandradio/10036702/The-Village-episode-six-BBC-One-review.html.

Laymon, Kiese (2019), *Heavy: An American Memoir*, London: Bloomsbury Publishing.

Leggott, James (2016), 'The Catherine Cookson Television Adaptation Cycle: Production, Reception, and Heritage', in Julie Anne Taddeo (ed.), *Catherine Cookson Country: On the Borders of Legitimacy, Fiction, and History*, Abingdon: Routledge, pp. 175–90.

LeMahieu, D. L. (1990), 'Imagined Contemporaries: Cinematic and Televised Dramas about the Edwardians in Great Britain and the United States, 1967–1985', *Historical Journal of Film, Radio and Television* 10 (3): 243–56.

Levine, Elana (2015), 'Introduction: Feminized Popular Culture in the Early Twenty-First Century', in Elana Levine (ed.), *Cupcakes, Pinterest, and Ladyporn: Feminized Popular Culture in the Early Twenty-First Century*, Urbana: University of Illinois Press, pp. 1–12.

Light, Alison (1991), 'Englishness', *Sight and Sound* (March).

Lindner, Katharina (2017), *Film Bodies: Queer Feminist Encounters with Gender and Sexuality in Cinema*, London: I.B. Tauris.

Littler, Jo (2005), 'Introduction: British Heritage and the Legacies of "Race"', in Jo Littler and Roshi Naidoo (eds), *The Politics of Heritage*, London: Routledge, pp. 1–17.

Littleton, Cynthia and Low, Elaine (2019), 'Adapt or Die: Why 2020 Will Be All about Entertainment's New Streaming Battleground', *Variety*, 17 December, https://variety.com/2019/biz/features/streaming-2020-dis ney-plus-netflix-hbo-max-apple-tv-amazon-1203439700/.

Long, Paul (2017), 'Class, Place and History in the Imaginative Landscapes of Peaky Blinders', in Beth Johnson and David Forrest (eds), *Social Class and Television Drama in Contemporary Britain*, London: Palgrave Macmillan, pp. 165–80.

Loughrey, Clarisse (2016), 'Ken Loach Criticises British TV's Reliance on "Fake Nostalgia" of Period Drama', *Independent*, 18 October, www.inde pendent.co.uk/arts-entertainment/tv/news/ken-loach-i-daniel-blake-bbc-nos talgia-downton-abbey-period-drama-a7367211.html.

Low, Elaine (2019), 'John Landgraf: Nearly 60% of FX's Writing Staff Are Now Not White Men', *Variety*, 26 October, https://variety.com/2019/tv/news/john-landgraf-usc-gould-entertainment-law-1203384643/.

Luckett, Moya (2017), 'Women's History, Women's Work: Popular Television as Feminine Historiography', in Rachel Moseley, Helen Wheatley and Helen Wood (eds), *Television for Women: New Directions*, Abingdon: Routledge, pp. 15–33.

Lyndon, Neil (1975), 'Years of Promise', *Radio Times*, 6 September.

McArthur, Colin (1980), *Television and History*, London: BFI Publishing.

MacCabe, Colin (1974), 'Realism and the Cinema: Notes on Some Brechtian Theses', *Screen* 15 (2): 7–27.

McCabe, Janet (2014), 'Shoulder to Shoulder: Female Suffrage, Second-Wave Feminism and Feminist TV Drama in the 1970s', *Women's Film and Television History Network-UK/Ireland* (blog), 17 June, https://womensfilmandtel evisionhistory.wordpress.com/2014/06/17/shoulder-to-shoulder-female-suf frage-second-wave-feminism-and-feminist-tv-drama-in-the-1970s-2/.

McCabe, Janet and Ball, Vicky (2014), 'The Nearly Forgotten 40 Year-Old BBC Mini-Series, "Shoulder to Shoulder" Reminds Us Why the Struggle for Gender Equality Still Matters', *British Politics and Policy at LSE* (blog), 4 June, https://blogs.lse.ac.uk/politicsandpolicy/why-remember-shoulder-to-shoulder/.

McDonald, Soraya Nadia (2019), 'With Billy Porter at Its Center, "Pose" Provides a Vital Reframing of Queer History', *The Undefeated* (blog), 23 August, https://theundefeated.com/features/with-billy-porter-at-its-center-pose-provides-a-vital-reframing-of-queer-history/.

McFarland, Melanie (2018), 'The Uplifting Realness of "Pose": Ryan Murphy's Revolutionary Drag Ball Drama Delivers', *Salon* (blog), 1 June, www.salon.com/2018/06/01/the-uplifting-realness-of-pose-ryan-murphys-revolutionary-drag-ball-drama-delivers/.

McHenry, Jackson (2019), 'The Story Behind Dickinson, a Sexy, Queer, Gothic, Millennial Apple TV+ Sitcom', *Vulture* (blog), 28 October, www.vulture.com/2019/10/emily-dickinson-apple-tv.html.

Mackenzie, Midge (1988), *Shoulder to Shoulder*, New York: Vintage.

Maciak, Phillip (2017), 'Perfect Manhattan', *Los Angeles Review of Books* (blog), 18 December, https://lareviewofbooks.org/article/marvelous-mrs-maisel-season-one/.

Mahoney, Cat (2015), '"Not Bad for a Few Ordinary Girls in a Tin Hut" – Re-imagining Women's Social Experience of the Second World War through Female Ensemble Drama', *Frames Cinema Journal* 7 (June), https://framescinemajournal.com/article/not-bad-for-a-few-ordinary-girls-in-a-tin-hut-re-imagining-womens-social-experience-of-the-second-world-war-thro ugh-female-ensemble-drama/.

Malik, Sarita (2001), *Representing Black Britain: Black and Asian Images on Television*, London: SAGE.

Martin, Alfred L. (2018a), 'Notes from Underground: WGN's Black-Cast Quality TV Experiment', *Los Angeles Review of Books*, 31 May, https://lareviewofbooks.org/article/notes-from-underground-wgns-black-cast-qual ity-tv-experiment/.

Martin, Alfred L. (2018b), 'Pose(r): Ryan Murphy, Trans and Queer of Color Labor, and the Politics of Representation', *Los Angeles Review of Books* (blog), 2 August, https://lareviewofbooks.org/article/poser-ryan-murphy-trans-queer-color-labor-politics-representation/.

Martin, Brett (2013), *Difficult Men: From The Sopranos and The Wire to Mad Men and Breaking Bad*, London: Faber & Faber.

Martin, Kevin H. (2018), 'Cinematographers M. David Mullen, ASC, and Eric Moynier on The Marvelous Mrs. Maisel's Retro NYC', *Studio Daily* (blog),

17 January, www.studiodaily.com/2018/01/cinematographers-m-david-mullen-asc-eric-moynier-marvelous-mrs-maisels-retro-nyc/.

Matthews-Jones, Lucinda (2013), 'Will the Real Esther Price Please Stand Up? Archival Fiction & The Mill', *Journal of Victorian Culture Online* (blog), 6 August, http://jvc.oup.com/2013/08/06/will-the-real-esther-price-please-stand-up/.

Mead, Matthew (2009), 'Empire Windrush: The Cultural Memory of an Imaginary Arrival', *Journal of Postcolonial Writing* 45 (2): 137–49.

Mendes, Ana Cristina (2017), 'Neo-Victorian Slumming on Screen', *Continuum* 31 (6): 912–22.

Mittell, Jason (2004), *Genre and Television: From Cop Shows to Cartoons in American Culture*, New York: Routledge.

Mohamed, Iman (2017), 'The Problem with Guerrilla and Its Erasure of Black Women', *Gal-Dem* (blog), 13 April, http://gal-dem.com/the-problem-with-guerrilla-and-its-erasure-of-black-women/.

Monk, Claire (1995), 'The British "Heritage Film" and Its Critics', *Critical Survey* 7 (2): 116–24.

Monk, Claire (2001), 'Sexuality and Heritage', in Ginette Vincendeau (ed.), *Film/Literature/Heritage: A Sight and Sound Reader*, London: BFI Publishing, pp. 6–10.

Monk, Claire (2002), 'The British Heritage-Film Debate Revisited', in Claire Monk and Amy Sargeant (eds), *British Historical Cinema: The History, Heritage and Costume Film*, Abingdon: Routledge, pp. 176–98.

Monk, Claire (2012), *Heritage Film Audiences*, Edinburgh: Edinburgh University Press.

Monk, Claire (2015), 'Approaches to the Costume Drama. Pageantry and Populism, Democratization and Dissent: The Forgotten 1970s', in James Leggott and Julie Anne Taddeo (eds), *Upstairs and Downstairs: British Costume Drama Television from the Forsyte Saga to Downton Abbey*, Lanham, MD: Rowman & Littlefield, pp. 27–44.

Moseley, Rachel (2013), '"It's a Wild Country. Wild ... Passionate ... Strange": Poldark and the Place-Image of Cornwall', *Visual Culture in Britain* 14 (2): 218–37.

Moseley, Rachel, Wheatley, Helen and Wood, Helen (2017), 'Introduction', in Rachel Moseley, Helen Wheatley and Helen Wood (eds), *Television for Women: New Directions*, Abingdon: Routledge, pp. 1–12.

Munden, Marc (2011), 'The Crimson Petal and the White: Subverting Expectations', *BBC TV Blog* (blog), 4 April, www.bbc.co.uk/blogs/tv/2011/04/the-crimson-petal-and-the-whit.shtml.

Murfitt, Nikki (2016), 'Primetime Porn BBC Calls "a Delicious Treat"', *Mail Online*, 12 March, www.dailymail.co.uk/tvshowbiz/article-3489581/Primetime-porn-BBC-calls-delicious-treat-shocking-images-21m-French-series-graphic-sex-scenes-British-TV.html.

Naidoo, Roshi and Littler, Jo (2003), 'White Past, Multicultural Present: Heritage and National Stories', in Helen Brocklehurst and Robert Phillips (eds), *History, Nationhood and the Question of Britain*, Basingstoke: Palgrave Macmillan, pp. 330–41.

Newman, Michael Z. and Levine, Elana (2011), *Legitimating Television: Media Convergence and Cultural Status*, London: Routledge.

Noor, Poppy (2019), 'Gurinder Chadha: Beecham House Is a "Flipping Radical Thing"', *The Guardian*, 18 June, www.theguardian.com/film/2019/jun/18/gurinder-chadha-beecham-house-is-a-flipping-radical-thing.

Nussbaum, Emily (2016), '"Call the Midwife," a Primal Procedural', 13 June, www.newyorker.com/magazine/2016/06/20/call-the-midwife-a-primal-procedural.

O'Connor, Joanne (2015), 'On Location: "Indian Summers"', *Financial Times*, 20 February, www.ft.com/content/eef56122-b5d3-11e4-a577-00144feab7de.

O'Falt, Chris (2017), 'Why Netflix Spent Millions so "The Crown" Could Shoot in Very, Very Big Rooms', *IndieWire* (blog), 16 August, www.indiewire.com/2017/08/netflix-the-crown-production-design-emmy-stephen-daldry-martin-childs-1201867229/.

Ofcom (2019a), *Media Nations 2019*, Ofcom, 7 August, https://www.ofcom.org.uk/research-and-data/tv-radio-and-on-demand/media-nations-reports/media-nations-2019.

Ofcom (2019b), 'Breaking the Class Ceiling – Social Make-Up of the TV Industry Revealed', Ofcom, 18 September, www.ofcom.org.uk/about-ofcom/latest/media/media-releases/2019/breaking-the-class-ceiling-tv-industry-social-makeup-revealed.

Oliete-Aldea, E. (2015), *Hybrid Heritage on Screen: The 'Raj Revival' in the Thatcher Era*, Basingstoke: Palgrave Macmillan.

Oltermann, Philip (2016), 'Deutschland 83 Has Wowed the World – Pity the Germans Don't Like It', *The Guardian*, 17 February, www.theguardian.com/commentisfree/2016/feb/17/deutschland-83-wowed-world-germans-dont-like-it.

Olusoga, David (2016), *Black and British*, London: Macmillan.

Padva, Gilad (2014), *Queer Nostalgia in Cinema and Pop Culture*, Basingstoke: Palgrave Macmillan.

Pensis, Eva (2019), '"Running Up that Hill": On Love, Sex, and Work in Pose', *Journal of Popular Music Studies* 31 (2): 15–24.

Perlman, Allison (2011), 'The Strange Career of Mad Men: Race, Paratexts, and Civil Rights Memory', in Gary R. Edgerton (ed.), *Mad Men: Dream Come True TV*, London: I.B. Tauris, pp. 209–25.

Petrie, Duncan J. (2000), *Screening Scotland*, London: BFI Publishing.

Pidduck, Julianne (2004), *Contemporary Costume Film: Space, Place and the Past*, London: BFI Publishing.

Pierson, Eric (2012), 'Producing Blackness. The Importance of Roots', in Beretta E. Smith-Shomade (ed.), *Watching While Black: Centering the Television of Black Audiences*, New Brunswick, NJ: Rutgers University Press, pp. 19–32.

Porch, Scott (2018), '"Good Girls Revolt" Was a Huge Failure for Amazon, but Not for the Reasons You Think', *Decider*, 19 March, https://decider.com/2018/03/19/why-amazon-cancelled-good-girls-revolt/.

Pribram, E. Deidre (2018), 'Felt History: Emotions, Gender, and Genre in The Bletchley Circle', *Gender & History* 30 (3): 755–68.

Primorac, Antonija (2018), *Neo-Victorianism on Screen: Postfeminism and Contemporary Adaptations of Victorian Women*, Cham: Palgrave Macmillan.

Rampton, James (1999), 'Television: A Class Act – Lucy Gannon', *The Independent*, 18 June, https://www.independent.co.uk/arts-entertainment/television-a-class-act-lucy-gannon-1101130.html.

Ravindran, Manori (2020), '"12 Years a Slave" Director Steve McQueen Dedicates Cannes-Selected Films to George Floyd', *Variety*, 3 June, https://variety.com/2020/film/global/12-years-a-slave-director-steve-mcqueen-dedicates-cannes-selected-films-to-george-floyd-1234624465/.

Regis, Amber K. (2012), 'Performance Anxiety and Costume Drama: Lesbian Sex on the BBC', in Beth Johnson, James Aston and Basil Glynn (eds), *Television, Sex and Society: Analyzing Contemporary Representations*, London: Continuum, pp. 143–56.

Robertson Wojcik, Pamela (2010), *The Apartment Plot: Urban Living in American Film and Popular Culture, 1945 to 1975*, Durham: Duke University Press.

Rolinson, David (2011), 'Small Screens and Big Voices: Televisual Social Realism and the Popular', in David Tucker (ed.), *British Social Realism in the Arts since 1940*, London: Palgrave Macmillan, pp. 172–211.

Rolinson, David (2017a), 'Call the Midwife Notes #1: Why Sunday Nights?', *British Television Drama* (blog), 31 January, www.britishtelevisiondrama.org.uk/?p=6553.

Rolinson, David (2017b), 'Call the Midwife Notes #2: Style and Meaning; or, Trixie's Fingernails', *British Television Drama* (blog), 28 February, www.britishtelevisiondrama.org.uk/?p=6871.

Rorke, Robert (2018), 'How "Marvellous Mrs. Maisel" Brought NYC Back to the 1950s', *New York Post*, 1 December, https://nypost.com/2018/12/01/how-marvelous-mrs-maisel-brought-nyc-back-to-the-1950s/.

Roxborough, Scott (2015), '"Deutschland 83" Debuts to So-So Ratings in Germany', *The Hollywood Reporter*, 27 November, www.hollywoodreporter.com/news/deutschland-83-debuts-ratings-germany-844053.

Roxborough, Scott (2018), 'How the "Babylon Berlin" Team Broke the Rules to Make the World's Biggest Foreign-Language Series', *The Hollywood Reporter*, 26 December, www.hollywoodreporter.com/news/how-babylon-berlin-team-broke-all-rules-make-worlds-biggest-foreign-language-series-1171013.

Rushdie, Salman (1992), *Imaginary Homelands: Essays and Criticism 1981–1991*, London: Granta.

Rushdy, Ashraf H. A. (1999), *Neo-Slave Narratives: Studies in the Social Logic of a Literary Form*, London: Oxford University Press.

Russell, Emma (2017), 'The Deuce's Set Designer on Her "Really Scrappy" Recreation of '70s NYC', *Bedford + Bowery* (blog), 30 October, https://bedfordandbowery.com/2017/10/the-deuces-set-designer-on-her-really-scrappy-recreation-of-70s-nyc/.

Ryan, Maureen (2016), 'FX Diversity: Hiring Directors of Color – CEO John Landgraf Interview', *Variety*, 9 August, https://variety.com/2016/tv/features/fx-diversity-directors-hiring-ceo-john-landgraf-interview-1201831409/.

Ryan, Maureen E. and Keller, Jessalynn (eds) (2018), *Emergent Feminisms*, New York: Routledge.

Ryan, Maureen and Littleton, Cynthia (2017), 'TV Series Budgets Hit the Breaking Point as Costs Skyrocket in Peak TV Era', *Variety*, 26 September, https://variety.com/2017/tv/news/tv-series-budgets-costs-rising-peak-tv-1202570158/.

St Felix, Doreen (2020), 'Reviving Phyllis Schlafly in "Mrs. America"', *The New Yorker*, 20 April, www.newyorker.com/magazine/2020/04/27/reviving-phyllis-schlafly-in-mrs-america.

Sali, Loredana (2014), 'Remediating Gaskell: North and South and Its BBC Adaptation, 2004', in Loredana Salis (ed.), *Adapting Gaskell: Screen and Stage Versions of Elizabeth Gaskell's Fiction*, Newcastle: Cambridge Scholars Publishing, pp. 123–48.

Samuel, Raphael (1994), *Theatres of Memory*, London: Verso.

Sanders, James (2002), *Celluloid Skyline: New York and the Movies*, London: Bloomsbury.

Sargeant, Amy (2000), 'Making and Selling Heritage Culture: Style and Authenticity in Historical Fictions on Film and Television', in Justine Ashby and Andrew Higson (eds), *British Cinema: Past and Present*, London: Routledge, pp. 301–15.

Schulz, Kathryn (2016), 'The Perilous Lure of the Underground Railroad', *The New Yorker*, 15 August, www.newyorker.com/magazine/2016/08/22/the-perilous-lure-of-the-underground-railroad.

Schwander, Lisa (2019), '"He's One of Us": Community, Imperialism, and the Narrative of Progress in Indian Summer (2015–2016)', in Caroline Lusin and Ralf Haekel (eds), *Community, Seriality, and the State of the Nation: British and Irish Television Series in the 21st Century*, Tübingen: Narr Francke Attempto, pp. 119–42.

Seid, Danielle (2019), 'Television Is Burning: Revolutionary Queer and Trans Representation on TV', *Flow Journal* 26 (1), www.flowjournal.org/2019/09/television-is-burning/.

Seitz, Matt Zoller (2018a), 'Pose Is a Deeply American Story of Self-Creation', *Vulture*, 22 July, www.vulture.com/2018/07/pose-season-1-finale-review.html.

Seitz, Matt Zoller (2018b), 'The Marvelous Mrs. Maisel Isn't Just a "Feel-Good Show"', *Vulture* (blog), 26 December, www.vulture.com/2018/12/mrs-maisel-season-2-palladino-interview.html.

Shacklock, Zoë (2019), 'Queer Kinaesthesia on Television', *Screen* 60 (4): 509–26.

Shine, Jessica (2017), '"One Minute of Everything at Once": How Music Shapes the World of BBC's Peaky Blinders (2013–)', *Musicology Research* 2 (Spring): 47–69.

Singh, Anita (2017), 'Riz Ahmed: We Will Lose Kids to Extremism if We Don't Make Them Heroes in Our Stories', *The Telegraph*, 2 March, www. telegraph.co.uk/news/2017/03/02/riz-ahmed-will-lose-kids-extremism-dont-make-heroes-stories/.

Singh, Anita (2019a), 'Beecham House: How ITV's "Delhi Downton" Will Challenge View of the Empire', *The Telegraph*, 27 March, www.telegraph. co.uk/news/2019/03/27/beecham-house-itvs-delhi-downton-will-challenge-view-empire/.

Singh, Anita (2019b), 'Andrew Davies Sexes Up Sanditon in "risqué" New Jane Austen Adaptation', *The Telegraph*, 27 July, www.telegraph.co.uk/news/2019/07/27/andrew-davies-sexes-sanditon-risque-new-jane-austen-ada ptation/.

Singh, Anita (2020), 'Vikram Seth Defends Choice of White Writer to Adapt A Suitable Boy', *The Telegraph*, 24 July, www.telegraph.co.uk/news/0/vikram-seth-why-chose-white-writer-a-suitable-boy/.

Sisson, Patrick (2016), 'How a New TV Show Recreates the Underground Railroad and Slave Experience', *Curbed* (blog), 17 March, www.curbed.com/2016/3/17/11256320/underground-slave-dwelling-underground-rail road-wgn.

Snoddy, Raymond (2016), 'Versailles: The Price of Success for French TV Drama', *Royal Television Society* (blog), 25 July, https://rts.org.uk/article/versailles-price-success-french-tv-drama.

Sonnet, Esther (1999), 'From Emma to Clueless: Taste, Pleasure and the Scene of History', in Deborah Cartmell and Imelda Whelehan (eds), *Adaptations: From Text to Screen, Screen to Text*, London: Routledge, pp. 51–64.

Spigel, Lynn (2013), 'Postfeminist Nostalgia for a Prefeminist Future', *Screen* 54 (2): 270–8.

Stevenson, Brenda E. (2018), 'Filming Black Voices and Stories: Slavery on America's Screens', *The Journal of the Civil War Era* 8 (3): 488–520.

Swaminathan, Srividhya (2017), 'The New Cinematic Piracy: Crossbones and Black Sails', in Srividhya Swaminathan and Steven W. Thomas (eds), *The Cinematic Eighteenth Century: History, Culture, and Adaptation*, Abingdon: Routledge, pp. 139–53.

Sweney, Mark (2017), 'French TV Company Behind Versailles to Invest in UK Drama', *The Guardian*, 15 May, www.theguardian.com/media/2017/may/15/french-tv-company-behind-versailles-to-invest-in-uk-drama.

Swinson, Brock (2017), '"This Is a Story that We Have to Honor." Misha Green on Underground', *Creative Screenwriting* (blog), 18 May, https://creativescreenwriting.com/underground/.

Taddeo, Julie Anne (2015), '"Why Don't You Take Her?": Rape in the

Poldark Narrative', in James Leggott and Julie Anne Taddeo (eds), *Upstairs and Downstairs: British Costume Drama Television from the Forsyte Saga to Downton Abbey*, Lanham, MD: Rowman & Littlefield, pp. 207–22.

Taddeo, Julie Anne (2018a), '"The War Is Done. Shut the Door on It!"': The Great War, Masculinity and Trauma in British Period Television', in Katherine Byrne, Julie Anne Taddeo and James Leggott (eds), *Conflicting Masculinities: Men in Television Period Drama*, London: I.B. Tauris, pp. 165–86.

Taddeo, Julie Anne (2018b), 'Let's Talk about Sex: Period Drama Histories for the Twenty-First Century', *Journal of British Cinema and Television* 16 (1): 42–60.

Tashiro, C. S. (1998), *Pretty Pictures: Production Design and the History Film*, Austin: University of Texas Press.

Thornton, Edith P. (1993), 'On the Landing: High Art, Low Art, and Upstairs, Downstairs', *Camera Obscura: Feminism, Culture, and Media Studies* 11 (1 (31)): 26–47.

Thorpe, Vanessa (1999), 'Costume War Declared on TV', *The Observer*, 28 November, www.theguardian.com/uk/1999/nov/28/vanessathorpe.theobserver1.

Tincknell, Estella (2013), 'Dowagers, Debs, Nuns and Babies: The Politics of Nostalgia and the Older Woman in the British Sunday Night Television Serial', *Journal of British Cinema and Television* 10 (4): 769–84.

Tomlinson, Hugh (2020), 'A Suitable Boy: How They Turned Vikram Seth's Doorstopper into a Must-See TV Drama', *The Times*, 9 July, www.thetimes.co.uk/article/a-suitable-boy-how-they-turned-vikram-seths-door stopper-into-a-must-see-tv-drama-jbd8wpgxs.

Tucker, Lauren R. and Shah, Hemant (1992), 'Race and the Transformation of Culture: The Making of the Television Miniseries Roots', *Critical Studies in Mass Communication* 9 (4): 325–36.

VanArendonk, Kathryn (2019), 'Dickinson Is a Different, Better Kind of Origin Story', *Vulture* (blog), 29 October, www.vulture.com/2019/10/dickinson-apple-tv-review.html.

VanArendonk, Kathryn (2020), 'The Great Is Nasty, Brutish, and Long – and Very, Very Good', *Vulture*, 13 May, www.vulture.com/2020/05/the-great-hulu-review.html.

VanDerWerff, Emily, Frank, Allegra and Grady, Constance (2020), 'Mrs. America's Many Brands of Feminism, Discussed and Dissected', *Vox*, 29 May, www.vox.com/culture/21271423/mrs-america-feminism-fx-hulu-review.

Vidal, Belén (2012a), *Figuring the Past: Period Film and the Mannerist Aesthetic*, Amsterdam: Amsterdam University Press.

Vidal, Belén (2012b), *Heritage Film: Nation, Genre and Representation*, New York: Wallflower.

Warner, Kristen (2016), '[Home] Girls: Insecure and HBO's Risky Racial Politics', *Los Angeles Review of Books* (blog), 21 October, https://lareviewof books.org/article/home-girls-insecure-and-hbos-risky-racial-politics/.

Wheatley, Helen (2005), 'Rooms within Rooms: Upstairs Downstairs and the Studio Costume Drama of the 1970s', in Catherine Johnson and Rob Turnock (eds), *ITV Cultures: Independent Television Over Fifty Years*, Maidenhead: Open University Press, pp. 143–58.

Wheatley, Helen (2016), *Spectacular Television: Exploring Televisual Pleasure*, London: I.B. Tauris.

Whelehan, Imelda (2012), 'Neo-Victorian Adaptations', in Deborah Cartmell (ed.), *A Companion to Literature, Film, and Adaptation*, Chichester: John Wiley & Sons, pp. 272–92.

White, Bonnie (2019), 'Britishness and Otherness: Representing and Constructing Identity in BBC's Land Girls', *Critical Studies in Television* 14 (1): 90–105.

White, Brion (2017), 'Boardwalk Empire, Shell Shock and the Great War: The Characters of Militarism', *Continuum* 31 (1): 138–49.

Wilson, Benji (2019), 'Beecham House – "The Delhi Downton Abbey" Covers a Racy Part of Indian History', 16 June, www.thetimes.co.uk/article/beecham-house-the-delhi-downton-abbey-covers-a-racy-part-of-indian-history-8wr5bjphj.

Winant, Johanna (2019), 'Despite the Twerking and F-Bombs, Dickinson Gets Emily Dickinson Right', *Slate Magazine* (blog), 8 November, https://slate.com/culture/2019/11/dickinson-apple-tv-accuracy-poetry.html.

Wollaston, Sam (2013), 'The Village; Arne Dahl – The Blinded Man; Catchphrase – TV Review', *The Guardian*, 8 April, www.theguardian.com/tv-and-radio/2013/apr/08/the-village-tv-review.

Wollen, Tana (1991), '"Over Our Shoulders: Nostalgic Screen Fictions for the 1980s"', in John Corner and Sylvia Harvey (eds), *Enterprise and Heritage: Crosscurrents of National Culture*, London: Routledge, pp. 178–93.

Wood, Helen (2017), 'Foreword', in Beth Johnson and David Forrest (eds), *Social Class and Television Drama in Contemporary Britain*, London: Palgrave Macmillan, pp. vii–ix.

Woodacre, Elena (2018), 'Early Modern Queens on Screen: Victors, Victims, Villains, Virgins, and Viragoes', in Janice North, Karl C. Alvestad and Elena Woodacre (eds), *Premodern Rulers and Postmodern Viewers: Gender, Sex, and Power in Popular Culture*, London: Palgrave Macmillan, pp. 27–50.

Woods, Faye (2016), *British Youth Television: Transnational Teens, Industry, Genre*, London: Palgrave Macmillan.

Woods, Faye (2019), 'Wainwright's West Yorkshire: Affect and Landscape in the Television Drama of Sally Wainwright', *Journal of British Cinema and Television* 16 (3): 346–66.

Zemler, Emily (2019), 'Stuffy? Hardly. How "Dickinson" and Others Blew Up the Period Piece', *Los Angeles Times*, 7 November, https://www.latimes.com/entertainment-arts/tv/story/2019-11-07/apple-dickinson-comedy-central-drunk-history-the-favourite-another-period.

Zhu, Ying (2005), 'Yongzheng Dynasty and Chinese Primetime Television Drama', *Cinema Journal* 44 (4): 3–17.

Index